FTCE FELE Florida Educational Leadership

Teacher Certification Exam

By: Sharon Wynne, M.S.
Southern Connecticut State University

"And, while there's no reason yet to panic, I think it's only prudent that we make preparations to panic."

XAMonline, INC.

Boston

To obtain permission(s) to use the material from this work for any purpose including workshops or seminars, please submit a written request to:

XAMonline, Inc.
21 Orient Ave.
Melrose, MA 02176
Toll Free 1-800-509-4128
Email: info@xamonline.com
Web www.xamonline.com
Fax: 1-781-662-9268

Library of Congress Cataloging-in-Publication Data

Wynne, Sharon A.
   FELE Florida Educational Leadership: Teacher Certification / Sharon A. Wynne. -3rd ed.
   ISBN 978-1-60787-001-2
   1. FELE Florida Educational Leadership.   2. Study Guides.   3. FTCE
   4. Teachers' Certification & Licensure.   5. Careers

Disclaimer:

The opinions expressed in this publication are the sole works of XAMonline and were created independently from the National Education Association, Educational Testing Service, or any State Department of Education, National Evaluation Systems or other testing affiliates.

Between the time of publication and printing, state specific standards as well as testing formats and website information may change that is not included in part or in whole within this product. Sample test questions are developed by XAMonline and reflect similar content as on real tests; however, they are not former tests. XAMonline assembles content that aligns with state standards but makes no claims nor guarantees teacher candidates a passing score. Numerical scores are determined by testing companies such as NES or ETS and then are compared with individual state standards. A passing score varies from state to state.

Printed in the United States of America   œ-1

FTCE: FELE Florida Educational Leadership
ISBN: 978-1-60787-001-2

Table of Contents

Proposed Florida Educational Leadership Examination Test Configuration Model Note: some adjustments to the number of questions and testing time may be made after pilot testing in the 2007 year.				
SUBTEST AREA	**COVERING STANDARDS**	**NUMBER OF ITEMS**	**SCORING**	**TESTING TIME**
Subtest #1: Instructional Leadership	• Instructional Leadership • Managing the Learning Environment • Learning, Accountability, and Assessment	Approx. 65 multiple choiceitems Testing 49 skills or approximately 2 items per skill	Scaled	Recommend 2 hours
Subtest #2: Operational Leadership	• Human Resource Development • Decision Making Strategies • Ethical Leadership • Technology	Approx. 65 multiple choice items Testing 29 skills or approximately 3 items per skill	Scaled	Recommend 2 hours
Subtest #3: School Leadership	• Community and Stakeholder Partnerships • Diversity • Vision	50 to 60 multiple choice items + written performance assessment Testing 13 skills or approximately 4 items per skill	Composite (70% multiple choice/30% written assessment)	Recommend 2.5 hours
* The proposed date of administration for the new FELE exam is January 2009. The level of difficulty of this exam will be approximately equal to the current FELE exam.				

Great Study and Testing Tips!

What to study in order to prepare for the subject assessments is the focus of this study guide but equally important is *how* you study.

You can increase your chances of truly mastering the information by taking some simple yet effective steps.

Study Tips:

1. <u>Some foods aid the learning process.</u>

Foods such as milk, nuts, seeds, rice, and oats help your study efforts by releasing natural memory enhancers called CCKs (*cholecystokinin*) composed of *tryptophan*, *choline* and *phenylalanine*. All of these chemicals enhance the neurotransmitters associated with memory.

Before studying, try a light, protein-rich meal of eggs, turkey or fish. All of these foods release memory-enhancing chemicals. The better the connections in your brain, the more you comprehend. Likewise, before you take a test, stick to a light snack of energy-boosting and relaxing foods. A glass of milk, a piece of fruit, or some peanuts all contain CCKs and help you to relax and focus on the subject at hand.

2. <u>Learn to take great notes.</u>
We learn best when information is organized. When it has a logical structure and we can see relationships between pieces of information helps us assimilate new information.

If your notes are scrawled all over the paper, it fragments the flow of the information. Instead, strive for clarity. Newspapers, for example, use a standard format to achieve clarity. Your notes can be much clearer through use of proper formatting. A very effective format is called the <u>*"Cornell Method."*</u>

Take a sheet of loose-leaf lined notebook paper and draw a line all the way down the paper about 1-2" from the left-hand edge.

Draw another line across the width of the paper about 1-2" up from the bottom. Repeat this process on the reverse side of the page.

Look at the highly effective result. You have ample room for notes, a left hand margin for special emphasis items or inserting supplementary data from the textbook, a large area at the bottom for a brief summary, and a little rectangular space for just about anything you want.

3. Get the concept and then the details.

Too often we focus on the details and don't grasp an understanding of the concept. However, if you simply memorize only dates, places, or names, you may well miss the whole point of the subject.

A key way to understand things is to put them in your own words. If you are working from a textbook, automatically summarize each paragraph in your mind. If you are outlining text, don't simply copy the author's words.

Rephrase them in your own words. You remember your own thoughts and words much better than someone else's, and will subconsciously tend to associate the important details to the core concepts.

4. Ask why.

Pull apart written material paragraph by paragraph – and don't forget the captions under the illustrations.

If you train your mind to think in a series of questions and answers, not only will you learn more, but you will also have less test anxiety because you are used to answering questions.

Example: If the heading is "Stream Erosion", flip it around to read "Why do streams erode?" Then answer the questions.

5. Read for reinforcement and future needs.

Even if you only have 10 minutes, put your notes or a book in your hand. Your mind is similar to a computer; you have to input data in order to have it processed. *By reading, you are creating the neural connections for future retrieval.* The more times you read something, the more you reinforce the learning of ideas.

Even if you don't fully understand something on the first pass, *your mind stores much of the material for later recall.*

6. <u>Relax to learn: in other words, go into exile</u>.

Our bodies respond to an inner clock called biorhythms. Burning the midnight oil works well for some people, but not others.

If possible, set aside a particular place to study that is free of distractions. Shut off the television, cell phone and pager, and exile your friends and family during your study period.

If you really are bothered by silence, try background music. Light classical music at a low volume has been shown to aid in concentration over other types of music. Music that evokes pleasant emotions without lyrics is highly suggested. Try just about anything by Mozart. It can relax you.

7. <u>Use arrows not highlighters</u>.

At best, it's difficult to read a page full of yellow, pink, blue, and green streaks. Try staring at a neon sign for a while and you'll soon see that the horde of colors obscures the message.

A quick note, a brief dash of color, an underline or an arrow pointing to a particular passage is much clearer than a cascade of highlighted words.

8. <u>Budget your study time</u>.

Although you shouldn't ignore any of the material, ***allocate your available study time in the same ratio that topics may appear on the test.*** In other words, focus on the areas that are most likely to be included in the test.

Testing Tips:

1. Get smart by playing dumb. Don't read anything into the question.

Don't make an assumption that the test writer is looking for something other than what is asked. Stick to the question as written and don't read anything into it.

2. Read the question and all the choices *twice* before answering the question.

You may miss something by not carefully reading, and then re-reading both the question and the answers.

If you really don't have a clue as to the right answer, leave it blank on the first time through. Go on to the other questions, as they may provide a clue as to how to answer the skipped questions.

If later on, you still can't answer the skipped ones . . . *Guess.* The only penalty for guessing is that you *might* get it wrong. One thing is certain; if you don't put anything down, you will get it wrong!

3. Turn the question into a statement.

Look at the way the questions are worded. The syntax of the question usually provides a clue. Does it seem more familiar as a statement rather than as a question? Does it sound strange?

By turning a question into a statement, you may be able to spot if an answer sounds right, and it may also trigger memories of material you have read.

4. Look for hidden clues.

It's actually very difficult to compose multiple-foil (choice) questions without giving away part of the answer in the options presented.

In most multiple-choice questions, you can often readily eliminate one or two of the potential answers. This leaves you with only two real possibilities and automatically your odds go to fifty-fifty with very little work.

5. Trust your instincts.

For every fact you have read, you subconsciously retain something of that knowledge. On questions that you aren't really certain about, go with your basic instincts. **Your first impression on how to answer a question is usually correct.**

6. Mark your answers directly on the test booklet.

Don't bother trying to fill in the optical scan sheet on the first pass through the test. *Just be very careful not to miss-mark your answers when you eventually transcribe them to the scan sheet.*

7. Watch the clock!

You have a set amount of time to answer the questions. Don't get bogged down trying to answer a single question at the expense of 10 questions you can answer more readily.

COMPETENCY 1.0   **Instructional Leadership**
Managing the Learning Environment
Learning, Accountability, and Assessment

SKILL 1.1   **Knowledge of instructional leadership standard as related to curriculum development and continuous school improvement process**

1. Given a scenario, assess the curriculum and school wide professional development needs of an instructional program.

2. Given a set of school data, identify appropriate objectives and strategies for developing, implementing, assessing, and revising a school improvement plan.

3. Given a school data set, determine an appropriate instructional improvement strategy.

4. Identify functions and implications of various curriculum designs.

5. Given grade-level data on reading, identify strategies to align curriculum, instruction, and assessment.

The school curriculum is an action plan to educate children. The aims and goals that shape education are generated from nationwide commissions and task forces comprised of educators, and other influential citizens, including politicians. An example was the 1983 report *A Nation-At-Risk* in which the Commission on Excellent in Education reported its findings on the quality of education in America and made specific recommendations. Another example is the effort made by President Bush and state governors with the Goals 2000 effort, which emerged in 1990.

At the local level, task forces of parents, educators, and community groups impact school curriculum similar to national groups. Change is affected by data including attitudinal surveys of the students, teachers, and parent and community groups. Another data source for curriculum selection is direct student information, such as interviews and conferences. These yield information related to dispositions for learning, likes and dislikes, as well as difficulties experienced by students due to the curriculum design or related situations. Additionally, anecdotal records held by teachers and the contents of student folders, such as testing results and report cards, may contribute to the development of profiles of students to aide in the decision-making process about curricula.

Research findings about curriculum principles and design, as well as content organization, are also valuable for decision-making. Societal expectations directly impact the objectives for learning. For example, Goal Four (4) of Goals 2000 states that "By the year 2000, U.S. students will be first in the world in science and mathematics achievement." The expectations of this societal goal affected the curriculum in every state, district, and school. Even if this goal was lofty and not fully attained, it has affected the selection and content of the local curriculum.

The Commission for Goals 2000 uncovered the deplorable student achievement in math and science. By disclosing these conditions, parent, teachers, and community groups endorsed these goals as a way of improving education. Thus, the commission influenced a chain reaction where objectives were identified at the lowest levels to change the outcomes in these subject areas. As a result, subject-area goals were clearly written and became the driving force of curriculum change.

The nation is also concerned with producing citizens who are prepared to transmit the ideals of a democratic society. Therefore, the school as a societal institution must include in its teaching and learning process objectives that will produce desirable learner outcomes.

The school curriculum should satisfy societal needs and goals to produce individuals who have the social, intellectual, moral, emotional and civic development to function as an integral part of our democratic society. However, selecting the best curriculum to meet all of these needs is not an easy task. It should be a collaborative effort, and necessary changes should be described clearly in relation to existing district and school goals. In developing and selecting curricula, administrators should also consider the motivation of students and instructional staff, feasibility of time and resources, and curriculum balance in terms of concepts, skills, and application.

Curriculum Design

The design of the curriculum accounts for the manner in which the elements of the curriculum are organized. The design must include the nature and organization of the aims, goals, and objectives, as well as the subject matter, learning activities, and evaluation. Curriculum design precedes instructional design. It is the phase concerned with the nature of the component parts, which is influenced by various philosophies, theories, and practical issues.

A curriculum designer must specify each of the elements included in the design and develop a blueprint before implementation. The goals and objectives should be specific so that all stakeholders clearly understand what will be done and what behaviors are expected of learners. The next step is to identify the resources needed to attain curricular goals and objectives. Required material and human resources must be identified and secured. Materials may include textbooks, charts, maps, and other technology and equipment, such as projectors, computers, calculators, sport equipment, and microscopes. Human resources include administrators, teachers, volunteers, support staff, and others. Facilities are classrooms, gyms, athletic fields, cafeterias, and auditoriums. The subject matter, methods of organization, and activities, as well as the methods and instruments to evaluate the program, must be determined.

The organization of the components of the curriculum consist of two distinct elements: horizontal and vertical organization. *Horizontal organization* is a side-by side course arrangement where the content of one subject is made relative to the concepts of another related subject. *Vertical organization* is concerned with longitudinal treatment of concepts within a subject across grade levels. The success of horizontal organization depends heavily on the collaboration of teachers of various disciplines at the same grade level, while the vertical organization depends heavily on collaboration and planning among teachers of various grade levels.

The dimensions within the curriculum content must also be considered in curriculum design. Therefore, attention should be given to curriculum scope, sequence, integration, continuity, articulation, and balance. *Curriculum scope* refers to the breadth and depth of the curriculum content, learning activities, experiences, and topics. *Curriculum sequence* refers to the order of topics to be studied over time. The sequencing of the curriculum is usually organized from simple to complex topics; however, it can also emphasize chronological, whole-to-part, or prerequisite learning. *Curriculum integration* refers to linking the concepts, skills, and experiences in the subjects taught. *Curriculum continuity* deals with the smoothness of knowledge repetition from one grade level to another in specific subjects or areas of study. *Curriculum articulation* is the interrelationship within and among subjects both vertically and horizontally. *Curriculum balance* refers to the opportunities offered for the learners to master knowledge and apply it in their personal, social, and intellectual life pursuits.

Curriculum content can be based on a number of different design principles. These include subject-centered, discipline, broad fields, and process-centered designs. *Subject-centered* designs reflect the mental discipline approach to learning. The curriculum is organized according to essential knowledge that must be learned in each different subject area.

The *discipline* design is based on the organization of content, which allows for in-depth understanding of the content and the application of meaning. It is used primarily in secondary schools to emphasize the organizational content inherent to disciplines such as science, math, and English. Using this approach, the emphasis becomes experiencing the discipline as learning takes place.

Unlike the subject field, where a subject is studied separately from other subjects that are related, in the *broad fields design*, related subjects are broadened into categories. For instance, in this design social studies encompasses history, geography, and civics, and physical science encompassing physics and chemistry. The intent of the broad field design is to integrate the traditional subjects so that the learner develops a broader understanding of the areas included.

The *process centered* design addresses how students learn and apply learning processes to the subject matter. This design focuses on the student thinking-process and incorporates strategies for children to gain knowledge regardless of the topic.

Learning Theories

Curriculum selection must also take into account the contribution from the field of psychology, which is responsible for the major theories of learning. Learning theories serve as the foundation for methods of teaching, materials for learning, and activities that are age and developmentally appropriate for learning. Major theories of learning include behaviorism, cognitive development, and phenomenology or humanistic psychology.

Behaviorism represents traditional psychology that emphasizes conditioning the behavior of the learner and altering the environment to obtain specific responses. As the oldest theories of learning, behaviorism focuses specifically on stimulus response and reinforcement for learning. The work of Thorndike led to the development of connectionism theories from which come the laws of learning. These are:

> *Law of Readiness: when the conduction is ready to conduct, satisfaction is obtained and, if readiness is not present, it results in dissatisfaction.*

> *Law of Exercise: a connection is strengthened based on the proportion to the number of times it occurs, its duration and intensity.*

> *Law of Effect: responses accompanied by satisfaction strengthens the connection, while responses accompanied by dissatisfaction weakens the connection.*

These laws also influenced the curriculum contributions of Ralph Tyler, Hilda Taba, and Jerome Brunner who discarded the view of specific stimuli and responses to endorse broader views of learning. For example, Taba recognized that practice alone does not transfer learning; therefore, rote learning and memorization should not be emphasized. Jerome Bruner, on the other hand, contributed the notion that learning is better transferred when students learn structure rather than by rote memorization.

Classical conditioning theories emphasized the elicited response aspect of learning through adequate stimuli. Pavlov and Watson taught a dog who learned to salivate at the sound of a bell. This was accomplished by presenting food simultaneously with a stimulus, the bell. Their experiment gave the notion that the learner could be conditioned for learning or training.

Operant conditioning is a behavioral theory promoted by B. Frederick Skinner. It emphasizes learning by following behavior with either positive or negative reinforcers. This theory uses "reinforcers" to increase desirable behavior and "punishments" to decrease unwanted behavior. Positive reinforcers give desirable stimuli and negative reinforcers take away unpleasant stimuli. In contrast, positive punishment gives unpleasant stimuli and negative punishment removes desirable stimuli.

Behavioral theories gave birth to behavior-modification approaches to discipline and learning. Albert Bandura's theory of *observational learning and modeling* focuses on children learning through modeling the behaviors of others. *Hierarchical learning theories* by Robert Gagne organize types of learning into a classical, hierarchical model of intellectual skills, information, cognitive strategies, motor skills, and attitudes learned through positive experiences.

Cognitive development theories focus on human growth and development in terms of cognitive, social, psychological, and physical development. These theories suggest that schools should not focus solely on children's cognitive development. The *developmental theory* of Jean Piaget proposes that growth and development occur in stages. Piaget identified four stages of development including the sensory-motor stage (birth to age two) in which the child manipulates the physical surroundings; the pre-operational stage (ages 2-7) in which complex learning takes place through experiences; concrete operational stage (age 7-11) in which the child organizes information in logical forms using concrete objects; and the formal operational stage (age 11 and above) in which the child can perform formal and abstract operations.

Phenomenology or humanistic psychology is not widely recognized as a school of psychology. Those who disregard it believe that psychology in-and-of-itself is humanistic in nature; therefore, there is no need for such school. However, those who believe in the theory regard it as a third grouping because it emphasizes the person as a total organism during the learning process rather than separating learning into the domains of behavior and cognition. *Gestalt psychology* is representative of phenomenology and humanistic psychology. In this theory, the end-product is a wholesome, happy and healthy child/person who is self-actualized and fulfilled, incorporating Maslow's hierarchy of needs.

Curriculum Development

Identifying the educational goals and setting priorities before developing the curriculum are essential aspects of planning. Additionally, setting and prioritizing the goals must be carefully linked to the performance of the learner. Next, the curriculum design occurs with careful selection of instructional materials and equipment, as well as methods to attain the pre-established goals and objectives. The final steps include organizing the personnel involved and implementing a plan to supervise and give direction and focus to the project. Finally, the product planning and implementation at the classroom level are followed by the evaluation process, which determines the effectiveness and attainment of the goals and objectives of the curriculum.

A needs assessment is always the initial step in program or curriculum planning. It provides the opportunity to survey stakeholders and identify the context in which the program will be developed. The needs assessment survey should focus primarily on the needs of the students. This focus can identify achievement problems, goals can be written for the initial planning stage, and specific instructional objectives can be formulated.

Systematic assessment of school needs may range from grade level surveys of needs to school-wide surveys. This practice will not have full impact unless careful attention is given to a cohesive set of goals developed jointly with administrators, teachers, parents, and members of the school community to address specific needs. It is important that the instrument gathers pertinent information related to students' needs and the program environment at the school.

In any assessment process, data gathering is a key step that gives meaning to what is being measured. Ornstein and Huskins (1993) identify five distinct phases for gathering data to assess program effectiveness. These include identifying the curriculum phenomena to be evaluated and collecting, organizing, analyzing, and reporting and recycling the data/information.

In the first phase, identifying the curriculum phenomena to be evaluated, the evaluator determines the design of the evaluation and specifies exactly what will be evaluated. The evaluators will determine if the entire school will be included or just selected grade levels or subject areas. Whatever is decided at this stage must include a clear delineation of the relationship between the variables. This includes establishing a clear relationship between the objectives, the constraints of the learning activities, and the expected outcomes.

In the collection phase, the evaluator must identify the sources of information, which is based on the design established in the previous phase. A plan must be developed to collect hard-data from various sources including parents, teachers, staff, students, and other members of the school community. Organizing the information leads the evaluator to arrange the data so that it is usable. This includes coding and storing the data in a system where it can be retrieved for analysis. The data is then analyzed based on statistical approaches that are suitable for the information collected.

Reporting the information requires the evaluator to decide the level of formality that will meet the needs of the various audiences. Finally, recycling the information shows that evaluation is a continuous process. The implication is that the information received from this process will provide feedback for program modification and adjustment, which will lead to continuous change in an organization that is itself continuously changing.

Curriculum and Program Evaluation

In the process of educational program evaluation or classroom instructional evaluation, outcomes are reflected in terms of aims, goals, and objectives. Aims are general statements that reflect value judgments that give overall direction of the curriculum. They guide the educational process to achieve future learning outcomes. Aims are the results of societal concerns, which usually are expressed through national commissions and task forces. Goals are more specific than aims.

Even though goals may be written in a general manner similar to aims, aims become goals when the statement of purpose gives specificity to particular areas of the curriculum. Objectives are the most specific statements of expected learner outcomes. Examples of goals are expressed in the 1990 national initiative *Goals 2000*. Goal one states "By the year 2000 all children in America will start school ready to learn. Goal two states "By the year 2000 the high school graduation rate will increase."

As observed, these goal statements are very general and they do not include specific behaviors or parameters for the behavior. Objectives are generally expressed in behavioral terms, which are measurable. Non-behavioral objectives, on the other hand, are generally used to express higher-order learning. This suggests non-quantifiable measurement, such as appreciation and understanding. In most schools, behavioral objectives are preferred to ones that are non-behavioral. Behavioral objectives state what is expected of the student at the conclusion of the unit or lesson. They state the terms for the behavior and the minimum expectancy. This is an example of a well-written behavioral objective: *after completing the unit on telling time, students will be able to complete 25 problems with 80% accuracy within a thirty minute time span.*

Objectives should be written in measurable terms. With specific objectives, attention is given to the *behavior* to be measured, the *situation* in which the performance will take place and the *criterion* for the performance. For example, students will be able to solve multiplication word problems (behavior) at the rate of one problem per minute (situation) with 80% accuracy (condition). Objectives can be written to give directions at various program levels including grade levels or subject levels.

Program effectiveness can only be measured through an evaluation. Program evaluation is the process of collecting and analyzing data to discover whether a design, development, or implementation is producing the desired outcomes as stated by the goals and objectives. This may lead to changing or eliminating aspects of the program or curriculum.

The CIPP (Content Input Process Product) developed by Daniel Sufflebeam is a popular program evaluation model. In a three-step process, information is provided for decisions, information is delineated for collection, obtained, and provided to stakeholders. These steps must then correspond with four distinct types of evaluation: content, input, process, or product (Ornstein and Hunskin 1993).

Content evaluation reviews the program environment and its met and unmet needs. *Context evaluation* is the diagnostic stage of the evaluative process. It provides baseline information related to the entire system of operation. *Input evaluation* provides information and determines how to utilize resources to attain the goals of the program. It focuses on whether the goals and objectives of the program are appropriate for the expected outcome or if the goals and objectives are stated appropriately. It also takes into account whether the resources to implement specific strategies are adequate, whether or not the strategies are appropriate to attain the goals, or if the time allotted is appropriate to meet the objectives set forth for the program.

In schools, *process evaluation* focuses on decisions regarding curriculum implementation. It is concerned with whether planned activities are being implemented, procedures are recorded as they occur, and monitoring is continuous to identify potential problems. Continuously identifying potential problems allows corrections to be made before or during the implementation of the program. For example, it might be necessary to establish special planning sessions or in-service workshops at specific grade levels to work on modifying strategies due to problems uncovered. Process evaluation is also known as the piloting process prior to the actual implementation of a school-wide or district-wide program (Ornstein and Hunskin, 1993). Finally, *product evaluation* takes into account whether the final product or curriculum is accomplishing the goals or objectives and to what degree.

At this point decisions must be made regarding the continuation, termination or modification of the program. Since the evaluation process is continuous, the evaluators may, at this point in the cycle, link specific actions back to other stages or make changes based on the data collected. The data obtained may indicate the need to delay full implementation of the program until corrections are made, or it may lead to the decision that the program is ready for large scale implementation.

In summary, the main purpose of the evaluative process is to diagnose strengths and weaknesses, and to provide feedback to make appropriate decisions for programs and schools. The data collection for the evaluation process originates from a number of sources, including classroom observations, interviews and discussions with students, discussion with teachers and parents, testing and measurement data, information from pupil services or guidance services, and surveys of the school and school community.

Communicating Curriculum Change

Successful curriculum implementation is highly dependent on effective communication of the changes that are occurring, especially when the new curriculum will upset the status quo. The channels of communication must always be open so that discussion and exchange are ongoing at all levels and across groups. Effective communication requires high quality exchange through two-way channels within a defined network. While the formal network remains the official way of communicating in organizations, the informal network should not be ignored or discouraged. It can be shaped into a very healthy system of communication between members of the organization.

School restructuring calls for communication models different from the traditional top-down approach. Curriculum implementation requires that administrators and support personnel not only understand the curriculum but provide support to the classroom. Effective lateral communication allows information flow among participants at varying levels. This shows value for their contribution and promotes involvement through the process of networking. While lateral communication is usually formal, informal channels tend to be lateral as well.

Informal lateral communication might be a small group of teachers deciding amongst themselves to get together and share ideas from an article that could be useful in their classroom, or it could be the development of a simulation project for the grade level. Formal lateral communication messages may be written and disseminated systematically through newsletters, bulletin, memos, and reports. Formal lateral communication may also be verbal and communicated through speeches, lectures, and oral reports where body language, tone of voice, and other physical expressions can enhance the message being communicated.

The mode of communication should be adjusted to meet the needs of the audience. Workshops, bulletins, lectures, and other written and oral reports are all appropriate formats for disseminating program information, but while each approach serves a definite purpose they must be adjusted to meet the needs of their intended audiences. The approach used with teachers may generally be in-service training. These sessions teach procedures and methods for curriculum implementation where well-defined educational terms are used and specific strategies are developed or practiced. Conversely, a presentation for parents, community groups, and other lay individuals should be free of educational jargon and adjusted to their educational levels and school experiences. Whatever the mode or approaches to communication, a steady flow of information exchange at every stage of program implementation is necessary.

Organizational Change Theories and Models

Understanding theories of organizational change can be very useful in the process of implementing new curricula. Kurt Lewin's force field model looks at how two groups of opposing forces, when equalized, acquire a balance or equilibrium. This model states once change begins (what is described as "unfreezing") there is a driving force and a restraining force. The driving force reduces the power of the restraining force, thereby increasing actions to attain change. The restraining force is generally governed by fear of the unknown, strong identification with traditional values of the organization, or obsolete knowledge, which helps to maintain the status quo. The driving force is armed with new knowledge, technology, societal values, processes, or institutional approval to initiate the change process.

Specific strategies for curriculum implementation, for example, depend greatly on the curriculum implementation model utilized for change. Among these are the Organizational Resistance to Change model (ORC model), the Organizational Development model, the Organizational Parts, Units, and Loops model, and the Educational Change model.

The *ORC Model* accepts that resistance to change is natural because individuals become very comfortable with what they know and are afraid of the unknown. Therefore, people resist change in order to preserve the status quo. However, this model sees change and innovation as inevitable and essential to organizational and curriculum growth and development. The model produces a high level of success because it levels the playing field for those involved by endorsing power equalization between administrators and teachers.

Change must be planned to involve all key players. The plan should address all levels of concerns whether personal or programmatic. Individuals may need to share their values and beliefs concerning the difference between the new program and the existing one. Such dialogue and exchange may be the starting point of building consensus and resolving critical issues. Participants may need to listen to the opinions and visions of other colleagues. Participants may have concerns regarding materials for program implementation, time lines, or strategies to be used. Whatever the concerns may be, they must be addressed. The plan of action should allow time for all individuals to buy in to the concept and take ownership for the successes and failures.

The *Organizational Development Model* uses a top down, vertical approach where the key players are the administrators, directors, and supervisors. This model uses the rational planning approach to change, which emphasizes teamwork focused on specific issues identified by the key players. The strategies used in this model are planned through careful deliberation and consideration of available alternatives to make sure the organization retains what is valued so that the new program fits within the organization.

The *Organization Parts, Units, and Loops Model* asserts that units and departments comprise the whole organization. According to Rensis Likert, persons in these overlapping workgroups are the linking pins between the groups in the organization. The interaction of the linking pins between the groups has direct impact on the attitudes and behaviors within groups, which also implies that they can influence administrators by gaining support, respect, and trust. Therefore, the change process utilizes group interaction to provide the links needed for administration and teachers to work together. The concept promoted by this model is that the organization can create the situation and atmosphere for change by influencing perceptions and involving key individuals in the process.

The *Educational Change Model* calls for a clear understanding of the characteristics of the change being implemented. Individuals should have clarity of the goals and means to implement the program. The complexity or difficulty of the program implementation is affected by the level of participant experience. in order to buy-in and provide support to the change process, participants must perceive that there is worth in the efforts being made, that there is a sense of quality control, and that the process and outcomes are practical.

Ongoing School Improvement

School improvement is a continuous process that must receive prime attention from every administrator. To assist educators in their efforts, the state of Florida has established several agencies including the Bureau of School Improvement (FLBSI). In order to implement Florida's system of school improvement and differentiated accountability a cross-agency, team-based delivery system has been developed. The goal is to collaborate with stakeholders to provide assistance and interventions so ALL schools can help ALL students maximize learning gains and reach their highest achievement levels.

According to the FLBSI, "Our focus is on student success and continuous improvement. Our VISION: Leave No School Behind!" To that end, the agency provides numerous resources including a sample school improvement plan. Go to http://www.flbsi.org/0809_sip_template/Public/print.aspx?uid=010000 for more information. A school improvement plan should include:

- School vision/mission/belief statements
- School profile demographics
- A match between schools needing assistance with high performance schools in order to learn improvement strategies
- A plan for recruiting and retaining high quality administrators and teachers
- A coordination and integration component required for Title I
- A School Wide Improvement Model selected by the school for use in its change efforts
- Information for parents about public school choice options, as required by the No Child Left Behind Act
- Staff improvement strategies including professional development plans
- Appropriate use of school and student assessment data, including formal and informal sources
- Teaching strategies required by the state including direct instruction, School Learning Communities, parental involvement, and academic and career planning
- Clear goals for readings, mathematics and science, with accompanying budget figures
- Attention to discipline, school safety, and student health and fitness
- Reporting issues

A sample school improvement plan is available at
http://www.fldoe.org/nclb/pdfs/response/2-4-2a.pdf.

Principals as Leaders of Curriculum and Instruction

The role of the principal has indeed changed in recent years. In prior years, principals were the managers of the school building. They made sure all aspects were working together according to specifications. They ensured that activities were safe and cost effective, all students had places to go during the day, students were behaving properly, and teachers had the resources they needed in order to teach.

Lately, there has been a shift to thinking of principals as leaders of curriculum and instruction. They are expected to be thoroughly aware of each classroom, the instructional styles of each teacher, and the learning outcomes of all students. In summary, they are held responsible for the quality of instruction and the depth of learning at their schools.

With this shift of responsibilities, though, comes a dilemma for most school leaders: Should they focus on subject-matter instruction at the expense of all other areas, or should they focus on other developmental domains, which tend to create a positive school culture? A third question is if they should try to balance both demands, an option that requires much more time, money, and effort?

Most principals would argue that both are necessary and that option three is the best choice. They realize that students, their families, and teachers need to see that all students' needs are met on a variety of levels. Schools are ideal places to provide various athletic, creative, and intellectual activities. Furthermore, these activities provide schools with a greater sense of community.

How do principals balance those two disparate roles, as well as facilitate the development, implementation, evaluation, and refinement of student services and activity programs to fulfill academic, developmental, social, and cultural needs?

First, principals must focus on the school's mission. Most schools think beyond test scores and student achievement in their mission statements. For example, a school that says that its mission is to prepare students to succeed in a changing world will ultimately acknowledge that achievement is important. However, such a school will also offer students opportunities to succeed socially, physically, and creatively.

Second, the principal must monitor how students are achieving in key domains and adjust the allocation of resources and curricular focus accordingly. Committees or domain-specific teams are efficient ways in which this can be accomplished. Involving a cross-section of stakeholders will provide more representative feedback; as such, groups should include teachers, parents, students, and members of the broader community. Periodic reports from these groups can then aid the principal in making informed and effective adjustments to the educational agenda for the school.

SKILL 1.2   Knowledge of instructional leadership standard as related to research-based best practices

1. Given school-based student assessment data on reading performance, identify research-based reading instruction to improve student achievement.

2. Given school-based student assessment data on reading performance, identify instructional strategies to facilitate students' phonemic awareness, phonics, fluency, vocabulary, and reading comprehension throughout the content areas.

3. Given a scenario, which may include data, identify programs or initiatives that are research based to integrate reading, writing, and mathematics across all subject areas to increase student achievement.

4. Given a description of recurring problems in student performance in a content area, select strategies for engaging teachers in ongoing study of current best practices.

5. Identify scientifically based research applications to effective teaching and learning methods.

6. Identify practices in teacher planning, instructional organization, and classroom management that enhance student learning and achievement.

7. Identify instructional delivery methods that enhance student learning and achievement

Scientifically Based Research (SBR)

The No Child Left Behind (NCLB) Act requires educational programs and practices to be grounded in scientifically based research. Scientifically based research (SBR) is defined in the NCLB legislation as "research that involves the application of rigorous, systematic, and objective procedures to obtain reliable and valid knowledge relevant to education activities and programs" (NCLB, 2002). The imperative for incorporating SBR is dictated not only by federal law, but by common sense as well. With budgets tighter and district demands greater, educators need to be able to evaluate the evidence for the effectiveness of costly programs and materials. SBR is the "gold standard" for such evidence (Coalition for Evidence-Based Policy, 2003).

NCLB Programs That Require SBR

- Title I directs funds toward improving the academic achievement of the disadvantaged. Title I funds are directed toward improving basic programs operated by school districts, Reading First and Early Reading First, Comprehensive School Reform, Even Start, and improving school libraries. All of these funds must be directed toward programs and materials that are grounded in SBR.

- Title II directs money toward preparing, training, and recruiting high-quality teachers and principals. It also provides grants for math and science partnerships. These funds may support only those interventions that show evidence of effectiveness in improving student performance.

- Title III addresses language instruction for limited-English-proficient and immigrant students. It mandates that all curricula for teaching these students be tied to SBR criteria.

- Title IV, also known as 21st Century Schools, funds programs that promote safe and drug-free schools and communities, as well as 21st Century Community Learning Centers. Both kinds of programs need SBR supporting their effectiveness.

The U.S. Department of Education (Comprehensive School Reform Program Office, 2002) has identified the following questions to ask when judging the quality of implementation and replicability:

- How many schools have used this practice or program?

- Did the schools using it fully implement the practice or program?

- In what settings has it been implemented?

- Has improved student achievement been convincingly demonstrated in a variety of settings?

The U.S. Department of Education (Coalition for Evidence-Based Policy, 2003) has provided guidelines for a school to judge whether the research base of an educational intervention provides evidence of effectiveness:

- Strong evidence of effectiveness requires experimental studies of high quality (i.e., studies that meet all the criteria detailed in the previous section). Moreover, the research must demonstrate effectiveness in at least two typical school settings (i.e., using regular schools and classroom teachers), including a setting similar to the school considering whether to implement the program.

- Possible evidence of effectiveness requires quasi-experimental studies of high quality (i.e., studies that carefully match the treatment and control groups and that meet the criteria discussed in the previous section), or experimental studies that do not meet all the criteria for quality.

Gathering, synthesizing, and using SBR are the steps to making good decisions about educational programs, products, and practices. Although studying the evidence base is time consuming, proper consideration of SBR gives educators greater confidence in their decision making and may lead to greater opportunity for students to succeed.

- Decision makers should understand the importance of research. Just as leaders in business and industry use research to improve their products and services, so too school leaders should utilize research to inform their decisions about school programs.

- Administrators and teachers should have a grasp on the fundamental principles of research. This will allow them to understand the strengths and limitations of the research behind a given school program or product. It is true that school leaders have neither the time nor training to offer expert critiques of educational research. Nevertheless, if they understand basic concepts of research—such as comparison groups, measurement quality, and replication—they will have the basic vocabulary to comprehend the critiques of those who are qualified to offer them. This will help school leaders make more informed decisions about how to select the right programs and products for their schools.

Pitfalls of SBR

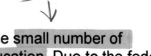

Perhaps the greatest pitfall to the use of SBR is the small number of experimental studies about important topics in education. Due to the federal requirements regarding SBR, many vendors are touting their products and services as "evidence based."

There is likely to be confusion between programs that are based on scientific research and programs which themselves have been rigorously tested (Slavin, 2003). This distinction is subtle yet important: The individual components of a program may all be supported by research, but the way that the program organizes and emphasizes the components may not be supported by research. The experience of the New York City schools in selecting a reading curriculum is a case in point. School officials selected a reading program whose major components were amply supported by research. Yet, in the view of some critics, the program *itself* had not been rigorously tested and, therefore, was not sufficiently scientifically based. As a result, the New York City school district had to switch its reading program in order to ensure federal funding (Manzo, 2004).

Another pitfall is overreliance on SBR. Potentially, a school can be so swayed by the evidence for the effectiveness of an educational program that it might fail to verify whether such a program is a good match for its own conditions and needs. Administrators must look beyond the evidence for a program's effectiveness and also consider evidence for successful implementation in schools similar to theirs.

Finally, the limited amount of time for educators to study the research can be a pitfall. Reviewing the research literature is a time-consuming process. One resource for identifying evidence-based practices is the What Works Clearinghouse (WWC), sponsored by the U.S. Department of Education.

Scientifically Based Research on Reading

Good reading programs

- use valid screening measures to find children who are at risk and provide them with effective, early instruction in phonology and oral language; in word recognition and reading fluency; and in comprehension and writing skills;

- interweave several components of language (such as speech sounds, word structure, word meaning, and sentence structure) into the same lessons;

- build fluency in both underlying reading skills and text reading, using direct methods such as repeated readings of the same text;

- incorporate phonemic awareness into all reading instruction, rather than treating it as an isolated element;

- go beyond the notion of phonics as the simple relationship between letters and sounds to include lessons on word structure and origins;

- build vocabulary from the earliest levels by exposing students to a broad, rich curriculum; and

- support reading comprehension by focusing on a deep understanding of topic and theme rather than just a set of strategies and gimmicks.

SKILL 1.3   Knowledge of instructional leadership standard as related to school culture

1. Given data from a school climate survey, identify appropriate strategies for improving student learning.

2. Given data from a school climate survey, identify factors contributing to morale and performance.

For the most part, an organization's goals and objectives are achieved through Motivation is defined by Baron (1992) as a force that energizes, sustains, and channels behavior toward a goal. Individuals have needs, desires, likes, and dislikes and these are related to their motivation; thus, an understanding of this and how it relates to work is important to understand. The question of how to get people motivated to achieve those goals and objectives, expeditiously and effectively, is at the heart of motivational theories.

Theorists maintain that there are two types of motivation. One is intrinsic motivation, which results from an individual's internal drive state and provides impetus toward goal attainment. The other is extrinsic motivation, meaning that the orientation toward goal achievement is influenced by incentives and rewards external to the individual. A number of theories have been developed to explain what influences individuals to work enthusiastically, to want to engage in professional growth, to contribute to goal attainment in organizations, and to act responsibly. According to Hoy & Miskel (1996) motivating individuals is a complex process of trying to facilitate desired motivational patterns. One strategy to influence motivation is providing for the needs, desires, and likes of individuals in an organizational setting, this in turn impacts the objectives of the organization.

Incentives and rewards are used by an organization to influence the motivation of its members; thus making them more productive. Of importance in any work environment are the environmental factors present, those things that tend to make the workplace enjoyable and those things that tend to make the workplace distasteful. Administrators' attention to these factors significantly affects the workplace and, subsequently, has an impact on the motivation of members to accomplish tasks and fulfill organizational goals.

The utilization of reinforcers to influence behavior then becomes an important element in motivational theory, specifically, *the behavioral approach*. The two other categories of motivation are *the cognitive* and *humanistic approaches*. While the behavioral approach to motivation suggests that motivation depends upon the effectiveness of reinforcers. Cognitive theory suggests that motivation consists of two personal factors, expectations and beliefs. When there is the expectation that one can succeed at a task, and value is attached to achieving that task, then a feeling of self-efficacy emerges. In organizations then, leaders may ask what can be done to help bring about emotions of self-efficacy in its members. The humanistic perspective views motivation as attempts by people to reach their potential. Motivation proceeds from internal mechanisms acting to cause individuals to achieve, grow and develop, and reach their potential.

Currently, educational policy relies on the idea of external motivation to improve instructional quality. The federal legislation commonly referred to as *No Child Left Behind* operates largely on the principle that rewards and punishments will increase motivational levels of teachers, principals, and students. Growth targets are incremental; however, when they are not met punishment may include staff being transferred to other schools in the district. We may not know until 2014, when all students are expected to be fully proficient, the effectiveness of this attempt at external motivation for improving the learning of all students across the country.

Creating a Positive School Climate

A fundamental task of in every school is to create a positive environment within which all students are respected and can thrive. The school administrator is the central figure whose leadership sets the tone, implements key policies, and models behavior that contributes to a healthy school climate. By setting an example and striving to be a transformational leader, the principal can create a positive environment that also enhances the ability of teachers to teach, and inspires all faculty and staff members to do their best.

Positive school environments share these qualities:

- Core values of respect, integrity, cooperation and care for one another.

- Adults strive to be caring, competent and "in charge" without abusing their power and authority.

- Clear and direct communication is valued, practiced and taught.

- Student success is measured not only by academic achievement but also by the physical, mental, social and emotional health of students.

- Avoidance of stereotyping and bias while still acknowledging and valuing diversity.

- An attitude of "we are all in this together" rather than an "us vs. them" mentality, including a sense of partnership with parent/guardians and the community.

- Opportunities for students to get to know and work with students who are different from them.

- Refusal to allow sexual and other forms of harassment and bullying.

- Conflict resolution, problem-solving skills and violence prevention programs built into the curriculum.

- Policies and procedures are proactive and preventive in nature, including but not limited to crisis management planning and the creation of a safe school climate.

These qualities should exist across the entire school community. In positive school environments, the values and characteristics described above are present among the student population, among the staff, faculty and administration, and between the students and the adults in the school. Ideally, these qualities are also present at the school board level and in all interactions with parents/guardians and community members.

Transformational Leadership

All members of staff, students, and parents/guardians can be leaders within the school as well as the community. This is the essence of transformational leadership: a school administrator who strives to be a transformational leader fosters the growth of the stakeholders and enhances their goals. This approach also helps to bring about greater professionalism and appropriate responsibility-taking within the school community.

By allowing teachers, students and parents/guardians a greater voice in the workings of the school, a principal will find that these groups are more willing to make extra efforts. Participants who believe that they have been successful, either alone or as part of a team, are more likely to apply what they have learned to bring about changes in the school. The principal can help to influence staff by providing a picture of what a successful school looks like. The principal can set feasible goals and help to interpret the data to determine success or failure.

Celebrating accomplishments and having high expectations for teachers, students and parents contribute to empowering groups and individuals to become leaders. Failures should be treated as learning experiences and opportunities to find out what works and what doesn't work. A positive attitude and effective communication (addressed in Skills 3.6 and 3.7) helps utilize and transform "failures."

As principals visit the classrooms and talk with teachers, students, and parents they can develop strategies, such as providing timely and accurate feedback. Exemplars of successful teamwork help those who are not quite sure of the process. Timetabling that allows teachers a chance to collaborate or observe each other increases teacher empowerment and makes it easier for them to become leaders. Such activities also help reduce teacher stress because they do not have to spend extra amounts of time in meetings after school hours.

A collaborative school culture that values the perspectives of staff, students, and parents will also enable them to problem-solve more effectively. Staff members who have experienced success, such as with new teaching strategies, for example, are more likely to view themselves as leaders, thus providing encouragement in future endeavors.

Measuring School Climate

Perceptions held by stakeholder groups (e.g., students, parents, and teachers) about the physical, social, and learning environments of a school may influence both the processes and outcomes that occur. Unlike measures of satisfaction in which each individual as *respondent* is asked to give a personal affective reaction, climate is measured by asking each individual to serve as an *informant*; i.e., to respond to each item in terms of what he or she believes *most people* hold to be true about that characteristic of the school's environment.

The shared perceptions of climate represent what most people believe, not the individual's personal reaction to the environment. These shared perceptions tend to be persistent and stable over time. Just as meteorological climate is largely unaffected by daily shifts in temperature, the climate of the school is a relatively stable phenomenon.

Measurement of the climate solely by what most people believe, rather than as a collection of climate and individual satisfaction responses, is the primary difference between the National Association of Secondary School Principals (NASSP) School Climate Survey and most other measures of climate. A second difference is the emphasis in the NASSP Model on the collection of perceptions of climate from all major stockholder groups. A third difference is the description of climate as a mediating variable rather than as an outcome measure.

As an example, the NASSP School Climate Survey is normed for use with students in grades 6-12, and for use with teachers and parent or citizen groups. Assessment of all major stakeholder groups, rather than a single group, is recommended. Broader assessment allows for comparison of perceptions between and among groups. These comparisons can be useful in discerning and planning for appropriate interventions to improve school environments.

The NASSP School Climate Survey collects data about perceptions on 10 subscales:

- **Teacher-Student Relationships**. Perceptions about the quality of the interpersonal and professional relationships between teachers and students.
- **Security and Maintenance**. Perceptions about the quality of maintenance and the degree of security people feel at the school.
- **Administration**. Perceptions of the degree to which school administrators are effective in communicating with different role groups and in setting high performance expectations for teachers and students.
- **Student Academic Orientation**. Perceptions about student attention to task and concern for achievement at school.
- **Student Behavioral Values**. Perceptions about student self-discipline and tolerance for others.
- **Guidance**. Perceptions of the quality of academic and career guidance and personal counseling services available to students.
- **Student-Peer Relationships**. Perceptions about students' care and respect for one another and their mutual cooperation.
- **Parent and Community-School Relationships**. Perceptions of the amount and quality of involvement of parents and community members in the school.
- **Instructional Management**. Perceptions of the efficiency and effectiveness of teacher classroom organization and use of classroom time.
- **Student Activities**. Perceptions about opportunities for and actual participation of students in school-sponsored activities.

SKILL 1.4 Knowledge of instructional leadership standard as related to instructional design, teaching, and learning

1. Given taxonomy of learning, identify instructional objectives to facilitate varying levels of learning.

2. Identify age-appropriate learning strategies based on principles of human growth and development.

3. Identify practices for evaluating the appropriateness of instructional strategies.

4. Identify practices for evaluating the appropriateness of instructional materials.

Helping Teachers Understand Best Practices

Even though new principals often inherit ongoing programs, as well as faculty members who have been at the school for many years, principals have significant responsibility for the quality of instruction that goes on within the school. This discussion will focus on two important elements in achieving high quality instruction: what high quality, flexible instruction looks like and methods principals can use to ensure that such instruction takes place.

High quality instruction focuses on research-based strategies of effective teaching. Such strategies are portrayed heavily in books and trade journals for teachers. Many colleges of education throughout the nation now regularly instruct students in these instructional methods. The methods, of course, will look very different for each grade level and each content subject. However, all good instruction ensures that standards for student learning are clear to the students. Students will know what it is they are expected to do and/or know. Furthermore, all instruction will focus on bringing students from where they are to where they need to be, in accordance with the standard(s).

Flexible instruction is the next step in the discussion of high quality teaching. Not all students will start out in the same place, and not all students will learn at the same rate—or in the same way. Teachers who are comfortable with lecturing and testing may need to be assisted as they learn new approaches so that all students will be guaranteed mastery of content. Lecturing, as many of us know, does not work for all students. Differentiation is a term often used to describe the work of teachers to meet various students' learning needs. For example, some students need more visual support than auditory support; others need extra time; some need extra assistance. Differentiation assists in ensuring that all students reach the same standard.

In addition to designing differentiated instructional activities so that all students can meet standards, teachers need sufficient materials in which to provide instruction. Often, technology is very important in the delivery of differentiated instruction. Furthermore, many students need additional out-of-class support that may be available through tutoring and pull-out services.

Principals can encourage high-quality, flexible instruction by providing the conditions it requires. These are: knowledge, encouragement, and support.

Knowledge refers to pedagogical and content knowledge. Many teachers are not familiar with all the pedagogical (teaching) strategies available. Learning such strategies is time consuming, but very important. Principals can support this learning by providing high quality professional development. With professional development funds, teachers can attend workshops and purchase trade books. Teachers can get a better understanding of content as well through professional development. Both pedagogical and content knowledge can be fostered through Professional Learning Communities. Such communities provide teachers time and space to discuss current teaching problems and generate solutions.

Encouragement is provided in two ways: First, teachers need to know that they can attain high standards. Schools that focus on providing teachers with a supportive, helpful climate have teachers who feel more positive about working toward difficult goals. Second, teachers need to know that they are indeed expected to work toward higher standards. For this to occur, principals must be highly visible on campus, doing walk-throughs, attending department meetings, and staying around for whole sessions of school professional development (When principals do not attend required professional development, teachers often view the training as unimportant.). Principals should engage teachers in discussion of their work, ask them about their lessons, and help them to focus on utilizing better instructional strategies.

Finally, *support* comes through assistance provided by the principal, on-site coaches, and teacher-leaders. Teachers need to feel safe in making mistakes. They need to know that it is okay to experiment with new strategies. Principals can encourage this particularly by sending positive signals about new classroom strategies they see teachers use.

Overall, it is critical that principals spend a considerable portion of each day on the improvement of instructional programs. They need to come across to teachers as highly concerned about providing students with the best instruction possible.

Over the last thirty years, many detailed lists of "best practices in teaching" have been compiled, beginning with Bloom's taxonomy for educational objectives and continuing with considerable research on teaching and learning,. Most lists of important "best practices" include the following:

- *Engage students in active learning experiences*
- *Set high, meaningful expectations*
- *Provide, receive, and use regular, timely, and specific feedback*
- *Become aware of values, beliefs, preconceptions; unlearn if necessary*
- *Recognize and stretch student styles and developmental levels*
- *Seek and present real-world applications*
- *Understand and value criteria and methods for student assessment*
- *Create opportunities for student-faculty interactions*
- *Create opportunities for student-student interactions*
- *Promote student involvement through engaged time and quality effort*

Domains of Instructional Strategies

There exist six core domains of instructional strategy and functioning. They are planning, management of student conduct, instructional organization and development, presentation of subject, communication, and testing. Each should be part of evaluating teacher effectiveness.

In the domain of *planning*, a course of action for teaching is formulated. The teacher organizes the subject matter to be taught, the materials to be used for instruction, the activities that will be implemented, and the method of assessing the learning outcome. Specific concepts included in this domain are content coverage, utilization of instructional materials, activity structure, goal focusing, and diagnosis. Effective indicators of planning included on the school district's formative assessment instrument may vary, but they will generally correlate with the selected concepts for the domain. For example, *"assesses students' needs before instruction"* might be used as an indicator of diagnosis, while *"presets goals for teaching"* might be used as an indicator of the concept of goal focusing.

The domain of *management of student conduct* is inclusive of teacher behavior that reduces student misconduct, halts disruptive student behaviors once they occur, and deals with serious misconduct. The effective teacher knows that student misconduct affects the behavior and learning of other students in the classroom. It is expected that the teacher will use appropriate and effective techniques to stop a deviancy with minimal disruption to other children. The effective teacher is aware that teacher behavior may also increase or decrease negative responses from students. Specific concepts included in this domain are rule explanation and monitoring, teacher with-it-ness, overlapping, quality of desists, group alertness, movement smoothness, movement slowdown, and praise. *"Stops misconduct while maintaining instructional momentum"* might be used as an indicator of movement smoothness on an assessment instrument.

The domain of *instructional organization and development* includes the specific concepts such as efficient use of time, review of subject matter, lesson development, teacher treatment of student talk, teacher academic feedback, and management of seatwork/homework. A formative assessment instrument for teacher performance may use an indicator such as *"circulates and assists students"* to assess the concept of management of seatwork or *"recognizes responses, amplifies and gives corrective feedback"* to assess treatment of student talk.

The domain of *presentation of subject* focuses on interaction with students as well as the treatment of the subject matter. Specific concepts include presentation of interpretive (conceptual) knowledge, explanatory (law or law-like) knowledge, academic rule knowledge, and value knowledge (statements about the worth of things). A formative assessment instrument for teacher performance may use *"develops concept, gives definition, attributes, examples and non-examples"* as an indicator to assess the concept of presentation of interpretive or conceptual knowledge.

The domain of *communication* (verbal and nonverbal) focuses on verbal and nonverbal skills to express information and establish personal relationships. While verbal interaction is important to successful teaching, body language and other nonverbal expressions are also crucial in establishing relationships and engaging students in meaningful learning. This domain includes the concepts of control of discourse, emphasis, task attraction and challenge, speech, and body language. A formative assessment for teacher performance may use an indicator to assess body language such as *"uses nonverbal expressions that show interest, such as smiles, gestures, etc."*

The domain of *testing* (student preparation, administration, and feedback) addresses the environment in which students are tested, as well as the feedback they receive about their test performance. Administrators are seldom present during direct student assessment periods so they may not have direct information about the teacher's competency at testing. Indicators for teacher testing competencies are usually initiated through the development of a school-wide plan for testing, but are individually assessed through conferences with teachers and feedback from parents and students.

Effective Planning Enhances Achievement

Effective teachers plan for instructional delivery even if they have taught the same lessons before. They continue to improve upon the presentation by finding new or additional materials to bring new energy. As part of teaching, planning is a deliberate act that can be long or short range, formal or informal. Long-range planning, such as unit or semester plans, takes into account milestones, standards, major goals, time periods, the nature of the content, the process in which the content will be covered, the activities to be used, and resources needed.

Short-term planning consists of daily, weekly, or even monthly lesson plans or units for instruction. Daily and weekly lesson plans are usually more detailed and specific, while unit plans can be more general and serve as the source for the daily lesson plans. Written daily or weekly lesson, or unit plans, grouping of students, instructional-materials selection, activities for specific experiences to attain specific goals, and student assessment are all part of the planning process.

The formal aspect of planning has greater breadth and scope, which includes long and short-term written plans. The informal aspect of planning is continuous and includes teachers ideas' that emerge (1) as resourceful teachers gather materials useful for learning, (2) as teachers consider varying experiences useful for specific students, (3) as they share ideas with other professionals, (4) and as they toy with ideas on how to do things better. Whether long or short-term, effective planning begins with specified learning goals and objectives. Next, instructional strategies and materials should be selected, followed by the appropriate evaluation techniques to assess learning.

Instructional Delivery Methods

Instructional planning also involves organizing students for learning. Whole group and small group instruction are beneficial in different ways. Whole group instruction is beneficial when the teacher is introducing new concepts and skills while small group instruction is recommended when teachers want to ensure that students' master the material. Students may be placed in ability groups for short-term activities. However, long-term ability grouping such as tracking should be avoided. Teachers should work to mix students who would have been placed in regular tracks and those identified as college bound. By learning together students benefit from each other.

Proponents believe that ability groups save time and allow teachers and learners to focus on the collective needs of the students. However, it is recognized that at all grade levels, cooperative, mixed-ability groups result in higher academic achievement. Other added benefits include improved time on task and increased interpersonal skills. Cooperative grouping as a dominant approach to instruction does not negate the need to use homogeneous grouping on a short-term basis. The teacher must be careful that ability groups are only used for the short-term and less proficient groups still receive high-quality instruction.

When teachers begin instruction they should be clear and focused. The lesson orientation and instructional objectives must be presented in terms that students can easily understand. The relationship between the current lesson and previous lessons should be made. Key points should be emphasized, concepts defined with examples and non-examples, cause and effect relationships established, and careful attention given to learning styles through the use of appropriate materials and strategies for learning. Students should be provided ample time for guided and independent practice in the form of class work and homework, and strategies to develop higher-level thinking skills should be used.

Effective teacher expressions are key in instructional delivery. Enthusiasm is as important as delivery of the instruction itself. Instruction, demonstrated through body language that expresses interest and caring, may also contribute to verbal effectiveness. The teacher should use good verbal skills for effective questioning to monitor understanding, to keep students focused, and to give feedback to reinforce learning progress.

Classroom Management

The dynamics of classroom management generally correspond to the leadership styles of individual teachers. An autocratic leadership style yields a punitive, harsh, and critical classroom environment. A laissez-faire leadership style, on the other hand, yields a permissive classroom environment where disorder and anarchy dominate. The democratic leadership style is more characteristic of today's school reform in which a participatory classroom is expected. This style yields a classroom that is firm but friendly, encouraging and stimulating, and caring and guiding. Most of all, fairness prevails as a way of resolving conflicts.

Regardless of the discipline model endorsed by the school, the effectively managed classroom follows basic principles generated by research. Various disciplinary models exist for the prevention and correction of misbehavior, any of which may produce good results based on the teacher's leadership/management style and philosophy. General knowledge of classroom management techniques can prevent behavioral problems and may prove much more effective than many leading models.

Current educational research suggests simple yet fundamental strategies for effective classroom management. These include beginning class on time, setting up classroom procedures and routines, and keeping desk and storage spaces clean and organized from the very beginning of the school year. Making smooth transitions from one activity to another, or from one class to another in a quick and orderly manner, is also important. This practice cuts down on idle time that generally encourages misbehavior. Making eye contact, being polite to students, and reinforcing positive interaction with and among the students all engender a healthy learning atmosphere.

"With-it-ness" is another component of good classroom management. This technique is often compared to "teachers having eyes behind their backs". Even though they appear to be doing something else, these teachers are always monitoring student behavior, especially when students are not paying attention. Having a general sense of what is going on in the classroom at all times, giving verbal and nonverbal encouragement, and stopping misbehavior in a firm and consistent manner as soon as it occurs without the use of threats, conveys consistent purpose and expectations. Careful instructional planning and pace of teaching may also reduce opportunities for problems in the classroom.

See Skill 1.1 for more information about **Evaluation of Instructional Programs.**

Principles of Human Growth and Development

There is a set of principles that characterizes the pattern and process of all human growth and development. Using these principles, we can predict how most children will develop. Although there are individual differences in children's personalities, activity levels, and the timing of developmental milestones, the principles and characteristics of development are universal patterns. A general knowledge of these principles allows for the development of appropriate learning strategies.

1. **Development proceeds from the head downward.** According to this principle, the child gains control of the head first, then the arms, and then the legs. Infants develop control of the head and face movements within the first two months after birth. In the next few months, they are able to lift themselves up by using their arms. By 6 to 12 months of age, infants start to gain leg control and may be able to crawl, stand, or walk. Coordination of arms always precedes coordination of legs.

2. **Development proceeds from the center of the body outward.** This means that the spinal cord develops before outer parts of the body. The child's arms develop before the hands and the hands and feet develop before the fingers and toes. Finger and toe muscles (used in fine motor dexterity) are the last to develop in physical development.

3. **Development depends on maturation and learning.** Maturation refers to the sequential characteristic of biological growth and development. The biological changes occur in sequential order and give children new abilities. Changes in the brain and nervous system account largely for maturation. These changes in the brain and nervous system help children to improve in thinking (cognitive) and motor (physical) skills. Also, children must mature to a certain point before they can progress to new skills (i.e., readiness).

   For example, a four-month-old cannot use language because the infant's brain has not matured enough to allow the child to talk. By two years of age, the brain has developed further and with help from others, the child will have the capacity to say and understand words. Also, a child can't write or draw until he has developed the motor control to hold a pencil or crayon. Maturational patterns are innate, that is, genetically programmed. The child's environment and the learning that occurs as a result of the child's experiences largely determine whether the child will reach optimal development. A stimulating environment and varied experiences allow a child to develop to his or her potential.

4. **Development proceeds from the simple (or concrete) to the more complex.** Children use their cognitive and language skills to reason and solve problems. For example, learning about relationships between things (how things are similar), or classification, is an important ability in cognitive development. The cognitive process of learning how an apple and orange are alike begins with the most simplistic or concrete thought of describing the two. Seeing no relationship, a preschool child will describe the objects according to some property of the object, such as color. Such a response would be, "An apple is red (or green) and an orange is orange." The first level of thinking about how objects are alike is to give a description or functional relationship (both concrete thoughts) between the two objects. "An apple and orange are round" and "An apple and orange are alike because you eat them" are typical responses of three, four and five year olds. As children develop further in cognitive skills, they are able to understand a higher and more complex relationship between objects and things; that is, that an apple and orange exist in a class called fruit. The child cognitively is then capable of classification.

5. **Growth and development is a continuous process.** As a child develops, he or she adds to the skills already acquired and the new skills become the basis for further achievement and mastery of skills. Most children follow a similar pattern. Also, one stage of development lays the foundation for the next stage of development. For example, in motor development, there is a predictable sequence of developments that occur before walking. The infant lifts and turns the head before he or she can turn over. Infants can move their limbs (arms and legs) before grasping an object. Mastery of climbing stairs involves increasing skills from holding on to walking alone. By the age of four, most children can walk up and down stairs with alternating feet. As in maturation, in order for children to write or draw, they must have developed the manual (hand) control to hold a pencil and crayon.

6. **Growth and development proceed from the general to specific.** In motor development, the infant will be able to grasp an object with the whole hand before using only the thumb and forefinger. The infant's first motor movements are very generalized, undirected, and reflexive, waving arms or kicking before being able to reach or creep toward an object. Growth occurs from large muscle movements to more refined (smaller) muscle movements.

7. **There are individual rates of growth and development.** Each child is different and the rate at which individual children grow is different. Although the patterns and sequences for growth and development are similar for all children, the rates at which individual children reach developmental stages will be different. Understanding this fact of individual differences in rates of development should cause us to be careful about using and relying on age and stage characteristics to describe or label children. There is a range of ages for any developmental task to take place. This dismisses the notion of the "average child". There is no validity to comparing one child's progress with or against another child. An understanding of the principles of development helps us to plan appropriate activities and stimulating and enriching experiences for children, and provides a basis for understanding how to encourage and support young children's learning.

SKILL 1.5   Knowledge of instructional leadership standard as related to instructional program for students with special needs

1. Given student special needs characteristics in a specific classroom and walk-through observation notes, identify an appropriate instructional adaptation/modification to provide for students with special needs in that classroom.

2. Given an IEP, determine whether or not provisions made are adequate to meet student needs.

The No Child Left Behind Act addresses accountability of school personnel for student achievement with the expectation that every child will demonstrate proficiency in reading, math, and science. For example, all students should know how to read by grade three. The general education curriculum should reflect state learning standards.

At the same time, flexibility and creativity may be required to help a student achieve. For example, teachers in grades K-3 are mandated to teach reading to all students using scientifically based methods with measurable outcomes. Some students (including some with disabilities) will not learn to read successfully unless taught with a phonics approach. Therefore, incorporating phonics into the reading program may be necessary.

Another example: Students are expected to learn mathematics. While some students will quickly grasp the mathematical concept of groupings of tens (and further skills of adding and subtracting large numbers), others will need additional practice. Research shows that many students with disabilities need a hands-on approach. Perhaps those students will need additional instruction and practice using snap-together cubes to grasp the grouping-by tens concept.
This means that students with special needs, such as those with a physical or mental disability or an emotional problem, generally require specific educational planning. Based on the unique needs of the child, such programs are documented in the child's Individualized Education Program (IEP), as dictated by the Individuals with Disabilities Education Act (IDEA).

In Florida, parents of students with disabilities can utilize the McKay Scholarships for Students with Disabilities Program. According to the provisions of s. 1002.39, it allows parents who are dissatisfied with their student's progress to request and receive a McKay Scholarship to then attend a private school. Such provisions typically exist because special education services at the district level may be ineffective or even negligent.

In the best case scenario, the school district and the principal ensure that all students who need special services receive them. Favorable outcomes result when there is effective collaboration between general and special education teachers, and the school works to develop a truly individualized plan. A team consisting of appropriate personnel – such as the special education coordinator, school psychologist, social worker, guidance counselor and/or nurse – along with the principal as needed, should work together with classroom teachers to develop a plan of action for each student. The team also needs to work collaboratively with parents, students, and community personnel in the development of clear, measurable goals and objectives that are aligned with district, state and federal standards.

Creating Effective Individualized Education Plans

Assessment results usually provide basic information contributing to the development of a good Individualized Education Plan (IEP). These results need to be clearly interpreted. When first looking at assessment results, it is most beneficial to identify skill areas closest to grade level expectations. Since the student is demonstrating some skills very close to grade level, the team needs to think of what simple adaptations can be made to the regular curriculum to allow the student to achieve success. There are numerous adaptations and modifications available from many different sources that could be implemented easily to provide success, from providing outline of the information to allowing extra time to complete written assignments.

Once all of the possible adaptations have been made then it is time to look further. Skills that are significantly below grade level require more than simple adaptations. The team needs to consider what strategy can be implemented that will help the student make up the lost ground. It is not enough for the student to simply progress; the goal is to catch the student up to grade level in the shortest amount of time possible and to achieve to the best of his or her ability.

After the plan has been made, it is imperative that the team continually monitor the progress the student is making. Using regular weekly or bi-weekly monitoring, the team can make timely adjustments to the student's educational plan. Further, regular assessment can also be valuable in ensuing that an IEP is adequate.

Students in grades 3 through 11 take the FCAT exams. These tests indicate how much the students have learned and help to indicate how well the school's instructional program is functioning. Other forms of assessment may also be needed, utilizing both school and community resources.

Students with disabilities (in all areas) may demonstrate difficulty in academic skills. A student with mental retardation will need special instruction across all areas of academics while a student with a learning disability may need assistance in only one or two subject areas. Students with disabilities may demonstrate difficulty with independence or self-help skills. A student with a visual impairment may need specific mobility training while a student with a specific learning disability may need a checklist to help in managing materials and assignments.

Teachers and administrators should be aware that although students with disabilities may demonstrate difficulty in similar ways, the causes may be very different. For example, some disabilities are due to specific sensory impairments (hearing or vision), some due to cognitive ability (mental retardation), and some due to neurological impairment (autism or some learning disabilities). The root causes of behavioral or emotional problems may be multi-faceted, including genetic disposition, traumatic stress, biochemical imbalances, current family issues and other factors. The reason for the difficulty should be a consideration when planning the program of special education intervention.

Additionally, educators should be aware that each area of disability has a range of involvement. Some students may have minimal disability and require no services. Others may need only a few accommodations and have 504 Plans. Some may need an IEP that outlines a specific special education program which might be implemented in an inclusion/resource program, self-contained program, or in a residential setting. A student with attention deficit disorder (ADD) may be able to participate in the regular education program with a 504 Plan that outlines a checklist system to keep the student organized and additional communication between school and home. Other students with ADD may need instruction in a smaller group with fewer distractions and would be better served in a resource room.

For more information about assisting students with disabilities related to learning and the Florida Sunshine State Standards, including the Standards for Special Diploma, go to http://www.cpt.fsu.edu/ese/.

SKILL 1.6 Knowledge of instructional leadership standard as related to federal and State law in education and schooling

1. Given a scenario, identify the State requirements for students to participate in interscholastic or extracurricular student activities.

2. Given a scenario, identify employee and student rights and responsibilities under federal statutes.

Federal Statutes

The following federal acts and case law decisions impact education in various ways. Familiarity with these is essential for all school leaders.

Title VI of The Civil Rights Act of 1964 extends protection against discrimination on the basis of race, color, or national origins in any program or activity receiving federal financial assistance (see *Clark v. Huntsville* and *Tyler v. Hot Springs* for more information).

Title VII of The Civil Rights Act of 1964 states that it is unlawful for an employer to discriminate against any individual with respect to compensation, terms, conditions, or privileges of employment because of an individual's race, color, religion, sex, or national origin. Some exceptions are noted in this statute. It does not apply to religious organizations that seek individuals of a particular religion to perform the work of that organization. Where suspect classifications (those classifications having no basis in rationality) represent bona fide occupational qualifications, they are permitted. Classifications based upon merit and seniority are also acceptable under this statute (see *Ansonia BOE v. Philbrook*).

Title IX, The Educational Amendments of 1972 states that no individual shall be excluded from participation in, be denied the benefits of, or be subjected to discrimination under any educational program or activity that receives or benefits from federal assistance on the basis of sex. This statute covers the areas of admission, educational programs and activities, access to course offerings, counseling and the use of appraisal and counseling materials, marital or parental status, and athletics (see *Marshall v. Kirkland*).

Section 504, The Rehabilitation Act of 1973 indicates that "No otherwise handicapped individual... will be excluded from the participation in, be denied the benefits of, or be subjected to discrimination under any program or activity receiving federal financial assistance solely because of his/her handicap (see *School Board of Nassau Co v. Arlin*).

The Age Discrimination Act of 1967 states that it shall be unlawful for an employer to fail or refuse to hire or discharge any individual or otherwise discriminate against any individual with respect to his/her employment because of an individual's age. This statute does allow an employer or employment to consider age as a Bone Fide Occupational Qualification (BFOQ) (see *Geller v. Markham*).

The Family Rights and Privacy Act of 1964 (FERPA) (also known as the Buckley Amendment) states that no funds will be made available under any applicable program to any state or local educational agency, any institution of higher education, any community college, any school, agency offering a preschool program, or any other educational institution, which has a policy of denying parents of students the right to inspect and review any and all official records, files, and data directly related to their children. This includes material incorporated into the student's cumulative folder such as identifying data, academic work completed, level of achievement, attendance records, testing results, health data, family background information, teacher or counselor ratings and observations, and verified reports of serious or recurring behavioral problems. Each educational organization must establish appropriate procedures for granting access requests within a reasonable period of time (not to exceed 45 days).

Under FERPA, parents have an opportunity for a hearing to challenge the record's contents, to ensure the record's accuracy, and to provide corrected or rebuttal information.

- Educational organizations must require written consent of the parent in order to release identifying information to external individuals and organizations. (The state can specify exceptions to this requirement.)

- All persons, agencies, or organizations seeking access to a student's record must sign a written form that must be included in the student file.

- Students who are 18 years-of-age or attending a post-secondary educational institution acquire the right of consent formerly held by the parent. "Directory information" can be released without consent. Such information includes the following: student's name, address, telephone listing, date and place of birth, major field of study, participation in officially recognized activities and sports, weight and height of members of athletic teams, dates of attendance, degrees and awards of attendance, degrees and awards received, and the most recent educational agency or institution attended by the student.

The Individuals with Disabilities Education Act (IDEA) (or The Education of All Handicapped Children Act) requires that states adopt policies that assure all children with disabilities receive a "free and appropriate public education." The statute requires that each student's unique needs are addressed through an Individualized Educational Plan (IEP) and that extensive procedural requirements are put into place. Requirements allow for the withholding of federal financial resources to states that fail to comply with the statute (see *Honig v. Doe* and *Hendrick Hudson Board of Education v. Rowley*).

The Equal Access Act of 1985 states that is will be unlawful for any public secondary school which receives federal financial assistance and which has a limited open forum to deny equal access, or a fair opportunity to or to discriminate against any students who wish to conduct a meeting within that limited open forum on the basis of the religious, political, philosophical, or other content of the speech at the meetings. A limited open forum exists whenever a school grants an opportunity for one or more non-curriculum-related student groups to meet on the school premises during non-instructional time. The criteria for a fair opportunity provide that:

- the meeting is voluntary and student initiated;
- there is no sponsorship by the school, the government, or its agents or employees;
- school agents or employees are present at the meetings only in a non-participatory capacity;
- the meeting does not substantially interfere with the orderly conduct of educational activities within the school;
- non-school persons may not direct, conduct, control, or regularly attend activities of student groups.

This statute does authorize the school and its agents or employees to maintain order and discipline on school premises, to protect the well-being of students and faculty, and to assure that the attendance of the students at the meeting is voluntary (see *Board of Education of Westside Community Schools v. Mergens*).

The federal constitutional amendments cited above all contain powerful clauses, and educators must be careful to ensure that a balance is struck between the individual's constitutional freedoms and the state's compelling interest (e.g., to provide an appropriate educational environment). Court cases that arise out of the federal constitution and/or federal statutes come under the jurisdiction of the federal court system. As noted earlier, when school administrators, teachers and school employees act in their official capacities, they represent the state. This has significant implications for analyzing actions performed in the course of official duties that could breach the constitutional and statutory rights of students, parents, teachers, and staff members.

Florida Law

In addition to the relevant federal statues, every principal and school administrator should be familiar with all Florida statutes related to education. These statutes can be found online at
http://www.leg.state.fl.us/statutes/index.cfm?App_mode=Display_Statute&URL=Ch1002/ch1002.htm.

Major categories of the Florida statutes include the following topics:

- Compulsory education, truancy and home schooling
- Educational choice, special and charter schools
- Health, immunization and medication issues
- Instructional environment guidelines
- Disabilities and special needs students
- Student records
- Disciplinary actions
- Religious issues
- Athletics and other extracurricular activities
- Parental notification, progress reports and due process
- Student-parent handbooks

Some important sections of Florida law are detailed below:

F.S. 228 Public Education: General Provisions sets forth the plan and scope of the state public-education system. It includes definitions of terms and the rules and objectives for specialized schools and programs that operate through the public-education system. The Florida Equity Act that covers issues concerning discrimination against students and employees is spelled out. Other provisions set forth in this statute cover the handling and retention of records, test security, and school food service.

F.S. 229 Functions of State Education Agencies consists of three parts. Part I outlines the key information about the State Board of Education: composition, operating procedures, powers, and its role and responsibility in handling resources. Part II describes the duties and powers of the commissioner, educational management procedures, school improvement processes, powers and duties of the commission, implementation of the school-to-work transition accountability, the career education program, educational partnerships, international education, and the school readiness pilot program.

F.S. 230 District School Systems specifically lays out the scope, authority and operational procedures for district school systems. It provides clear guidelines for the management, control, operation, administration, and supervision of the school district.

F.S. 231 Personnel of School Systems spells out personnel qualifications, selection processes, certification processes, the operation of the Educational Standards Commission and the Educational Practices Commission, leave policies, and contractual and termination procedures.

F.S. 120.50-.73 Administrative Procedures Act specifies the administrative operations of governmental units. The units affected by the statute are defined and their duties and responsibilities regarding meetings, rulemaking, decision-making, and hearings are explained.

F.S. 119.18-.15 Public Records states the penalties for violation of the public records statute and describes the victim protection procedures, the guidelines for accelerated hearings, and the assessment of attorney's fees. The "Open Government Sunset Review Act of 1995" is part of this statute.

F.S. 228.092-A93 Student Records details the rules for the retention of records of students attending nonpublic schools. Definitions, transfer procedures, Department of Education responsibilities and intent are provided. The procedures for compliance with FERPA are included in this statute.

F.S. 231.29-.291 Assessment Procedures and Criteria Personnel Files provides specific criteria and procedures involved in the assessment process. The hearing process is outlined and the criteria and procedures for accessing and maintaining personnel file contents are presented.

F.S. 231 Personnel spells out personnel qualifications, selection processes, certification processes, the operation of the Education Standards Commission and the Education Practices Commission, leave policies, and contractual and termination procedures. It is a key statute because it provides a detailed description of every aspect of the professional personnel area.

Florida Constitution, Article IX, Uniform System of Public Schools focuses specifically on education and contains six sections. The first section states that adequate provision shall be made by law for a uniform system of free public schools. Section 2 describes the makeup of the State Board of Education. Section 3 states the terms of service for appointed board members. Section 4 identifies the scope and duties of school districts. Section 5 states the manner in which, superintendents come to office and the terms of office. Section 6 identifies the use of the income from the state school fund.

F.S. 229.555 Educational Evaluation Procedures identifies student performance standards in the various program categories and grade levels. The standards apply to language arts, mathematics, science, social studies, the arts, health and physical education, foreign language, reading, writing history, government, geography, economics, and computer literacy.

F.S. 232 Compulsory School Attendance covers all areas pertaining to the enrollment and attendance of students in the Florida public school system. Attendance policies, school health and immunization policies, truancy, transfer, graduation, and issues of child welfare are included. For example, the mandatory school attendance ages are from six to sixteen.

F.S. 232.425 Interscholastic and Extracurricular Activities describes the governance of athletic programs in schools, including involvement with Florida High School Athletic Association, Inc. (FHSAA), insurance issues, parental permission, academic and other requirements for participation in athletics.

F.S. 233 Courses of Study sets forth the instructional programs that are to be offered, the guidelines for their implementation, and the duties of school personnel in providing the instructional program.

F.S. 235 Educational Facilities provides inclusive information regarding the acquisition and maintenance of physical facilities, the role of the Department of Education and the local boards, funding information, building code guidelines, and contract information. This statute is known as the 'Educational Facilities Act'

F.S. 236 Finance and Taxation details the finance and taxation issues for all aspects of the Florida educational system. The specifics of the Florida Education Finance Program (FEFP) are spelled out. Fund allocation and distribution and taxation requirements are also detailed.

SKILL 1.7   **Knowledge of managing the learning environment standard as related to tort and contract liability in the operation of Florida public schools**

> 1. Given a scenario, identify legal standards of negligent tort liability applicable to school employees and districts.
>
> 2. Given a scenario, identify legal standards of intentional tort liability applicable to school employees and districts.
>
> 3. Given a scenario, identify legal standards that are applicable to site administrators in negotiating contracts for goods and services.

Negligence

Negligence constitutes the failure to exercise ordinary prudence and foresight that results in injury to another person, specifically, another person to whom some duty is owed. When determining negligence, the facts must be analyzed for the following elements: (1) a legal duty to conform to a standard of conduct for the protection of others, (2) a failure to exercise an appropriate standard of care, (3) a causal connection (proximate cause) between the conduct and the resultant injury, and (4) actual loss or damage as a result of the neglect. An actionable case for negligence requires a positive response to each of the elements. A defense can be made if the elements were not present. Other defenses include contributory negligent and assumption of risk, see *Rupp v. Bryant, Collins v. SB of Broward,* and *Donohue v. Copiague Free Union SD.*

This has implications for schools and educators because of the nature of the relationship between the educator and the student. The level of that relationship rises to *In loco parentis,* by its very nature this implies a heightened duty of care. It is crucial that all school administrators have a clear understanding of this duty and the ways in which schools and school personnel may be held liable.

Intentional torts

A tort is a civil wrong. This means that one person can bring a lawsuit against another person or entity (such as a school district). Assault and battery are the most common intentional torts that educators experience. Battery is the unpermitted and unprivileged contact with another person. Actual harm is not necessary. Assault is the placing of someone in apprehension of immediate harm; physical contact is not required (LaMorte, 1996, p.389). (See *Neff v. Ploetz* and *Vinson v. Linn-Mar Community SD* for more information.)

Statutory liability

Federal Title 42, Section 1983 of the Civil Rights Act of 1871 (statutory liability) provides for liability if a "person" operating under the color of the state violates another person's "rights, privileges, or immunities secured by the Constitution, and laws...." The federal courts have addressed the liability of school officials and school districts under this federal statute (42 U.S.C. s 1983) and have determined the extent of resultant damages (see *Wood v. Strickland, Carey v. Piphus,* and *Monell v. Dept. of Social Services).*

F.S. 231.17 Official Statements of Eligibility and Certificates describes the application process for statements of eligibility, the temporary certificate, and the professional certificate. Exceptions for the issuance of certificates, the demonstration of professional competence, examination requirements, and certificate denial are also addressed.

F.S. 232.50 Child Abuse and Neglect Policy outlines the requirements for all schools regarding the child abuse and neglect policy. Notice must be posted that all employees or agents of the district school board have an affirmative duty to report all actual or suspected cases of child abuse or neglect. It also stipulates that the superintendent or a designee will act as a liaison to the Department of Health and Rehabilitative Services and the child protection team.

F.S. 236.0811 Educational Training provides for the development and maintenance of an educational training program in all districts. Classroom teachers and guidance counselors, are required to participate in in-service training for child abuse and neglect prevention, alcohol and substance abuse prevention education, and multicultural sensitivity education.

F.S. 415.501, .5015, 504, .509, .513 Protection from Abuse, Neglect, and Exploitation addresses the guidelines for educators regarding the prevention of abuse and neglect of children; it mandates the reporting of child abuse or neglect by any person and specifically by a school teacher or official. The protective services for abused and neglected children are also outlined.

F.S. 237 Financial Accounts and Expenditures for Public Schools describes guidelines for uniform record keeping and the handling of accounts. It sets forth the procedures for establishing budgets, levying taxes, incurring indebtedness, the obligation to eliminate emergency conditions, handling school funds, and auditing procedures.

SKILL 1.8   Knowledge of managing the learning environment standard as related to funding of Florida schools

> 1. Given an FTE report, identify, interpret, and apply each formula factor used in computing the Florida Education Finance Program allocation.

> 2. Given a school budget, identify funding categories available to a school beyond the Florida Education Finance Program allocation.

> 3. Given a school budget, identify or apply the processes of planning, developing, implementing, and evaluating a budget.

Background Information on School Funding

Every state has its own funding formula to allocate general distribution of funds to local school districts. This formula can be complex because of the efforts of state legislatures to provide uniformity of support. While some public school programs are fully funded by the state, others may rely on flat grants, foundation programs, or a variety of tax-base-equalization programs.

Florida uses the foundation program where the state defines the level of funding for basic education. The state and the school district in partnership provide the funds required for the educational programs. Unlike the flat grant model, where the state alone provides per pupil funding, in the foundation program both the state and the districts act in partnership to determine the required level of local participation.

Major sources of support for public education come from revenues generated from taxes. Property tax at the local level, sales tax at the state level, and income tax at the federal level constitute primary sources of revenues for education. Legal provisions for funding public education come from the constitution. The lack of clear language and specificity of public school funding results in school funding litigations, which historically have led to major school finance reforms. Legislative enactment, regulations, decrees, or rulings are outgrowths of school finance litigations. These reforms originated from the basic values and beliefs of the citizens and leaders at the national, state, and local levels.

Early litigation of school finance alleged that the methods of financing education at the state level violated the equal protection for certain classes of people under the constitution. Allegations were also made that the reliance on local revenues to support a large portion of the total public school budget was unfair because of the disparity in property tax wealth among the school systems. There are four landmark court cases that built on each other to produce significant school financing reform.

In *McInnis v. Shapiro -1969*, the plaintiffs contended that the Illinois method of financing public education was inequitable because it permitted a wide variation in expenditures per student. This method of financing did not apportion funds according to the educational need of students. The court rejected the plaintiff's contention and stated that the controversy was unjustifiable because it lacked judicially manageable standards. The court further stated that equal expenditures per student were inappropriate as a standard. The court was ill-prepared to provide advice on an plan to equitably finance public schools because it lacked specific understanding of cost-effectiveness.

Serrano v. Priest -1971 emerged after the precedence set by the previous case. In this situation, the plaintiffs contended that the California system of school finance allowed substantial disparities between the various districts in the amount of revenues available for education. They further contended that this method denied equal protection of the laws under the constitution of the United States and the constitution of California and that this system required some parents to pay taxes at a higher rate than taxpayers in many other districts in order to provide the same or lesser educational opportunities for their children. In this landmark decision, the court contended that education is a constitutionally protected fundamental interest and that wealth was a suspect classification. The court established the Standard of Fiscal Neutrality as a measurement to determine whether or not a school finance program was constitutional. Under this standard, the quality of the child's education could not be based on the wealth of the local school district, but on the wealth of the state as a whole.

In *Rose v. The Council of Better Education -1989*, the plaintiffs contended that the system of financing schools by the Kentucky General Assembly was inadequate because it placed too much emphasis on local school board resources which result in inadequacies and inequalities throughout the state. This resulted in an inefficient system of common school education, which violated the state constitution. The court ruled in favor of the plaintiffs and appointed a committee to review relevant data, provide additional analysis, consult with financial experts, and propose remedies to correct the deficiencies in the common school financing system.

Another landmark case in school finance is *San Antonio Independent School District v. Rodriguez - 1973*. The plaintiffs contended that the dual system of public school financing in Texas violated the equal protection clause of the Constitution of the United States and Texas. The initial ruling in 1971 held the state financing system of Texas unconstitutional under the equal Protection clause of the Fourteen Amendments. An appeal of this decision reversed the ruling because of unanswered questions concerning the constitution of Texas. But in the second ruling, the court found substantial disparities among the districts' school expenditures, which were largely attributed to the differences in the amounts of the dollars collected through property taxes. The court concluded that the dual system of public school finance in Texas indeed violated the equal protection clause.

Overall, the courts have found that education is both a public and a private good because it enhances the individual as it brings important benefits to society. At an individual level, education provides the ability to enjoy a higher standard of living by earning more money and living a better quality of life. Society benefits because the individual makes a contribution to the economy. Education supports the production of a skilled workforce for the efficient functioning of a society that is stimulated by economic growth and development.

Educational Budgeting

A main educational function of the state governor is to formulate budgetary recommendations for the legislature. In Florida, the governor depends on his or her appointed advisors and the elected Commissioner of Education as the main support in policy discussions and recommendations. While the governor has many powers, the position holds some limitations in personnel decisions. All Commissioners, the Secretary of State, and the Comptroller make up the Cabinet. The Cabinet approves State Board Rules. The Governor and each member of the Cabinet has only one vote. In Florida, the governor does not appoint the Commissioner of Education; the citizens do so through the electoral process. The governor also has veto power which serves to discourage the state legislators from enacting laws considered detrimental to education.

The process of financing schools is a yearly one. It is continuously reviewed to identify strengths and weaknesses so that meaningful and deliberate planning can take place to meet the needs of students. School administration has evolved into an inclusive and cooperative endeavor. The structure endorses a participatory model to include not only administrators and teachers, but also parents, business partners, and other interested citizens in the community.

Therefore, the planning process must be ongoing and systematic to allow time for the development of unity of purpose, methodology, and desirable outcome. At both the district and school-building levels, planning must be continuous and methodologies and applications may overlap. Planning follows a very logical sequence to accomplish organizational goals. It begins with setting goals, which includes articulating the mission of the organization and clarifying specific goals to be attained. It also means setting long and short-term plans of action that including general projections and details to carry out the actions deemed necessary. The evaluation process provides feedback for improvement and the process is repeated.

School financial management requires specific budgetary techniques for appropriate fiscal accountability. There are three commonly used techniques:

Incremental budgeting begins with the budget for the current term and examines each line item against expected revenues. By addressing expenditures by items and categories, there is a failure to observe the impact of the budget as a whole on the goals of the organization and the needs of children. It also hinders creativity and change.

Zero-based budgeting is another planning technique that produces similar outcomes as the incremental budgeting approach. It focuses on the current budgetary cycle and begins with zero dollars in all accounts to then justify the continuation of a program, activities, or expenditure.

In contrast, the *Planning, Programming, Budgetary, and Evaluation System* (PPBES) integrates long-range planning, the resources provided through funded sources are used to achieve institutional goals on the basis of annual fund allocations (Drake and Roe, 1994). This process requires the periodic collection and analysis of data to inform the decisions to be made about programs and to project needs to be met. The evaluation component that is built into the process not only assesses the effectiveness of the goal, but it also measures the level of goal attainment over specific periods of time.

Funding Education in Florida

Early in the history of our nation, education became a local and state responsibility. The responsibility is granted to the legislature of each state through plenary power, which enables the enactment of laws it considers appropriate and desirable for education. Under this premise, the Florida legislature enacted the FEFP (Florida Education Finance Program) in 1973 to equalize the educational opportunities for every child in the state. Florida Statute section 236.012 defines its purpose as follows:

> "To guarantee to each child in the state of Florida public educational system the availability of programs and services appropriate to his educational needs which are substantially equal to those available to any similar student notwithstanding geographic differences and varying local economic factors."

Until the early 1970s, previous formulas for public school funding were generally based on a school system's wealth, which took a ratio of school taxable property and allocated it equally to each child in the system. This resulted in either wealthy school systems or poor school systems. The higher the taxable property, the wealthier the school system became and conversely, the lower the taxable property, the poorer the school system became. To equalize the available resources to all children in Florida, the FEFP recognizes in its formula, the following components:

- varying program cost factors to account for district cost differentials

- differences in per student cost for equivalent educational programs due to scarcity and dispersion of student population

- varying local property tax bases

Each year the Florida Legislature determines the minimum efforts of taxation on district property tax roils, as well as the program cost factors, to determine the base funding for each student. For participation in the state allocation of funds, each school board must levy the millage set for its required local efforts. Each district's share is determined by certification of the property tax valuations by the Department of Revenue and the Commissioner of Education. Assessment ratios are used to equalize the effects of the FEFP on differing levels of property appraisals in each county. Millage rates are also adjusted to ensure that the required local rates do not exceed 90% of the district total FEFP entitlement. Ultimately, the state's appropriation is used to fund the difference between the amount raised for each student through the required local millage, times the property tax roll, plus the established base student allocation.

Since a key feature of the FEFP is based upon student participation in a particular educational program, the varying program cost factors set by the legislature are essential to the formula when determining base funding. To better understand the formula, here are definitions to key terms:

   FTE: A full-time equivalent student

   Weighted FTE: An FTE multiplied by a program cost factor

   Base student allocation: a fixed amount determined each year by the legislature

   District cost differential: The Commissioner of Education annually averages each district's Florida Price Level Index for the last three years and applies the prices of salary on district operating cost to reduce its impact on the district.

The base student funding is calculated by multiplying the full-time equivalent student (FTE) by the program cost factor, which gives the weighted FTE. The weighted FTE is then multiplied by the base student allocation and the district cost differential to produce the base student funding as seen below.

FTE x program cost factor = weighted FTE

Weighted FTE x base student allocation x district cost differential = BASE STUDENT FUNDING

Other FEFP factors authorized by the Legislature are added to adjust and finalize the distribution of funds to each school district. These adjustments include declining enrollment supplements, sparsity supplements, safe school allocations, remediation reduction incentives, discretionary tax equalizations, and hold-harmless and disparity-compression adjustments.

Apart from the FEFP formula, each district may levy discretionary millage, which is a level of additional discretionary taxes. This amount is authorized by the legislature with a proportion of it equalized with dollars from the state for categorical funds including instructional materials, student transportation, instructional technology, and food services. Another categorical fund outside the FEFP formula is preschool funding which comes from lottery proceeds. All of these considerations make the FEFP a model program for the equalization of educational opportunities for all children in the state of Florida. To participate in the FEFP, every district must provide annual evidence of its efforts to maintain an adequate school program throughout the district and must meet at least the following requirements:

1. Maintain adequate and accurate records including a system of internal accounts for individual schools, and file with the Department of Education correct and proper forms, on or before the date due, each annual or periodic report which is required by state Board of Education Rules.

2. Operate all schools for a term of 180 actual teaching days or the equivalent on an hourly basis. Upon written application, the State Board may prescribe procedures for altering this requirement.

3. Provide written contracts for all instructional personnel and require not less than 196 days of service for all members of the instructional staff.

4. Expend funds for salaries in accordance with a salary schedule or schedules adopted by the School Board in accordance with the provisions of the laws and rules of the State Board.

5. Observe all requirements of the State Board relating to the preparation, adoption, and execution of budgets for the district school system.

6. Levy the required local effort millage rate on the taxable value for school purposes of the district. In addition, collect fees for adult education courses.

7. Maintain an ongoing systematic evaluation of the educational program needs of the district and develop a comprehensive annual and long-term plan.

Sources of Funding

There are three major sources of school funding for the school districts in the State of Florida. Approximately 50% of the financial support comes from state sources, 42% from local sources, and 7% from the federal government. The state support for education comes from the state's general revenue funds (mainly from taxes), state school trust fund, Florida Lottery, and other funds that are appropriated to meet the needs of categorical programs and specific allocations. Other state funds come from proceeds from licensing of motor vehicles, gross utility taxes (which support capital outlay), racing commission funds, and other minor sources such as mobile home licensing.

Local support for education originates when the school boards levy the millage required for the local tax effort, which is determined by the state statutory process. The greatest source of funds is "Ad valorem" taxes (taxes levied on real estate or personal property). Additionally, voters may approve other tax levies such as maintenance bonds and operation-user fees. Federal funds to support education are administered by the Board of Education. These funds are provided to support federal mandates such as the National School Lunch Act, the Americans with Disabilities Act, and others.

Proceeds from the lottery are used to finance both district discretionary lottery funds and preschool projects. Education's share of the revenue is 38% which goes into the Educational Enhancement Trust Fund and is distributed at a rate of 70% for public schools, 15% for community colleges, and 15% for universities.

Future resources for education are planned through student enrollment forecasts. This is a joint effort between the Florida Department of Education, the Governor's Office, the Legislature, and the school districts. The forecast input is essential for the FEFP appropriation, primarily because it is used to compute district allocations and make actual payments until the student membership can be determined through certified surveys. This process is defined by Florida Statute section 216.136(4).

Local Budgeting and Accounting

From the appropriated funds, the district builds its budget. At this point, the budget becomes an important device for translating the educational plan into a financial plan. The budget is, in effect, the translation of prioritized educational needs into a financial plan. Ideally, the budget is interpreted for the public in such a way that, upon adoption, it expresses the kind of educational program the community is willing to support financially and morally for a one-year period.

The budget must be managed through a financial system of accounting. In the state of Florida this system is predetermined for the school districts and is managed through the Financial and Program Cost Accounting and Reporting for Florida Schools, also known as The Red Book. It deals only with revenues and expenditures. Revenues are categorized by sources. Sources of revenues can be federal, state, or local. Expenditures on the other hand, are categorized by dimensions, which include funds or account groups, objects, functions, facilities, projects, and reporting.

The funds or account groups are accounting entities with a self-balancing set of accounts that supports specific school activities to attain specific objectives. Therefore, funds or accounts can only be used for specified purposes. There are eight major funds or account groups: General Funds, Debt Services Funds, Capital Project Funds, Special Revenues Funds, Enterprise Funds, Internal Services Funds, Trust and Agency Funds, General Fixed Assets, and General-Long-Term Debt. Of all the funds, the General Fund is perhaps the most important to schools and school districts because it deals with the day-to-day operations of school.

The budget of the district is generally comprised of the account groups or funds established by the Red Book. Since many of the accounts held by the district are not appropriate to the school operation, the school account differs from that of the district. For example, most districts are responsible for salaries and benefits, utilities and services, therefore, these accounts are not included in the school-based budget.

A predetermined local formula allows expenditures from the General Fund to be used for the day-to-day operations of schools. Additionally, the school may have an Activity account and a School Internal account. The Activity account is derived from class fees, athletic contests and events, plays, yearly photos, and other special programs. While the proceeds belong to the school, they must be used for students' learning benefits such as award ribbons, trophies, and the like. These proceeds must be identified and accounted for in the same manner as any other funds of the school.

The School Internal account usually originates from vending machine sales in the teacher's lounge and from related faculty activities and must be used to benefit faculty and staff. Again, these proceeds must be identified and accounted for in the same manner as any other funds or accounts of the school.

For more information about FTE go to the Miami Dade County Public Schools website:
http://attendanceservices.dadeschools.net/fte.asp. It includes a helpful PowerPoint presentation with samples from an actual FTE report entitled 2007-2008 Elementary Training FTE Self-Review PowerPoint Presentation

SKILL 1.9   Knowledge of managing the learning environment standard as related to financial accounting and auditing

1. Given an FTE audit report (e.g., State, district, or school), identify categories that are out of compliance with Florida Statutes (e.g., attendance records, teacher certification, vocational time cards, ESE and ESOL student records).

2. Given a school internal funds audit report, identify violations of the State Board of Education policies and procedures for the administration and accounting of internal funds (e.g., fund-raisers, purchases, monthly financial reports, bonding of the treasurer).

Methods for cost accounting and reporting are contained in the Florida Department of Education's publication "Financial and Program Cost Accounting for Florida Schools" (also known as The Red Book). The content of this publication also reflects the requirements of Rule 6A-1.001 of Florida's Administrative Code and Sections 237.01 and 237.02 of Florida's Statutes.

To provide appropriate fiscal management for the economic and efficient operation of the school, school administrators must be knowledgeable of basic accounting principles. Accounting is the process used by administrators to record, present, summarize, and interpret accurate records of the financial data collected by the school through its daily operation. These basic accounting principles lead practicing administrators to be cognizant of revenues and expenditures for the pre-established accounts of the school.

General principles of school cost-accounting use an accrual rather than a cash basis accounting system. Using the accrual basis of accounting, financial transactions of the school must be recorded as revenues or expenditures at the time the transaction occurs. There should never be cash exchanged for goods or services. In this process, revenues earned at the time of the transaction become assets, and expenditures become liabilities, regardless of when the cash receipt or reimbursement occurs. Assets are inventory, investments, accounts receivable, building and fixed equipment, furniture, motor vehicles, etc. while liabilities are salaries, benefits, accounts payable, construction contracts, etc. Unlike private enterprises for profit where there is owners' equity, schools are owned by the taxpayers. Therefore, balances are known as fund equity, which include reserves, retained earnings, and contributed capital.

Schools must adhere to specific rules governing their internal funds as prescribed by State Board Rules. All school organizations must be accountable for receipts and expenditures of funds obtained from the public. Additionally, sound business practices are expected for all financial transactions of the school. For example, in an effort to raise money to benefit programs of the school, fund-raising activities should not conflict with the programs administered by the school board.

All purchases from internal funds must be authorized by the principal or designee and require the district's pre-approved, serially numbered receipt forms to record any cash received and to record the accounting transaction. Each school must have a bank checking account and each monthly statement must be reconciled as soon as it is received. Each account should have two authorized check signers, one being the principal. The principal should never pre-sign checks, under any circumstances. Monthly written financial reports must be made for the purpose of school decision-making, and annual reports must be made for the district's annual financial statement.

The sponsors of classes, clubs, or departmental student activities (such as athletic events, music groups, math club, etc.) are responsible for providing the financial documents and records to the principal or designee. The collection received must be deposited in the school internal fund in the respective classified account. All disbursements by the club or organization must be made by check from internal funds. A financial report must then be filed with the principal's office at the close of each fundraising activity.

Records and documents of school financial transactions used for its internal fund and accounts must be examined periodically through the auditing process. Whether internal or external, audits provide an adequate safeguard to preserve the property of the public school system. This process secures evidence of propriety of completed transactions; it determines whether all transactions have been accurately recorded in the appropriate accounts, and whether the statements have been drawn from the accounts.

Good auditing reviews are the result of excellent accounting practices. Drake and Roe (1994) define the accounting cycle as continuous and inclusive of documenting, analyzing, recording, and summarizing financial information. *Documenting* involves recording all financial transactions including the authority or initiator of the transaction, ensuring that the debt incurred is within the limit of allotment, that every financial transaction is identified with a unit or fund, and that each fund is restrictive and limited in use. The process of *analyzing* requires that each transaction is analyzed and classified into debits or credits, and that each debit or credit is referenced to a specific account under the affected fund. It also requires that a clear understanding is held of how a debit or a credit affects the balance in an account, and that budgetary accounts are restricted in purpose and amount of expenditure. The *recording* and *summarizing* processes require that all transactions of a fund or account be recorded and that summaries be provided to allow comparisons and analyses of the changes that are taking place within the budget.

The school operation must be very conscious of its fiscal control to avoid over-expenditure and maintain a positive balance in each of its accounts. Therefore, an encumbrance system must be used to charge each purchase order, contract or salary to an appropriation. Once paid, these transactions are canceled and they cease to be an encumbrance as soon as the liability is recorded.

SKILL 1.10 Knowledge of managing the learning environment standard as related to facilities management

1. Given a State request for a school room utilization update, identify the requirements of the Florida Inventory of School Houses as specified in Florida Statutes (e.g., space requirements for ESE, vocational courses, class size reduction).

2. Given a school building's security plan, determine compliance with Florida Statutes and State Board of Education rules.

Florida Statutes Governing Facilities Management

The statutes that follow detail the management of educational facilities.

1013.04 *School district educational facilities plan performance and productivity standards; development; measurement; application.*

(1) The Office of Educational Facilities and SMART Schools Clearinghouse shall develop and adopt measures for evaluating the performance and productivity of school district educational facilities plans. The measures may be both quantitative and qualitative and must, to the maximum extent practical, assess those factors that are within the districts' control. The measures must, at a minimum, assess performance in the following areas:

(a) Frugal production of high-quality projects.
(b) Efficient finance and administration.
(c) Optimal school and classroom size and utilization rate.
(d) Safety.
(e) Core facility space needs and cost-effective capacity improvements that consider demographic projections.
(f) Level of district local effort.

(2) The office shall establish annual performance objectives and standards that can be used to evaluate district performance and productivity.

(3) The office shall conduct ongoing evaluations of district educational facilities program performance and productivity, using the measures adopted under this section.

1013.05 *Office of Educational Facilities and SMART (Soundly Made, Accountable, Reasonable, and Thrifty) Schools Clearinghouse.*

(1) The SMART Schools Clearinghouse is established to assist school districts that seek to access School Infrastructure Thrift (SIT) Program awards pursuant to ss. 1013.42 and 1013.72 or effort index grants pursuant to s. 1013.73. The office must use expedited procedures in providing such assistance.

> *(2) The office shall prioritize school district SIT Program awards based on a review of the district facilities work programs and proposed construction projects.*

1013.10 *Use of buildings and grounds.*

The board may permit the use of educational facilities and grounds for any legal assembly or for community use centers or may permit the same to be used as voting places in any primary, regular, or special election.

For more information, go to the section of the Florida Code that governs school facilities at
http://www.leg.state.fl.us/Statutes/index.cfm?App_mode=Display_Statute&URL=Ch1013/titl1013.htm&StatuteYear=2008&Title=%2D%3E2008%2D%3EChapter%201013.

The SMART Schools Act

In a special session in 1997, the Florida legislature passed a school construction program called "The SMART Schools Act." Under the act, the state agreed to spend a total of $2.7 billion in state bonding over five years to build and repair schools. The state will borrow money by issuing in school construction bonds over 30 years and will pay back the bonds using money from the state lottery formerly earmarked for education operating funds. To make up for the annual shortfall from the lottery, the state increased general fund spending for education by a corresponding amount.

In addition, as part of the plan, the legislature allocated $600 million for an Effort Index Grant Fund, which will distribute money according to a formula to districts that have unmet school construction needs after meeting a specified level of local effort. The law also provides incentives to encourage districts to be frugal in building schools using state specifications or to employ innovative practices to reduce the cost of building and maintaining school facilities. Finally, $31.5 million was earmarked for classroom supplies to support student learning in the form of a $250 grant to each classroom teacher in the state.

The law establishes a five-year facilities planning process at the school district level, creates a special clearinghouse to review district work programs, administer state responsibilities for school construction, and provide technical assistance; and establishes local school construction advisory councils to help districts that are unable to meet the needs identified in their five-year plans.

The law limits construction costs on a per-student basis to $11,600 for elementary schools; $13,300 for middle schools; and $17,600 for high schools. These amounts, which are set in 1997 dollars, must be adjusted annually by the increase in the Consumer Price Index to allow for changes in construction costs.

The education commissioner may waive certain state requirements relating to surveys, need projections, and cost ceilings. Movable classrooms that meet certain standards may be counted as permanent classroom space. The Education Department must establish guidelines for use of such classrooms based on student enrollment and the capacity of a district's core space. Finally, the law makes it clear that districts can use revenue from the local school tax for maintenance projects.

School Safety and Security

School leaders are charged with providing students a safe, efficient, comfortable school building. While school districts and funding levels play significant parts in the aesthetics of a school building, basic safety and comfort issues are the responsibility of a school's administrative team. Various strategies can be put into place in order to promote satisfactory levels of building safety and efficiency.

A principal—or designee, such as an assistant principal—should be responsible on a <u>daily</u> basis to make rounds on a campus in order to verify a checklist of items. Such items might include visiting restrooms to ensure that everything is working properly and that students have clean, well operating facilities to use. A checklist might also include examining blacktop in the athletic areas to ensure that students would be safe running or playing on outside surfaces.

The school building must be in an operable condition. Any broken item that could pose a safety risk should be dealt with. Furniture that gets in the way of door areas must be moved. All doors should be completely operable and able to be opened quickly in an emergency. Windows should be able to be opened. Air conditioners, heaters, gas systems, plumbing, and electricity should all be able to be turned off easily and quickly if the need arises. This last point is a particular concern for many schools. If a specific custodian knows how to complete all those procedures, other individuals also need to learn how to operate such equipment in the case of that custodian's absence.

The principal must also advocate for building comforts at the district and community level. For example, while not all districts can afford air conditioning, principals can make needs clear to local taxpayers (with superintendent approval). While many school districts pay for utilities, school building leaders can examine utility usage for efficiency. Problems may be noted in terms of air drafts, heating duct problems, and plumbing.

Finally, school leaders should report problems that pose safety or privacy concerns to the district buildings manager. For example, if a bathroom stall door does not work properly, either a building level custodian must fix it, or if the building level resources are not available, a district support staff member should fix it. The same is true for issues of safety, such as a ceiling panel that is about to fall off in a classroom.

For information on assessing your school's risk during a crisis event see the website of the National Clearinghouse for Educational Facilities: http://www.ncef.org/pubs/mitigating_hazards.pdf.

SKILL 1.11   Knowledge of managing the learning environment standard as related to student services

1. Given a school guidance report, determine compliance with Florida Statutes.

2. Given a faculty handbook, identify the duties of school administrators governing student discipline and school safety per Florida Statutes (e.g., zero tolerance, discipline of exceptional students, emergency management plan, Student Code of Conduct).

3. Given a parent request to administer medication, identify the guidelines in Florida Statutes regulating the administration of prescribed medications to students by public school employees.

School Guidance Services

In 2004, the Florida Legislature signed into law House Bill 769 that amended several laws related to career and technical education. This was in response to goals to ensure that every Florida high school graduate is prepared to be successful in postsecondary education and the workplace. To successfully transition from middle school to high school and on to postsecondary education or the world of work, all students within the system must be supported by rigorous and relevant curriculum.

This bill also created Section 1006.025, Florida Statutes (Guidance Services) that requires district school boards to submit a guidance report to the Commissioner of Education by June 30 of each year. The guidance report must include the following:

- Examination of student access to guidance counselors
- Degree to which a district has adopted or implemented a guidance model program
- Evaluation of the information and training available to guidance counselors and career specialists to advise students on areas of critical need, labor market trends and technical training requirements
- Progress toward incorporation of best practices for advisement as identified by the department
- Consideration of alternative guidance systems or ideas, including, but not limited to, a teacher-advisor model, mentoring, partnerships with the business community, web-based delivery, and parental involvement
- Actions taken to provide information to students for the school-to-work transition
- A guidance plan for the district.

School Discipline

Principals are ultimately responsible for all school disciplinary measures. They must work with other school personnel to ensure that student behavior is monitored and managed in order to provide a safe and functional environment that encourages learning. In Florida, there exists a zero tolerance policy for crime, substance abuse and victimization of students. This policy is detailed in Florida statute 1006.12 (available at http://www.fldoe.org/safeschools/zero.asp).

A proactive approach can be very useful in preventing crime and victimization, and needs to be part of the overall plan for managing student discipline. One element of a proactive approach is establishing clear policies including but not limited to the following:

1. Weapons on school grounds
2. Homicidal and/or suicidal intent
3. Use of drugs and alcohol
4. Self-harm
5. Sexual harassment
6. Bullying
7. Violent threats

However, policies are not enough. Various prevention efforts can be effective in eclipsing student misbehavior, encouraging positive student interactions, and decreasing crime, violence and victimization in the school setting. Programs on bullying, sexual harassment and substance abuse need to be a regular part of the school curriculum.

Further, preventing violence and victimization is fundamentally related to resolving conflicts in interpersonal relations. Violence prevention efforts must be accompanied by programs of constructive conflict resolution so students can learn methods of positive interactions with others. Not only do these programs help create a safe environment in the schools, but they also teach students the skills to resolve future conflicts in their careers, family, and community as adults.

The National Youth Violence Prevention Resource Center offers resources on bullying and violence prevention and addresses substance abuse and other safety issues for teens at **www.safeyouth.org/scripts/topics/school.asp**. Other bullying and violence prevention resources are available at www.cdc.gov/ncipc/dvp/YVP/YVP-data.htm, mentalhealth.samhsa.gov/15plus/aboutbullying.asp, **and** stopbullyingnow.hrsa.gov/index.asp.

Emergency Response Planning

The best method of keeping students and staff safe is careful planning. It is crucial that all school community members are familiar with all emergency response plans. To ensure student and personnel safety, various levels of planning must be implemented. Plans must exist for ensuring safety in a variety of situations. Local natural disasters must be accounted for, as should plans for ensuring safety when, for example, the police are searching for a loose criminal in the surrounding neighborhood. Many schools may even have to consider safety plans for local terrorist attacks, particularly if the school is located near a busy or popular area.

Plans should include methods for getting students in a safe area, as well as communication among staff members and between administrative personnel and parents or media. Strategies for dealing with crisis reactions also need to be in place and are addressed in the next section (Crisis Management and Intervention Planning).

In planning for evacuation, routes should be drawn so that each hallway has the least amount of students walking through it possible, with no student having to walk too far. The quickest route out of a building may clog a hallway, thereby making the route much slower. However, it would also be unwise to have a whole classroom full of students walk far around a particular hallway and still be in a potentially dangerous location. Often, fire departments or safety consultants can assist in designing solid, quality evaluation plans.

A lock-down plan is the opposite of an evacuation plan, and consists of various rules and procedures for getting or keeping all students in a secure location, such as a classroom. Often communication suffers during a lock-down, so many schools now insist that school personnel look at their email accounts as soon as a lock-down occurs, to give the administration an efficient way to communicate to many people quickly.

The next level of ensuring safety concerns communicating those plans to staff, parents, students, and the district. Fire drills, for example, do not command great attention from most staff and students, typically because most people have never experienced a fire in a large institution. However, good administrators find creative ways to ensure that all staff members and students know the procedures. Clear directions should be posted all over campus for clarification when events occur. Directions and procedures should be mailed home to parents annually, as well.

When disasters or safety concerns occur, school leaders must behave like flight attendants: calm and collected, but decisive and clear. People in the school community will behave in a positive, productive manner during an emergency when the leadership gives clear instructions, is open and honest, and maintains a sense of peace while acting decisively.

After events that compromise safety, school leaders must do a few things. First, they must report all factors immediately to district administrators, local police, parents, students, and sometimes media. Second, they must sit down with other staff members and discuss the performance of the school community in responding to the crisis. From that discussion, the team can then make informed modifications to the plans. New plans, of course, must then be communicated to all stakeholders.

Crisis Management and Intervention Planning

Crisis and emergency situations such as those described above are events beyond the realm of every day life. They always involve some degree of surprise, shock, loss and emotion. The unpredictability of crises, the experience of loss that invariably accompanies such situations and the strong feelings that are evoked all make crisis and emergency events particularly potent and challenging for everyone involved. It falls on the shoulders of the building principal, in many cases, to manage the response to such traumatic situations.

Pre-planning and training in basic crisis management skills can be extremely helpful in responding effectively. Although the events themselves may be unpredictable, there is a body of information about how people react to crisis and what responders can do to ameliorate and manage the aftermath of crisis. This is important in school settings, where there are a large number of people congregated in one place and contagion is a concern. Anxiety and misinformation can spread like wildfire, exacerbating the short and long term effects of traumatic events.

Creating and training a crisis response team can be quite beneficial. Comprehensive crisis management training as well as ongoing refresher courses are necessary for a team to function well. A clearly designated leader (generally not the building principal who has enough to do in a crisis) should be chosen to head the team.

In addition to a crisis team, schools need to have clearly defined crisis response plans. They should include as much detail as possible, with specific recommendations for different situations as needed (as noted above regarding evacuation and lock-down), although a general plan is applicable in many circumstances. The plan should incorporate the following:

- delineate the school's goals in crisis situations (such as maintaining as normal a school day as possible, or providing timely information),
- identify key players on the crisis response team,
- specify how communication will be handled,
- describe what interventions will be used with students,
- note how interactions and referrals to outside agencies will be managed,
- detail what follow-up is needed.

Further, it helps to have handouts about traumatic stress reactions, sample letters to parents and guardians, press releases (when appropriate) and other useful documents ready prior to any event.

Prescription Medications Policy

The following statute addresses the administration of medication by school personnel to students. This is an example of the range of issues that principals face in attending to student needs on a day-to-day basis.

Florida Statute 232.46   *Administration of medication by school district personnel.*

Each district school board shall adopt policies and procedures governing the administration of prescription medication by school district personnel. The policies and procedures shall include, but not be limited to, the following provisions:

1. For each prescribed medication, the student's parent or guardian shall provide to the school principal a written statement which shall grant to the principal or the principal's designee permission to assist in the administration of such medication and which shall explain the necessity for such medication to be provided during the school day, including any occasion when the student is away from school property on official school business. The school principal or the principal's trained designee shall assist the student in the administration of such medication.

2. Each prescribed medication to be administered by school district personnel shall be received, counted, and stored in its original container. When the medication is not in use, it shall be stored in its original container in a secure fashion under lock and key in a location designated by the principal.

(2) There shall be no liability for civil damages as a result of the administration of such medication when the person administering such medication acts as an ordinarily reasonably prudent person would have acted under the same or similar circumstances.

SKILL 1.12 Knowledge of managing the learning environment standard as related to student and parental rights

> 1. Given the student-parent handbook, determine compliance with Florida Statutes governing parents' rights and responsibilities and/or students' rights and privacy to access student educational records (e.g., deny, release, challenge content, FERPA).

> 2. Given a scenario, identify standards and procedures applicable to United States Citizenship and Immigration Services and students attending public schools.

All school leaders must be cognizant of student and parental rights and responsibilities as outlined by the Florida education statutes. Specifically, section 1002.23 details the Family and School Partnership for Student Achievement Act. This part of the statute provides clear guidelines regarding the content of parent handbooks, parental rights and responsibilities, and information schools must share with parents and guardians.

By providing written information (such as handbooks, regular announcements and letters, and report cards) and by maintaining open channels of communication with parents through various means (such as open houses, parent-teacher conferences, new student-parent nights, and website access), school leaders can establish and develop solid partnerships with parents and students. This helps create an environment in which students and parents exercise their rights in positive ways, and take appropriate responsibility, contributing to a healthy school environment.

Further, there are federal laws that are also relevant to student and parent rights. They include the following key acts.

Title VI, The Civil Rights Act of 1964 extends protection against discrimination on the basis of race, color, or national origins in any program or activity receiving federal financial assistance. *Clark v. Huntsville, Tyler v. Hot Springs*

Title VII, The Civil Rights Act of 1964 states that it is unlawful for an employer to discriminate against any individual with respect to compensation, terms, conditions, or privileges of employment because of an individual's race, color, religion, sex, or national origin. Some exceptions are noted in this statute. It does not apply to religious organizations that seek individuals of a particular religion to perform the work of that organization. Where suspect classifications (those classifications having no basis in rationality) represent bona fide occupational qualifications, they are permitted. Classifications based upon merit and seniority are also acceptable under this statute. *Ansonia BOE v. Philbrook*

Title IX, The Educational Amendments of 1972 states that no individual shall be excluded from participation in, be denied the benefits of, or be subjected to discrimination under any educational program or activity that receives or benefits from federal assistance on the basis of sex. This statute covers the areas of admission, education programs and activities, access to course offerings, counseling and the use of appraisal and counseling materials, marital or parental status and athletics. *Marshall v. Kirkland*

Section 504, The Rehabilitation Act of 1973 indicates that "No otherwise handicapped individual... will be excluded from the participation in, be denied the benefits of, or be subjected to discrimination under any program or activity receiving federal financial assistance solely because of his/her handicap. *School Board of Nassau Co v. Arline*

The *Age Discrimination Act of 1967* states that it shall be unlawful for an employer to fail or refuse to hire or discharge any individual or otherwise discriminate against any individual with respect to his/her employment because of an individual's age. This statute does allow an employer or employment to consider age as a bone fide occupational qualification (BFOQ). *Geller v. Markham*

The *Family Rights and Privacy Act of 1964 (FERPA)* (also know as the Buckley Amendment) states that no funds will be made available under any applicable program to any state or local educational agency, any institution of higher education, any community college, any school, agency offering a preschool program, or any other educational institution which has a policy of denying parents of students the right to inspect and review any and all official records, files, and data directly related to their children. This includes material incorporated into the student's cumulative folder such as identifying data, academic work completed, level of achievement, attendance date, testing results, health data, family background information, teacher or counselor ratings and observations, and verified reports of serious or recurring behavior problems. Each educational organization must establish appropriate procedures for granting access requests within a reasonable period of time (not to exceed 45 days).

- Parents have an opportunity for a hearing to challenge the record's contents, to ensure the record's accuracy, and to provide corrected or rebuttal information.
- Educational organizations must require written consent of the parent in order to release identifying information to external individuals and organizations. (The state specifies exceptions.)
- All persons, agencies or organizations seeking access to a student's record must sign a written form that must be included in the student file.
- Students who are 18 years of age or attending a post-secondary educational institution acquire the right of consent formerly held by the parent. "Directory information" can be released without consent. Such information includes the following: student's name, address, telephone listing, date and place of birth, major field of study, participation in officially recognized activities and sports, weight and height of members of athletic teams, dates of attendance, degrees and awards of attendance, degrees and awards received, and the most recent educational agency or institution attended by the student.

The *Individuals with Disabilities Education Act* (IDEA) requires that states adopt policies that assure all children with disabilities receive a "free and appropriate public education." The statute requires that each student's unique needs are addressed through an "individualized educational plan (IEP) and that extensive procedural requirements are put into place. Requirements allow for the withholding of federal financial resources to states that fail to comply with the statute. *Honig v. Doe, Hendrick Hudson Board of Education v. Rowley*

The *Equal Access Act of 1985* states that is will be unlawful for any public secondary school which receives federal financial assistance and which has a limited open forum to deny equal access or a fair opportunity to or discriminate against any students who wish to conduct a meeting within that limited open forum on the basis of the religious, political, philosophical, or other content of the speech at the meetings. A limited open forum exists whenever a school grants an opportunity for one or more non-curriculum-related student groups to meet on the school premises during non-instructional time. The criteria for a fair opportunity provide that

- the meeting is voluntary and student initiated;
- there is no sponsorship by the school, the government, or its agents or employees;
- school agents or employees are present at the meetings only in a non-participatory capacity;
- the meeting does not substantially interfere with the orderly conduct of educational activities within the school;
- non-school persons may not direct, conduct, control or regularly attend activities of student groups.

This statute authorizes the school, its agents or employees to maintain order and discipline on the school premises, to protect the well-being of students and faculty, and to assure that the attendance of the students at the meeting is voluntary. *Board of Education of Westside Community Schools v. Mergens.*

SKILL 1.13 Knowledge of managing the learning environment standard as related to federal law for education and schooling

1. Given a scenario, identify exceptional education entitlements, equal access for students and staff with disabilities, and related rights under federal statutes.

Once school principals have an understanding of the important issues affecting teaching and learning, they must deal with them using existing legal guidelines. These guidelines exist with the sole purpose of protecting the rights of students and staff.

The No Child Left Behind (NCLB) Act is one such guideline designed to help schools improve by focusing on accountability for results, freedom for states and communities, proven education methods, and parental choice. Some important terms associated with NCLB include adequate yearly progress (AYP), standardized assessments, and Title I.

As noted previously, the Individuals Disability Education Act (IDEA) was enacted to make sure that children with disabilities had the opportunity to receive a free appropriate public education. The intent is to improve accountability, expand services, simplify parental involvement, and provide earlier access to services and supports for students with disabilities. There is a continuous goal of educating students with special needs in the least restrictive environment.

During the 2001-2002 school year, nearly one in 12, almost 4 million public school children, received special assistance to learn English. This number continues to steadily increase. These students, like all others, are protected by Title VI (of the Civil Rights Act). This act states "school systems are responsible for assuring that students of a particular race, color, or national origin are not denied the opportunity to obtain the education generally obtained by other students in the system". Additionally, a section of the U.S. Equal Educational Opportunities Act (EEOC), the federal agency responsible for interpreting and enforcing Title VI, adds that states are mandated also to protect and help students "overcome language barriers that impede equal participation by its students in its instructional programs."

Maintaining confidentiality is of utmost importance in the school setting. Students, parents, or staff members must feel that important information is kept confidential to promote more active participation in the school community. FERPA, the Family Educational Rights and Privacy Act, is a Federal law that addresses confidentiality in the schools and governs the disclosure of student education records.

See Skills 1.6 and 1.12 for more details of federal laws related to education.

SKILL 1.14 Knowledge of learning, accountability, and assessment standard as related to State law for education and schooling

1. Given a scenario, identify legal standards and procedures applicable to school accountability legislation.

2. Given a scenario, identify the standards and procedures applicable to the META Consent Decree.

Florida's school accountability program consists of state statutory educational goals, requirements for both state and local school improvement plans, deadlines for achieving the goals, measurement of progress, and provisions for addressing problems with schools that fail to make adequate progress. Responsibility for developing specific implementation strategies is delegated to a separate independent commission created to oversee the program. Florida law requires each school to have an advisory council and gives the council authority over school improvement projects, backed up by funding authority. It earmarks a percentage of state education aid for school improvement and spending by the councils.

The Florida school accountability law was first adopted in 1991 and has been amended several times since. The FL DOE's Division of Accountability, Research and Measurement (http://www.fldoe.org/arm/) oversees accountability and school improvement efforts.

Florida established the following goals to guide school improvement:

- That communities and schools work to prepare children and families for school success
- That students who graduate are ready to enter work and postsecondary education
- That students compete successfully at the highest national and international levels and are ready to make well-reasoned, thoughtful, and healthy decisions throughout life
- That school environments are conducive to teaching and learning
- That schools provide environments that are safe, healthy, drug-free, and protect students' civil rights
- That teachers and staff are professional
- That adults are literate and have the skills and knowledge to compete in the global economy and exercise the rights and responsibilities of citizens
- That communities, school boards, and schools give parents the opportunity to be actively involved in achieving school improvement and educational accountability (Fla. Stats. 229.591).

It is important to remember that in education, the main purpose of assessment is to guide instruction. Therefore, tests must measure not only what a child has learned, but also what a child has yet to learn and what a teacher must teach. Although today's educators utilize many forms of assessment, testing remains an integral part of instruction and evaluation.

META Consent Decree

A consent decree is the state of Florida's framework for compliance with the following federal and state laws and jurisprudence regarding the education of English language learner students:

The META Consent Decree addresses the civil rights of ELL students, foremost being their right to equal access to all education programs. In addressing these rights, the Consent Decree provides a structure that ensures the delivery of the comprehensible instruction to which ELL students are entitled.

Section I: Identification and Assessment
All students with limited English proficiency must be properly identified and assessed to ensure the provision of appropriate services. The Consent Decree details the procedures for placement of students in the English for Speakers of Other Languages (ESOL) program, their exit from the program, and the monitoring of students who have been exited.

Section II: Equal Access to Appropriate Programming
All ELL students enrolled in Florida public schools are entitled to programming appropriate to their level of English proficiency, their level of academic achievement, and any special needs. ELL students shall have equal access to appropriate English language instruction, as well as instruction in basic subject areas, which is understandable to the students given their level of English proficiency, and equal and comparable in amount, scope, sequence and quality to that provided to English language learner (or non-ELL) students.

Section III: Equal Access to Appropriate Categorical and Other Programs for ELL Students
ELL students are entitled to equal access to all programs appropriate to their academic needs, such as compensatory, exceptional, adult, vocational or early childhood education, as well as dropout prevention and other support services, without regard to their level of English proficiency.

<u>Section IV: Personnel</u>
This section details the certificate coverage and in-service training teachers must have in order to be qualified to instruct ESOL students. Teachers may obtain the necessary training through university course work or through school district provided in-service training. The Consent Decree details specific requirements for <u>ESOL certification and in-service training</u> and sets standards for personnel delivering ESOL instruction.

<u>Section V: Monitoring Issues</u>
The Florida Department of Education is charged with the monitoring of local school districts to ensure compliance with the provisions of the Consent Decree pursuant to federal and state law and regulations including Section 229.565, Florida Statutes (Educational Evaluation Procedures) and Section 228.2001, Florida Statues (Florida Educational Equity Act).

<u>Section VI: Outcome Measures</u>
The Florida Department of Education is required to develop an evaluation system to address equal access and program effectiveness. This evaluation system is to collect and analyze data regarding the progress of ELL students and include comparisons between the LEP population and the non-ELL population regarding retention rates, graduation rates, dropout rates, grade point averages and state assessment scores.

SKILL 1.15 Knowledge of learning, accountability, and assessment standard as related to measurement of effective student performance

1. Given data (e.g., national, state, district, school, classroom, individual student), analyze student achievement.

2. Given a scenario, determine aspects of adequate progress of the lowest 25% in reading and mathematics at the school level.

3. Given school data sets with differing accountability designations, compare and contrast multiple measures of data to analyze school needs.

4. Given school data, analyze or develop a plan to address statewide requirements for student assessment (e.g., science, reading, mathematics, writing).

5. Given school data, analyze or develop a plan to address national requirements for student assessment (e.g., NCLB science, reading, mathematics, writing).

Educational accountability has taken on a whole new meaning for administrators and teachers in the past decade. Large scale assessment of students at the end of the school year can make or break a school. Schools that do not perform well on these assessments are often subjected to sanctions or decreased funding and even the firing of teachers and administrators. Test results are published so that schools and school districts are compared with one another and where school choice is permitted, parents often decide to place their children in schools with high scores on the tests.

For administrators, this presents a challenge. Every classroom is different and high scores one year do not necessarily translate into high test scores in the following year. The first step is to analyze the scores and determine where there are successes to celebrate and where more work needs to be done. It is imperative that there be internal accountability so that all teachers take responsibility for the students' learning. The social studies teacher, for example, can work with the English teacher, so that the same objectives are covered in both classes.

The administrator should not only analyze the test scores to see where changes can be made, but test results should also be analyzed in order to determine the school's potential. Then, through consultation with the teachers, a plan can be devised to help bring about school growth and improvement. By comparing the practices of high achieving schools with those of your school, you can bring about gradual change that will improve the instruction in your building. Best practices will become part of the school setting as teachers meet to discuss problems and areas where they have experienced success.

By using best practices, schools can recognize areas of concern and take steps to effect change. This may mean adjusting practices in the classroom so that they meet the needs of all students. Ongoing assessment is a necessity to help teachers determine what students know and what they still need to learn. Through using the data from classroom assessments, teachers are better equipped to help students succeed.

Scores on the FCAT

The Florida Comprehensive Assessment Test (FCAT) is the primary measure of students' achievement of the Sunshine State Standards. Student scores are translated into a school grading scale in order to ascertain how well a school is functioning. Score are classified into five achievement levels, with 1 being the lowest and 5 being the highest. Schools earn one point for each percent of students who score in achievement levels 3, 4, or 5 in **reading**, one point for each percent of students who score 3, 4, or 5 in **mathematics,** and one point for each percent of students who score 3, 4, or 5 in **science**.

SCHOOL GRADING SCALE

A

525 points or more

Meet adequate progress of lowest students in reading and mathematics

Test at least 95% of eligible students

B

495-524 points

Meet adequate progress of lowest students in reading and mathematics within two years

Test at least 90% of eligible students

C

435-494 points

Meet adequate progress of lowest students in reading and mathematics within two years

Test at least 90% of eligible students

D

395-434 points

Test at least 90% of eligible students

F

Fewer than 395 points OR

Less than 90% of eligible students tested

Making Annual Learning Gains

Since FCAT **reading and mathematics** exams are given in grades 3 – 10, it is possible to monitor how much students learn from one year to the next. Students can demonstrate learning gains in any one of three ways: *Improve* achievement levels from 1-2, 2-3, 3-4, or 4-5; **or** *Maintain* within the relatively high levels of 3, 4, or 5; **or** *Demonstrate more than one year's growth* within achievement levels 1 or 2 (does not include retained students).

Special attention is given to the reading and mathematics gains of students in **the lowest 25%** in levels 1, 2, or 3 in each school. Schools earn one point for each percent of the lowest performing students who make learning gains from the previous year in reading and mathematics. It takes at least *50%* in both reading and mathematics to make "adequate progress" for this group. Schools that fall short of 50% can still meet the requirement if they show annual improvement in this percentage.

Schools that do not make adequate progress with their lowest students in reading and mathematics must develop a School Improvement Plan that addresses this need. If a school, otherwise graded "A", does not demonstrate adequate progress in the current year, the final grade will be reduced by one letter grade. If a school, otherwise graded "B" or "C", does not demonstrate adequate progress in either the current or prior year, the final grade will be reduced by one letter grade.

For more information on Florida's School Grading System see:
http://schoolgrades.fldoe.org/pdf/0708/SGGuide2008.pdf

SKILL 1.16 Knowledge of learning, accountability, and assessment standard as related to assessment instruments and their applications

1. Given a scenario, identify the appropriate type of formal assessment instrument (e.g., norm referenced, criterion referenced) to determine student strengths and needs.

2. Given a scenario, identify the appropriate informal assessment instrument (e.g., observations, checklists, inventories, interviews) to determine student strengths and needs.

The evaluation of students is a very important aspect of the teaching and learning process for individual students. Periodic testing measures learning outcomes based on established objectives. It also provides information at various stages in the learning process to determine future student needs such as periodic reviews, re-teaching, and enrichment. As the end process, the evaluation of students' performance measures the level of goal attainment, which is operationalized through the learning activities planned by the teacher. At varying stages of the teaching and learning process, the intended outcome must be measured, the level of goal attainment established, and this continuous cycle of student evaluation proceeds.

Evaluation and measurement are often used interchangeably to imply the same process. However, while closely related, they should be differentiated. *Evaluation* is the process of making judgments regarding student performance and *measurement* is the actual data collection that is used to make judgments of student performance. Evaluation is related to student performance when the focus is on how well a student carries out a given task or when student work is the focus of the measurement.

The purpose of the student evaluation will determine the type of process to use. Diagnostic, formative, and summative evaluations are the three types most commonly used.

Diagnostic evaluation is provided prior to instruction to identify problems, to place students in certain groups, and to make assignments that are appropriate to their needs. While it is important to address the specific needs of students, teachers must be cautious of the ramifications of grouping children in homogeneous groups versus heterogeneous groupings. It may appear time-effective to group and work with children of similar abilities, yet it often fails to foster students' intellectual and social growth and development. In fact, it has been shown that children in mixed groups benefit from the diversity within the group.

Formative evaluation is used to obtain feedback during the instructional process. It informs teachers of the extent to which students are really learning the concepts and skills being taught. The information should lead to modifications in the teaching and learning process to address specific needs of the students before arriving at the end of the unit. Therefore, it must be done frequently using the specific objectives stated for learning outcomes.

Summative evaluation is used to culminate a unit or series of lessons to arrive at a grade. Knowing the content studied and having the specific skills required to score well on tests are two different endeavors. Successful performance requires not only learning content, but also following the format of the assessment. Often, standardized tests are considered to be summative evaluations. Therefore, teachers must train students in test taking skills such as following directions, managing time effectively, and giving special attention to the type of tests and the skills required.

Regardless of the type of assessment, educators must gather and analyze the information they yield to determine strengths and weaknesses. The problem areas uncovered should be discussed with students collectively and individually and with parents at parent-teacher conferences. Whether diagnostic, formative, or summative, the evaluation of student performance should be a continuous process.

The accuracy of student evaluation is essential. Accuracy is determined by the usability of the instrument and the consistency of measurement, which is observed through reliability and validity of the instruments.

Validity is the extent to which a test measures what it is intended to measure. For example, a test may lack validity if it was designed to measure the creative writing of students, but it is also used to measure handwriting even though it was not designed for the latter.

Reliability refers to the consistency of the test to measure what it should measure. For example, the items on a true-false quiz, given by a classroom teacher, are reliable if they convey the same meaning every time the quiz is administered to similar groups of students under similar situations. In other words, there is no ambiguity or confusion with the items on the quiz.

The difference between validity and reliability can be visualized as throwing darts at a dart board. There is validity if the dart hits the target (an assessment measures what it is intended to measure), it is reliable if the same spot is hit time after time (the assessment consistently measures what it should measure). The goal should be to develop assessments that are both valid and reliable (every time the assessment is administered, it measures what it is intended to measure).

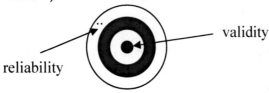

Usability is another factor in the evaluation process, which refers to practical considerations such as scoring procedures, level of difficulty, and time to administer the test. The usability is questionable if, for example, the scoring procedures had to be changed to accommodate local financial circumstances or if the allotted time for the test had to be reduced because of other circumstances.

Since the purpose of assessment instruments is data gathering, it is important to use various forms of information-gathering tools to assess the knowledge and progress of students. As previously noted, standardized achievement tests have become a central component of education today. The widespread use of standardized achievement tests to provide information for accountability to the public has driven many teachers to "teach to the test" and embrace more objective formats of teaching and learning. These tests are limited in what they measure and too often they are used to make major decisions for which they are not designed.

Standardized achievement tests can be norm-referenced or criterion-reference. In *norm-referenced* measurements the performance of the student is compared with the performance of other students who also took the same test. The original group of students who took the test establishes the norm. Norms can be based on age, sex, grade level, geographical location, ethnicity, or other broad classifications.

Standardized, norm-referenced achievement tests are designed to measure what a student knows in a particular subject in relation to other students of similar characteristics. The test batteries provide a broad scope of content area coverage so that it may be used on a larger scale in many different states and school districts. However, the questions may not measure the goals and content emphasized in a particular local curriculum.

Norm-reference, standardized achievement tests produce different types of scores that are useful in different ways. The most common types of scores are the percentile ranks or percentile scores, grade equivalent scores, stanines, and percentage of items answered correctly. The percentile score indicates how the students' performance compares to the norming group. It tells what percentage of the norming group was outscored by a particular student taking the test.

For example, a student scoring at the eightieth percentile did better than 80% of the students in the norming group. Likewise, 20% of the norming group scored above the particular student and 80% scored below. The scores are indicative of relative strengths and weaknesses. A student may show consistent strengths in language arts and consistent weakness in mathematics as indicated by the scores derived from the test. Yet one could not base remediation solely on these conclusions without a closer item analysis or a closer review of the objectives measured by the test.

The grade equivalency score is expressed by year and month in school for each student. It is used to measure growth and progress. It indicates where a student stands in reference to the norming group. For example, a second-grade student who obtained a grade equivalent score of 4.5 on the language arts section of the test is really not achieving at the fourth grade five month level as one may think. The 4.5 grade equivalence means that the second grader has achieved at about the same level of the norming group who is in the fifth month of the fourth grade, if indeed such a student did take the test. However, when compared to other second graders in the norming group, the student may be about average.

A point of consideration with grade equivalence is that one may never know how well the second grader might do if placed in the fourth grade or how poorly the second grader might do if given the fourth grade test compared to other second graders in the norming group.

Stanines indicate where the score is located on the normal curve for the norming group. Stanines are statistically determined but are not as precise as percentile ranking because it only gives the area in which the score is located, but not the precise location. Using stanines to report standard scores is still found to be practical and easy to understand for many parents and school personnel. Stanines range from one to nine (1-9) with five being the middle of the distribution.

Finally, achievement test scores can be reported by percentage of items answered correctly. This form of reporting may not be very meaningful when there are only a few questions/items in a particular category. This makes it difficult to determine if the student guessed well at the items, was just lucky at selecting the right answers, or knowingly chose the correct responses.

Criterion-Referenced Standardized Achievement Tests are designed to indicate that the student's performance is directly related to specific educational objectives, thus indicating what the student can or cannot do. For example, the test may measure how well a student can subtract by regrouping in the tens place or how well a student can identify the long vowel sound in specific words. Criterion-referenced tests are specific to a particular curriculum, which allows the determination of the effectiveness of the curriculum, as well as specific skills acquired by the students. They also provide information needed to plan for future student needs. Because of the recognized value of criterion-referenced standardized achievement tests, many publishers have developed tailor-made tests to correlate with state and districts' general goals and specific learning objectives. The test scores are reported by percentage of items answered correctly to indicate mastery or non-mastery.

Aptitude tests are another standardized form of testing that measures the cognitive abilities of students. They also measure potential and capacity for learning. While they do not test specific academic ability, the ability level is influenced by the child's experiences in and out of the academic setting. Aptitude tests are used to predict achievement and for advanced placements of students.

Teacher-made tests are also evaluative instruments designed by classroom teachers to measure the attainment of objectives. While they may lack validity, they serve the immediate purpose of measuring instructional outcomes. Teacher-made tests should be constructed to assess specific objectives, but they also take into account the nature of the behavior that is being measured. Among teacher-made tests are multiple choice, essay, quizzes, matching, alternative choices (yes/no, agree/disagree, etc.), and completion items (fill in the blanks).

Portfolio assessment is fast becoming a leading form of assessment, in which the student and teacher collect sample work in a systematic and organized manner to provide evidence of accomplishments and progress toward attaining specific objectives.

Certainly, testing is very important in the assessment of students' progress, but there are other sources of information that can be used for assessment as well. For example, conferencing and cumulative records of a child may also provide factual information for cognitive and psychomotor assessments. Other information sources may include interviews, diaries, self-assessments, observations, and simulations.

SKILL 1.17 Knowledge of learning, accountability, and assessment standard as related to diagnostic tools to assess, identify, and apply instructional improvement

1. Given a data set of reading test results for students in ESE or ESOL, identify diagnostic tools appropriate for assessing student learning needs.

2. Given a data set of reading test results for students in ESE or ESOL, identify appropriate instructional strategies to improve student performance in reading.

As was discussed in the prior section, diagnostic evaluations are administered prior to instruction. The results help teachers make instructional decisions based on where students are currently and where they want them to be. By identifying strengths and weaknesses, diagnostic tools allow instruction to be individualized and improved upon.

Teachers may find that assigning students to groups facilitates the dissemination and retention of content taught at various levels. In homogeneous groupings teachers may allow beginning students to perform basic tasks until they become more proficient. Students who performed at the expected level can work in a group and can be given more challenging tasks. Likewise, there can be high-level assignments given to those who have excelled on the diagnostic tool. It is wise for administrators to encourage heterogeneous groupings as well. This strategy capitalizes on the different levels of attainment and can be beneficial for all students in the group from the least to most proficient.

To encourage heterogeneous groupings, it is important that administrators conduct walk-throughs with each teacher on an on-going basis. This will allow the principal to make notes concerning student groups. If an instructor maintains the same type of groupings or always group the same students together, coaching may be necessary.

COMPETENCY 2.0   **Operational Leadership Technology Human Resource Development Ethical Leadership Decision-Making Strategies**

SKILL 2.1   **Knowledge of technology standard in the use of technology for teaching and learning**

> 1. Given a technology plan, identify hardware, software, and related technologies appropriate to design and delivery of instruction.

> 2. Given a technology plan to integrate technology to improve student performance in a subject area, identify appropriate technology applications to address student performance needs.

The last few decades have witnessed the debut of a number of electronic devices in America's public schools. These devices are grouped under the heading of technology. Each of these devices, however, has particular capabilities and advantages that can make the interactive experience of teaching and learning process stimulating, relevant, and constructive. Further, when these electronic tools are applied to administrative tasks, they yield results specific to administrative goals.

Given the assortment of technology available to schools and the range of capabilities of specific devices, a challenge facing school administrators is to identify the capabilities of technological devices and make a determination regarding the utility of that technology in the school environment and its ability to ultimately accomplish school objectives.

It is rarely useful to have technology in a school if it cannot be applied to solving school problems. Since technology is expensive to acquire and maintain, it is important that the introduction of technological devices be related to addressing specific school goals and objectives. Very little benefit, if any at all, accrues for students, teachers, and administrators when technology not used effectively.

The physical components of a computer system are called the hardware. The software consists of the program applications that tell a computer what to do. In effect, a computer system is delineated by the software which provides instructions to the computer and the hardware which executes the commands. In a computer system, various components accomplish certain tasks. There are certain functions and operations that cannot be conducted when components are missing from the system.

The use of technology in schools by teachers and students is contingent on an understanding of the capabilities of various technologies and an ability to integrate these capabilities into the curriculum framework of a school. The application of technology to curriculum goals and objectives is an important function of school leadership. Involving students in learning sequences that utilize technology provides a new and motivating context to learning. Computer technology offers teachers and students a constructivist learning environment, an opportunity for students to engage in hands-on learning.

The placement of computers in individual classrooms offers the most benefit. This placement maximizes both teacher and student access to technology. Computers can be used in schools for achieving a number of instructional objectives: remediation, drill and practice, and to simulate real world activities. Effective teaching utilizing technology is available. Understanding the appropriate application of technology to specific curriculum and learning objects is a key administrative skill. Knowing which applications of technology advance student learning is necessary.

Computers can only be significant in the teaching and learning process when the advantages and applications are carefully thought out and implemented. Traditional uses of computers in classrooms, such as drill and practice, games, and remediation under-use the capabilities of computers and software applications, which can be a versatile teaching tool with infinite potential. Computer technology can be used to support students in analysis, creative thinking, and problem solving. Specifically, information management, writing, and mathematical concepts can all be taught using the computer.

Video also has a powerful potential for education. Moving images have an advantage over still visuals in the teaching and learning process. Video can be used in the learning environment for both affective and cognitive learning. Video technology comes in a variety of formats. DVD, videodisc, videocassette, (U-matic and VHS), videocassette (8 millimeter), and compact discs are common media being used in the instructional process today.

Each of these formats presents advantages and disadvantages in the instructional environment. Video technology can be used to analyze human interactions, enhance the mastery of skills through repeated observations, and address values and attitudes, among other topics. However, in the classroom, it can promote inactive learning if not employed thoughtfully. Teachers need to ensure that their use of video technology in the classroom is appropriated for deep learning.

Each school must develop a technology plan in order to match needs and resources, identify appropriate technological advances, and provide adequate training, evaluation and follow up. Florida-specific resources for creating a technology plan can be found at http://www.flinnovates.org/.

SKILL 2.2   Knowledge of technology standard related to school operations

    1. Given a school technology plan, assess compliance with State technology goals (e.g., copyright law, Internet usage, digital learning environment, instructional leadership, Florida's digital educators, access to technology, infrastructure, support).

    2. Given a scenario, select computer hardware and software appropriate to school operations.

    3. Given a scenario, identify components of a technology infrastructure related to school and student safety.

    4. Given a scenario, select Web-based communication applications.

    5. Given a scenario, select presentation software applications.

Technology can be applied to make time-saving and organizational differences in scheduling, accounting, purchasing, inventory, attendance, grading, testing, and library automation. The appropriate use of technology in these areas can make a difference in personal productivity, efficiency, and time expenditure. In addition, there are communication and presentation programs that are changing the way school districts operate.

While a lack of knowledge about how to use technology has been common in the educational world in the past, this is rapidly changing. A leadership role in technology requires an ability to describe major hardware and software components and to be a role model for teachers. In many districts, technology professionals work with school leaders to assess and make decisions about technology needs. However, in some smaller districts, it falls to the principal or other administrator to choose software programs.

The school administrator must distinguish between software designed for accounting, scheduling, information management, and communication purposes. An administrator needs to be aware of what software programs can and cannot do. At minimum, school leaders must have knowledge of computer terminology, knowledge of instructional and administrative applications, and an understanding of the impact of technology in the school environment.

Here are some guidelines for selecting software:

- identify the objectives that are to be accomplished by introducing the software in the school environment.
- determine if the features and capabilities of the software match administrative goals and objectives.
- determine if the software actually does what it describes and if what it does is what is needed.
- be sure to ascertain that the software is compatible to the computer system in operation at the school.

Further, the right application must be applied to the appropriate task. Seldom can curriculum applications be applied to school administrative functions with desirable results, and visa versa. For example, the efficiency and effectiveness of the accounting software to handle school budget matters does not translate to the teaching and learning environment of the classroom.

Legal and Ethical Considerations

In an effort to protect the interests of originators, producers, and distributors of original works of art, information, and now technology, governments enact copyright laws. Copyright laws protect the originator from unlawful infringement upon a creation and specifies the conditions under which a work or idea may be copied. This area of law is constantly evolving, and consulting the school solicitor may be important when developing policies regarding copyright issues.

In 1976, Congress enacted the most recent copyright law. It included provisions for technological developments. Guidelines regarding computer software and television broadcasts were also included. Both criminal and civil penalties are a part of the copyright law. In 1990, Congress amended the copyright law which, in effect, took away a public institution's immunity from being sued. An employer as well as the employee can be held liable for infringing upon the copyright. Educators who intentionally and deliberately violate copyright law are subject to criminal penalty, which can be a fine up to $1000.00 and a year in jail.

The information age brings with it considerations of privacy and confidentiality of group and individual information. Who does and does not have access to certain records are important determinations. The question of security is always an issue when significant amounts of information are stored in one location. Not only are enormous amounts of information stored on computers, but that information is often sensitive in nature, meaning, not everyone needs to have access to it. Information can be used in inappropriate ways especially if that information is student data.

A breach of professional ethics occurs when student data is disseminated publicly to those who do not need the information. The confidentiality of school records is a paramount issue. In this age of computer hackers, the security and safeguard of school records becomes a high priority. Computer viruses are also an issue. Vigilance must be exercised and access monitored to prevent the possibility of a virus and the destruction of school records. The ways in which this can be accomplished are an important part of the professional skills of an administrator.

SKILL 2.3   **Knowledge of human resource development standard as related to recruitment, selection, induction, and retention of staff**

1. Given policies for teacher recruitment, selection, induction, professional development, and retention, determine compliance with Florida Statutes and No Child Left Behind legislation.

2. Given an out-of-field teacher report, identify various methods for acquiring Florida Teacher Certification (e.g., highly qualified teachers, critical shortage, special needs).

3. Given a sample of an interview, identify violations of federal and State laws that protect an applicant from job discrimination (e.g., AIDS, civil rights, Americans with Disability Act).

The educational leader in schools has a myriad of duties and tasks. The most time-consuming involves human resource management and development. Educational leaders must know and understand human relations since schools are labor intensive and use 80% to 90% of a school's budget. Over time, the personnel management roles of school administrators have expanded. Therefore, an understanding of the many aspects and importance of personnel management is essential in creating and maintaining a successful and efficient school organization.

The role of the principal in selecting instructional and non-instructional personnel is often considered the most important aspect of the position. It is through people that the principal is able to achieve the mission of the school; therefore he or she should lead the staff in a collegial environment. The administrator should convey that school personnel are of greatest importance and the principal should do all that is within his or her power to provide the best working conditions. Once they are empowered, the personnel will subsequently be empowered to do what is best for the students.

Hiring Personnel

In selecting instructional personnel, the principal has many responsibilities. Planning, recruitment, and selection are essential aspects of securing personnel. Planning requires the principal to look at the current staff and plan for future short-term and long-term personnel needs. Using site-based management, the principal involves current personnel in developing and revising the personnel plan for the school.

During this process, consideration must be given to current staff, students, parents, the community, school district, and state and federal rules and regulations. Planning must be comprehensive, take place well in advance of the need, and allow sufficient time to prepare papers and get approval through the district system. The principal must know the process used in the school district to select personnel, including how assignments are determined and the impact of the collective negotiation contract (if there is one in the district). The plan must also provide for emergencies such as unexpected promotions, illnesses, resignations, and terminations.

Once the plan is completed, recruitment can begin; this is a critical component of successful human resource management. First, the principal must understand the procedure in his or her district. Recruitment must occur early whether the principal has control of the entire process and uses a selection committee or whether the district does the recruiting and has to give approval to fill the positions. Second, the administrator must identify sources for qualified applicants with staff diversify factoring in to the hiring mix. College and university career offices, schools of education, and career fairs at the state and local levels are among popular recruitment options   Dialogue with colleagues and current school staff also offer opportunities to recruit new employees

The selection process involves screening the paperwork, interviewing candidates and checking references. The selection committee must understand the confidential nature of applicant information and must be charged with maintaining the integrity of the process. Using a job-related matrix for the position, each applicant's papers are evaluated against the criteria. Unqualified applicants are removed from the candidate pool. Although certification in field is one of the most crucial factors to consider, the quality of the application is also judged for training competencies, job stability, comprehensiveness, grammar, and neatness.

Qualified applicants are then interviewed, the most time–consuming phase of personnel selection. After candidates are notified of the time and location for the interview, the committee determines questions to be asked and criteria to judge the responses. Each candidate for a position must be asked the same questions and judged by the same criteria. The committee then submits to the principal the names of the most qualified applicants, usually three to five individuals.

The principal reviews the work of the committee, interviews the potential employees, and conducts reference checks. Notification is sent to candidates informing them of their selection or non-selection. Another good strategy is to visit the person's current or most recent place of employment. Principals often contact the institutions that trained the potential employee to obtain professional judgments about the candidate. Retrieving fingerprint records ensures that known criminals are not employed. Last, the principal recommends to the superintendent the person who should be employed.

Highly Qualified Teachers

Administrators are responsible for recruiting, selecting and inducting effective school personnel. The significance of this responsibility can be seen in the current national research that shows that of all high school graduates only about 72% enrolled as freshman. The drop-out rate for high school students is estimated to be around 20-30%. The cost of securing the best teachers is directly translated into high graduation rates and lowered drop-out rates for students who have demonstrated proficiency and knowledge acquisition during their high school career.

With *No Child Left Behind* and its emphasis on "highly qualified teachers," principals have to abide by state and federal laws regarding licensure/certification and degrees. For example, all secondary subject-area teachers must have a degree (or demonstrate extensive competency, usually through a very rigorous exam) in the subjects they will be teaching.

In Florida, all instructional personnel must be certified. This generally occurs by state testing after the potential teacher achieves the appropriate educational degrees. Specific information about certification for both in-state and out-of-state applicants can be found at http://www.fldoe.org/edcert/.

Retention of Qualified Personnel

An effective compensation and reward system is required in any organization. A compensation program attracts, maintains, and motivates quality employees. It also creates incentives for continual growth, and maintains budgetary control in school districts. Merit pay, paid leave, child care, cost of living increases, salary schedules, extracurricular stipends, early retirement plans, tax-sheltered annuities, and medical plans are types of compensation and rewards. In addition, social security benefits, retirement plans, severance pay, transportation allowances and leaves of various types (sick, annual, sabbatical, religious, military, and professional) are included. Supply and demand often determine the package available to employees.

Many districts are currently experimenting with pay for performance plans, where bonuses are given to teachers who increase test scores. This has been highly controversial, because statistical models to determine teacher impact on student test scores is rather complicated and imprecise.

A good induction process is also crucial to successful hiring and retention. Newly hired employees receive assistance because they usually need more support than experienced individuals. The first part of orientation is to introduce the procedures, paperwork required, teaching and learning expectations, rules, and other aspects of the school culture. In some systems the district conducts the orientation, with the school providing additional orientation for those factors unique to the school. The socialization process is another critical facet, it can determine how well new personnel adapt and contribute to the teaching/learning community. The induction process typically ranges from 90 days to a full school year. The best approach lasts a year and pairs a neophyte teacher with a mentor who teaches the same grade level and subjects.

SKILL 2.4 Knowledge of human resource development standard as related to performance assessment procedures

1. Given an instructional assessment instrument, determine compliance with Florida Statutes and State Board regulations for employee evaluation (i.e., management of students, maintenance of discipline, knowledge of subject matter, pay for performance, use of technology, and criteria for continual improvement).

2. Given an unsatisfactory performance evaluation, identify the Florida statutory requirements to facilitate employee growth (i.e., the performance improvement plan, notification of deficiencies, conference for the record).

3. Given an individual professional development plan, determine compliance with Florida Statutes governing the School Community Professional Development Act (i.e., requirement to establish and maintain an Individual Professional Development Plan for each teacher).

Employee Evaluation

When the evaluation process is conducted properly, teachers grow professionally and students benefit from increasingly effective instruction. Teachers should set professional development goals based on weak areas and should receive recognition for areas of strength. The processes for gathering the data used to rate teachers should also be published and discussed. Most often, there are formal, planned classroom observations, as well as informal walk-throughs and other informal methods for viewing a teacher's work.

In Florida, teacher evaluations are required by law, and are linked to compensation increases. Teacher performance ratings should be directly tied to student achievement, so student achievement data should be included in determining appraisal scores.

For administrators, the staff evaluation process must be met in a timely manner. This means conducting classroom visits and observations as noted above, and, at least once a year, completing a written evaluation using a designated appraisal tool. This written evaluation must be signed off on by an administrator and the employee, and is placed in the employee's personnel file. Evaluations for teachers include the following:

- Professional skills
- Classroom management and discipline
- Active engagement in student learning
- Possessing effective instructional practices
- Knowledge of subject content area
- Use of technology
- Engagement in professional development

A principal's goal is to improve the staff so that student achievement will be optimized. Underperforming teachers need assistance, and should agree with two or three improvement goals and concentrate on making progress in these areas before moving on to other areas of need. Document the improvement plan and progress, or lack of progress, toward the selected goals. Poorly trained teachers need to observe excellent models, so allow release time for observations in other classrooms. Conferencing with them after the observation will assist them in applying what they observed in their own classroom situation. When a teacher is working through an improvement plan, the principal should make more frequent visits to the classroom and look for signs of improvement. Document every visit and intervention. Ineffective teachers can improve with a principal's support, training and mentoring.

The appraisal process is also a way to provide recognition for outstanding teachers. When a teacher's performance is highly rated, this provides encouragement to continue instructional practices that benefit students. Appraisal systems allow the structured feedback that teachers need to improve instruction and grow professionally.

Teacher mentor programs provide assistance to new and experienced teachers new to teaching. The assistance of a peer teacher and a variety of induction activities enable teachers to receive assistance without the implied threat of evaluation. This open system enables these teachers to seek help when or before it is needed.

Professional Development for Instructional Staff

The School Community Professional Development Act of the Florida statutes requires that each school principal "establish and maintain an individual professional development plan (PDP) for each instructional employee." This means that the principal will work with each teacher to set goals for improvement in the performance of the students assigned to the teacher. These goals will include measurable outcomes in student performance, define related in-service objectives, and have an effective evaluation component. The PDP and the employee's regular performance evaluation should be integrated, as they are two facets of the same process designed to improve classroom instruction.

Professional development is a crucial component of successful school change. New standards and accountability systems demand more of teachers than ever before, and many teachers simply do not have the skills or knowledge to implement the many requirements for which they are now responsible. Significant research on professional development has concluded that among the worst ways of helping teachers learn new skills or knowledge is by putting them through a "one-shot" staff in-service. A staff in-service is a session that focuses on a particular strategy or technique for the classroom. Sometimes, these sessions are one to two hours. Other times, they are five to six hours. In either case, these sessions give teachers no reason to utilize their new learning, nor do they take into account adult learning theory.

Adult learning theory suggests that adults learn best when they have an immediate application of their learning. Since most staff in-services have no follow-up (i.e., discussion about how the strategy worked, one-on-one coaching, etc.), most teachers will not try the new strategies. After all, they feel safe and comfortable with their current procedures.

Effective professional development consists of deep learning across time with significant opportunities for follow-up, discussion, assistance, and reflection. Often, when professional development sessions, on one topic, are spread out over a whole year (perhaps, one three-hour session per month), teachers have more reason to follow through with trying new ideas in the classroom. Consistently, teachers report in surveys that they never have enough time to learn new strategies. Therefore, it is crucial that professional development not be limited to just a couple hours per year. Schools must provide teachers with multiple opportunities, often by re-arranging the school day, so that teachers can interact with each other and with new teaching ideas on a more regular basis.

SKILL 2.5   Knowledge of human resource development standard as related to managing personnel records

1. Given a sample of content from an employer's personnel file, determine compliance with Florida Statutes governing personnel files.

2. Given public information requests, determine compliance with Florida Statutes governing access to personnel files and records (e.g., medical records, complaints related to investigation, payroll deduction records, Social Security numbers).

Elements of a teacher's professional record are kept on file, usually in locked cabinets in the principal's office. They generally include information such as professional credentials, necessary clearance forms, hiring details, evaluations, disciplinary actions, and demographic information. Such records are, obviously, private; however, principals and district administrators can use this information when necessary. For example, if problems occur with a teacher's performance his or her record would be reviewed and updated. It is essential that this information be used only in appropriate circumstances, particularly as many districts have contracts with teachers' unions that stipulate how such information should be used.

Typically, district office personnel keep records of basic employment facts on each staff member. This can help when determining seniority and subject-area qualifications. Many districts now utilize computerized databases that allow varying levels of access to staff information. For example, human resources staff members might be able to view certification information for all teachers, while principals might only be able to access information for staff in their building.

Florida statute 1012.31 delineates the management of public school employee personnel files, including what may and may not be included in the files, the rights of the employee to respond to items in the file, privacy and confidentiality rights and other issues. The complete text of this statute can be found at http://www.leg.state.fl.us/statutes/index.cfm?mode=View%20Statutes&SubMenu =1&App_mode=Display_Statute&Search_String=employee+data&URL=CH1012/ Sec31.HTM.

SKILL 2.6 **Knowledge of human resource development standard as related to processes and procedures for discipline, dismissal, and nonrenewal of school employees**

1. Given a recommendation to terminate an employee's contract, identify the school site administrator's responsibilities regarding termination as required in Florida Statutes (e.g., union contract, professional service contract, annual contract, continuing contract).

2. Given case studies with accompanying documentation, identify and apply the Standard of Just Cause for any adverse employment decision as required by Florida Statutes (e.g., dismissal, suspension, demotion, reinstatement).

The Florida statute *F.S. 231 Personnel* spells out the qualifications, selection processes, certification processes, the operation of the Education Standards Commission and the Education Practices Commission, leave policies, and contractual and termination procedures relating to school personnel. Reviewing this law in detail is necessary for a principal to adequately manage disciplinary issues under his or her purview.

Termination is one of the most difficult tasks that a school principal must perform. The guiding principle question should and must be: Is this teacher permanently harming children because of incompetence or marginal teaching and learning outcomes? There are only a few of these teachers for whom the answer would be yes; however, these few individuals can consume a high percentage of a principal's time. Thus, the principal must follow clear guidelines, maintain a careful record, and provide due process to the teacher.

First, the principal must identify the teachers who need support and notify them in a timely manner. Next, they should be offered assistance; the Employee's Assistance Program is one resource. The teachers can be counseled into other positions if they cannot become high-quality instructors. If the issues require punitive action, the teacher must be notified of charges in writing, adequate time must be given for the teacher to prepare a rebuttal. The teacher must be permitted counsel of his or her choice. During an impartial hearing, the teacher must be able to examine any evidence. When a decision is made based on the evidence, a transcript of the hearing must be given to the teacher. Lastly, he or she is allowed an appeal if there is a decision to terminate him or her or if there is a severe loss to the teacher.

SKILL 2.7 Knowledge of human resource development standard as related to collective bargaining agreements

1. Given a collective bargaining agreement, identify the role of the administrator in managing the contract per Florida Statutes (e.g., grievances, school policies, enforcement, and punitive actions related to all classifications of school personnel).

Collective bargaining is the process of negotiating a contract between the management of a school district and the teachers' union, which represents the teachers within a district. Although monetary matters comprise the majority of issues in most collective bargaining sessions, other facets of working conditions (such as job duties, hours on campus, etc.) are negotiated, as well.
A principal may serve on the school district's management team during a collective negotiation. The negotiation process is usually lengthy, involves multi-year contracts, team determination, unit recognition, planning and preparation, agreement and implementation, strategies to reach agreement, and counterproposals. While collective bargaining has typically been viewed as a divisive process, progressive unions and sensitive school districts have found that working together can be more beneficial to both sides.

SKILL 2.8 Knowledge of human resource development standard as related to data analysis

1. Given school or classroom data, analyze teacher performance over time.

Goal setting is one way to bring about change in the instructional techniques used by teachers. It is also instrumental in school growth and improvement. At the beginning of each school year the whole staff should set at least three goals that are in line with the school mission statement or focus for the year.

Goals should be measurable, which means they should be specific. Applying the SMART method will ensure that the goals are achievable and can be evaluated.

The SMART method is:

- S – specific
- M – measurable
- A – achievable
- R – relevant
- T – time-framed

When goals are specific, it is easy to evaluate whether or not they have been achieved. The planning process should also identify resources the teachers need or will use to help achieve the goals.

At regular intervals throughout the year, the administrator should meet with each teacher to discuss the goals and how achievement is progressing. The administrator, through visitations to the classroom, will also be able to comment on what is happening and offer advice to the teacher on how to proceed.

Measurable goals means that data are collected and analyzed in order to determine success or failure. Teachers need to be part of the process in reviewing the data, so they can understand the links between their teaching approaches and the students' performances. Engagement in the process from planning through data analysis and subsequent planning will help teachers embrace the goals and the change process.

SKILL 2.9 Knowledge of human resource development standard as related to State law for education and schooling

1. Given a scenario, identify standards and procedures applicable to State certification, selection, evaluation, discipline, and reappointment of school district employees.

See Skills 2.3, 2.4, and 2.6

SKILL 2.10 Knowledge of ethical leadership standard as related to ethical conduct

1. Given the Code of Ethics of the Education Profession in Florida, identify violations of ethical conduct as stated in Florida Statutes (e.g., conviction of a crime involving moral turpitude; gross insubordination; misconduct in office; neglect of obligations to students, public, school personnel).

Principals are leaders. Their behavior, stated communication, and implied communication have a tremendous impact on those with whom they work. Others often follow the lead of the principal. If a principal is calm in difficult situations, the students, parents, staff, and faculty will often reflect back similar behavior; the reverse is also true. A principal who resolves conflict in a systematic, fair manner promotes this kind of behavior within the school. The means a principal uses to share information and reach decisions are closely observed and followed.

The principal who shows partiality or insists that his or her position is the only one will not obtain meaningful input from those with whom he or she is working. In this type of environment people will say what they expect the principal to say, say nothing, or agree with the principal's views. The result is that the best results are not achieved since the best collective thinking of the learning community is not a part of the planning, implementation, and evaluation of the work of the school. If the principal appears to close or open up discussion, others in the environment will respond accordingly. A strong principal realizes that there are times when decisions must be made and makes them in a timely fashion. For example, if a person enters the campus with a gun, the principal must take action to provide safety for everyone. If teachers have conflict, the principal must find means to resolve the problem before it becomes a major deterrent to achievement of organizational goals.

The state of Florida has assembled a variety of statements to guide the professional conduct of school employees. While the specific details can be found online (http://www.firn.edu/doe/dpe/publications.htm), the basic concept is that because public school educators work with children all day long, they must conduct themselves in an appropriate manner. Furthermore, when certain concerns about students arise, educators are mandated by the state to submit reports. For example, indications of child abuse or indications that the student has attempted suicide would require that a teacher follow specified reporting procedures. Principals must remind teachers of this regularly.

SKILL 2.11 Knowledge of ethical leadership standard as related to federal and State law for education and schooling

1. Given a scenario, identify judicially recognized rights and responsibilities guaranteed under the Constitution (e.g., First, Fourth, Fourteenth Amendments).

2. Given a scenario, identify the statutory powers and duties of the Florida Board of Education, Commissioner of Education, local school boards, superintendents, and principals.

3. Given a situation, identify standards and procedures of State administrative law, public disclosure, record keeping, and child welfare.

Knowledge of legal issues at they pertain to education is crucial for effective ethical functioning. Without a basic grounding in relevant law, school leaders cannot act ethically in complex situations where conflicting needs or the pressure for quick action is required. In order to act effectively and ethically in difficult situations, school administrators need to have basic legal knowledge and also be willing to call on the school solicitor whenever he or she is uncertain about the law, potential liability, or the most appropriate action under the circumstance.

Fundamental knowledge of key Constitutional amendments – such as freedom of expression, citizenship, school desegregation, and freedom from unreasonable searches – is important. See http://www.usconstitution.net/ for the text of the US Constitution and all subsequent amendments. Further, principals should have a basic understanding of Florida education law. An excellent resource regarding Florida statutes and the state board of education can be found at http://www.fldoe.org/ese/pdf/1b-stats.pdf. This guide details relevant statutes for special programs. For a list of all federal and state laws governing education in the State of Florida, see Skill 1.6.

SKILL 2.12   Knowledge of decision-making strategies standard as related to federal and/or State law for education and schooling

1. Given a scenario, identify standards and procedures applicable to federal and/or State statutory provisions for accomplished practices, pupil progression, compulsory school attendance, sexual harassment, charter schools, alternative schools, safe schools, curricula, and facilities.

As noted previously, school leaders must be grounded in all federal and state laws pertaining education and school in order to function effectively. This baseline provides key information affecting many decisions that principals and other administrators must make on a daily basis. Such legal data will also impact various aspects of planning, including the development of curricula, budgeting, and facilities management.

See **Skills 1.6, 1.7, 1.10, 1.11, 1.12, 1.13, and 1.14** for more information about federal and state statutes affecting decision-making.

SKILL 2.13   Knowledge of decision-making strategies standard as related to change

1. Apply current concepts of leadership (e.g., systems theory, change theory, situational leadership, visionary leadership, transformational leadership, learning organizations).

2. Select examples of organizational conditions or leadership actions that create positive attitudes toward change.

Today, the school principal is recognized as a critical person for impacting instructional change and bringing to fruition the goals and objectives of a school. The kind and quality of leadership exercised by those invested with the authority to supervise school operations makes a difference in the lives of students, the community, and ultimately the nation. Hence, the role of the principal and the competencies that an individual brings to this position are key elements in creating dynamic and effective school organizations.

There are various approaches to understanding the qualities of good leaders, qualities that principals may want to emulate. The *trait approach* to leadership focuses on the personality traits of leaders. The *situational approach* postulates that leadership is a result of understanding the idiosyncrasies and characteristics of specific groups. Finally, another approach to understanding leadership emerged, known as the *contingency approach*. The contingency approach specified that the kind of leadership to be exerted depends upon a number of variables, including personality, task, group dynamics, and the situation. "Collaborative leadership requires a new notion of power...the more power we share, the more power we have to use." It is the skillful and mission driven management of important relationships. Collaborative leadership is the point at which organization and management come together. Additionally, collaborative leadership uses supportive and inclusive methods to ensure that all stakeholders affected by a decision are part of the change process. Collaborative leaders must strive to build relationships with numerous stakeholders and create structures to support and sustain those relationships over time.

A review of leadership theories and styles, as well as links to more information about the large field of leadership theory, can be found at http://en.wikipedia.org/wiki/Leadership.

Organization Dynamics and Change Processes

Many theorists have proposed frameworks as they attempt to understand the dynamics that take place in organizations. To form its foundation, educational administration has borrowed extensively from organizational theorists.

Early organizational theorists were more concerned with how well people performed given tasks in the enterprise than with the well-being of the individuals in the organization. These theories and beliefs about organizations and individuals were soon challenged by another set of theories and beliefs, which focused on the quality of relationships and the importance of people in the organization. This evolutionary pattern was followed by critical analysis of the formal and informal structures existing in organizations. The conceptualization of organizations as a system, with internal and external influences, further contributed to the base of knowledge for educational administration and leadership.

A particularly salient view of leadership within organizations was developed by Bolman and Deal (1997). Their view is that people within organizations operate within one (or more) of four organizational frames: structural, human resources, political, and symbolic. These authors argue that most leaders operate in the structural frame (focusing on hierarchies, rules, regulations, procedures, etc.) or the human resources frame (focusing on the needs of people; within schools, this could either be teachers, students, or both). The authors also argue that the two remaining frames, often ignored, are highly important for the proper running of an organization. The political frame focuses on sources of power, and the symbolic frame focuses on the symbols of organizational culture and history that are so important to employees, students, and others.

Change is a consistent element of organizational vitality. Determining when to change and what to change in the organizational milieu presents difficulties for a leader. People resist change for a variety of reasons. Perhaps the most prominent barrier to change is the threat it poses to individual roles and the perceived security individuals have in an organization. Human beings resist change almost instinctively. Regardless of the way a certain task is being performed, individuals engaged in performing it are familiar with the details and comfortable using the existing format.

Change is viewed as disruptive because members of an organization have devoted energy and resources to accomplishing certain tasks in prescribed ways. To alter the methodology suggests a threat to competency—given a new way of doing it, individuals are not sure they can accomplish the task. So much has been invested in the old way that it is very difficult to acknowledge another method. As well, there is the perceived legitimacy of the old versus the unknown qualities of the new.

Organizational change occurs in three stages. The first stage is *initiation*, in which ideas are formulated and decisions are made regarding the nature and scope of change. The second stage is *implementation*, in which the change is applied in the environment. During the third stage, *integration*, the change is stabilized in the environment.

Several points are advised for individuals seeking to be change agents. The change that is to be introduced should not be done abruptly, but rather mentioned and discussed over a period of time preceding its intended implementation. Considerable support for the change should be marshaled so that it has sufficient sustaining force within the organization. Details must be shared regarding the specific goals to be addressed by the change.

Furthermore, when change is top-down, or driven entirely be a school principal, for example, change is viewed as a threat. Successful change comes from allowing teachers in a school to be central in the decision-making and implementation process. While studies of decentralized decision making (or site-based management) are mixed on the impact of involving teachers in management decisions, in general principle, top-down or imposed change causes more anxiety and is less effective at effecting real and significant change.

Doll (1996) discusses the process of change from three different perspectives. First, change is viewed as *technical*; that is, technical assistance can be employed to carefully design and implement an innovation. Second, change is *political*, there are special interests of individuals at work in the planning of change. Third, change is *cultural*, each change has the potential for disturbing or altering the cultural context.

In a plan called the *research utilizing problem solving process*, the Northwest Regional Educational Laboratory used a modified version of the classic five-step change process. It concentrates primarily on the initiation phase of a change process and the steps are (a) identifying a need for change, (b) diagnosing the situation in which change is to take place, (c) considering alternative courses of action, (d) testing the feasibility of a plan for change, and (e) adoption, diffusion, and adaptation for a successful change effort.

Irrespective of the chosen theory of change, school leaders must understand that certain factors can either support or stifle change. Generally, a school leader should develop a support system for change in the school environment. Teachers are often the ones expected to implement innovations and sustain change; therefore, attention must be paid to their emotional and professional needs. In addition, there is a greater likelihood of change becoming legitimized in the school if the change is made in a non-punitive, unpressured, supportive environment.

SKILL 2.14 Knowledge of decision-making strategies standard as related to data analysis

1. Given school data, perform procedural measures for school grade calculation.

2. Given a school improvement plan, identify criteria for learning gains of varying subgroups using disaggregated data.

School administrators must implement appropriate assessments to measure individual student growth during the school year, and from year to year, rather than measuring student achievement at a single point in time. Implementing a system like this assures that teachers and administrators can understand and influence growth for all students, regardless of achievement status, age and class groupings. Analyzing these growth measures over time will also help to determine how student achievement is aligned with district or state standards. Teachers should also be able to determine if classroom instruction is challenging individual students appropriately.

Teachers must be encouraged to shift from assessment of learning to assessment for learning. Assessment for learning is the process of seeking and interpreting evidence for use by learners and their teachers to decide where the learners are in their learning, where they need to go and how best to get there (http://www.aaia.org.uk/pdf/AFL_10principlesARG.pdf). Assessment for learning is an on-going process whereas assessment of learning is done at a point in time for the purpose of summarizing the current status of student achievement.

Additionally, research shows that assessment is most effective when it includes the following characteristics:

- student centered
- congruent with instructional objectives
- relevant
- comprehensive
- clear (in purpose, directions, expectations)
- objective and fair
- simulates "end" behavior/product/performance
- incites active responses
- shows progress/development over time

COMPETENCY 3.0   **School Leadership Community and Stakeholder Partnerships Diversity Vision**

SKILL 3.1   **Knowledge of community and stakeholder partnerships standard as related to community relations**

1. Select strategies to promote community cooperation and partnerships.

Public information management is a systematic communication process between an educational organization and its public, both within and outside the schools. It is the exchange of two-way information, designed to encourage public interest in and understanding of, education. The principal competency *"concern for image"* in the consensus management area specifies that a principal shows concern for the school's image. This is accomplished by monitoring impressions created by students and staff. The principal manages both these impressions and public information about the school by (1) advertising successes and (2) controlling the flow of negative information.

To be effective, communication between school leaders and the public must be open, honest, and unbiased. The attitudes of parents and members of the community at large have been adversely affected by reports of the decline of American education and negative media coverage. Despite the general perception of poor public education, the majority of parents surveyed nationally expressed satisfaction with their children's schools and teachers. The most positive feedback resulted when parents felt that their concerns were being heard and addressed and that they were involved in the decision-making process.

Community relations must be carefully organized. Information deliverers must have accurate information, understand their roles in the disseminating of the information, and provide appropriate channels for feedback. The public must perceive that they are being given complete, timely information by officials who respect their feelings and sincerely want feedback. School spokespeople must have a clear frame of reference; they need to know and be able to articulate the schools' vision/mission statements, goals and objectives, as well as current topics such as legislative issues that affect local education.

The Public Relations Process

Public information management requires analyzing the community attitude toward educational issues. The required school improvement surveys conducted each spring in many schools provide not only feedback on the issues but priorities for addressing them. Public workshops and meetings allow community members to become involved in learning about budgetary, disciplinary, and academic issues. Information gathering should be structured to obtain the most scientific results. For instance, a representative sampling is more likely from mailing surveys than from entrusting their delivery and return to students.

The planning phase requires setting specific goals and designing the campaign to achieve these goals. During this phase, educational leaders should determine the audiences, forums, and time frames in which their message(s) will be delivered to the public. For instance, presentations to senior citizens concerning a tax increase may require a different slant than a presentation to people who have children in the schools. Issues that require voter decisions should be presented with ample time for study and cooperative decision-making or at least discussion.

Equally important is whether information is delivered internally or externally. Student groups are a segment of the internal public and should be treated with the same open respect as other stakeholders. The information campaign must be encoded with specific audiences in mind. Also important is selection of the media (or transmission methods) to convey the message. First-level media are usually in the form of newsletters to parents, press releases, and annual reports—any written document that can be distributed to the intended audiences. Follow-up transmissions include open houses, school committees or school board meetings, and educational fairs—any face-to-face communication that brings the public and school representatives together for a two-way exchange.

Finally, school/district officials must evaluate the results of the public relations effort. Some evaluation is immediate, as in the defeat of a candidate or the passage of a bond issue. Less timely feedback can be obtained through periodic evaluations such as brief questionnaires in school newsletters, telephone surveys, or written assessments at the end of public meetings can help test the public's understanding and the level of community support.

Considerations Regarding the Media

Schools must establish good relationships with the media. When there are more educationally-focused complaints in the "Letters to the Editor" section of the newspaper than there are news articles about school events, there is obviously a poor interaction between media and schools. Of course, there are other reasons for the amount of educational coverage provided by various media.

- Small, hometown newspapers give broader coverage to local issues/events. They may devote a whole page or section to school/classroom events.

- Newspapers have to evaluate the "newsworthiness" of stories. Local spelling bees get better coverage than Mrs. Clarke's debate class' mock trial because one spelling bee winner in each district will compete nationally. Most newspapers consider a story of vandalism or fire at a school or a union walkout to be more newsworthy than a piece about students working at an animal shelter. Large city newspapers and television stations focus more on national and state news and regrettably often focus on educational issues that have negative or sensational.

- Local radio and television stations may be a better venue for school news; interviews with school officials, teachers, or students; or debates on education issues that have local impact.

Other Aspects of Community Relations

Building and maintaining positive community relations involves more than media coverage and press releases. It is about relationships – with local businesses, citizens, politicians, and other stakeholders. Keeping this in mind, school leaders are always "on" to some extent, and their behavior in the community impacts how the school is perceived overall. Therefore, being a good leader, as described in other sections, is critical for positive community relations.

Specific strategies that can build community relations include:

- School/district publications can be useful in providing a positive link with the community, e.g., newsletters, information brochures, handbooks, and annual reports.

- Displays of student work in public places provide visual evidence of student achievement, e.g., in malls, building lobbies, and business waiting rooms.

- Offering the use of the school building for community events (as regulated by statute) can bring community members into the school.

- School leaders can participate in community task forces and citizen groups to build relationships outside the context of school-related issues.

SKILL 3.2   Knowledge of community and stakeholder partnerships standard as related to assessment instruments and their applications

1. Given an audience, interpret standardized test results (e.g., percentiles, stanines, raw scores, scale scores).

Various community members are interested in how successful schools are. This means that they often want to know about various assessment methods used by the schools. School leaders need to be able to speak fluently and clearly about assessment methods and results when called upon by the school board, community groups or local foundations.

Being prepared for such opportunities involves comprehensive knowledge of assessment (see **Skill 1.16** for detailed information about assessment) and good communication skills (see **Skills 3.6 and 3.7**). Familiarity with the Florida School Grading program is also essential. Referring community members to the school grades website is a resource that might be useful as well (http://schoolgrades.fldoe.org/pdf/0708/SGGuide2008.pdf).

SKILL 3.3   Knowledge of community and stakeholder partnerships standard as related to State law for education and schooling

1. Given a situation, identify reporting procedures of the Florida Department of Law Enforcement's Missing Children program.

2. Given a scenario, interpret school advisory committee requirements as identified in State statutes.

School Advisory Councils

Florida Statute 1001.452 establishes the School Advisory Council (SAC), which "shall be composed of the principal and an appropriately balanced number of teachers, education support employees, students, parents, and other business and community citizens who are representative of the ethnic, racial, and economic community served by the school." The council is an integral component of the school and provides guidance and supervision in various aspects of its operation including assisting in the preparation of the school improvement plan and the annual budget.

Such advisory councils are an ideal opportunity to enhance partnerships with all stakeholders, including community members. It is the school leader's responsibility to ensure that the advisory council receives necessary information and coordinates its efforts with the school administration. An attitude of collaboration and inclusion is most effective and productive. Good communication is essential.

More information about School Advisory Councils can be obtained from the online network of SAC members at http://florida-family.net/SAC/.

The Missing Child Program

Numerous national and state laws have been discussed in various other sections. An additional law that needs to be addressed is The Missing Children Program established by Florida Statute 937.023 and Florida Administrative Code, Rule 6A-6.083. This initiative enlists local and state agencies, the Florida Department of Education (DOE), and individual school districts in pursuing investigations of reported missing children.

The following statement describes the procedure (taken from http://www.fldoe.org/eias/eiaspubs/missing.asp):

> Each month, the Florida Department of Law Enforcement (FDLE) provides the DOE with a data file comprising the names of children who have been reported missing to local law enforcement agencies and entered in the Florida Crime Information Center (FCIC) database. The DOE then makes this data available for school districts to access through the Northwest Regional Data Center (NWRDC).
>
> School districts are responsible for comparing this information with their own student database records to establish any matches between the names of children reported as missing and names of students in the district. Districts then report possible matches, using the ESE 092 form, both to the local law enforcement agency which originated the case and to the DOE. As the children in question are identified and located, the original law enforcement agency can then remove the solved cases from the FCIC database.

SKILL 3.4 Knowledge of community and stakeholder partnerships standard as related to student services

1. Given case studies of students with disabilities, identify the accommodations and services required per Florida Statutes (e.g., diagnostic and learning resource centers, ADA facilities, interagency support services).

Strong symbiotic relationships can develop between schools and their community partners. This is particularly the case with resource centers, which provide information, training, and resources to enhance the educational outcomes of students. Among them are Learning Resource Centers (LRCs), Diagnostic Resource Centers (DRCs), and School Choice Resource Centers (SCRCs). These organizations serve a range of stakeholders including administrators, teachers, paraprofessionals, and parents.

In its goal of educating all students, schools may need to help students and families access other services. Students who are gifted and talented may benefit from one group of educational agencies; those who need intervention support will be aided by another group of knowledge workers. Even if an agency serves the entire spectrum of student needs, it is good for administrators to be familiar with as many partner organizations as possible.

When a teacher or counselor refers a student for diagnosis of a disability or special services, the principal cannot delay the analysis because an agency is overbooked. The administration must be able to select from a list of service providers in order to meet student needs in a timely manner. Administrators will find it much easier to recruit assistance when they have ongoing relationships with external stakeholders.

In addition, an effective strategy involves developing strong partnerships with key groups such as churches, universities, health service providers, and law enforcement agencies. The school can provide useful service-learning opportunities for the organizations and in turn, the organizations are able to provide services to the school, its students, and their families.

For instance, Florida Statute 1008.25(4) mandates that when students do not meet specified levels of proficiency in reading, writing, mathematics, or science, the school district must develop a Progress Monitoring Plan (PMP). The process involves diagnostic assessments, individualized or school-wide Academic Improvement Plans (AIPs), frequent monitoring, academic progress updates to the student(s) and his or her/their parents, and the "closing" of the PMP annual contract by the last day of school.

During this process, the principal may need to reach out to psychologists, tutors, volunteers, and agencies designed to assist students needing academic remediation. Supporting students to succeed academically may require the utilization of other community resources. Students and families may need a variety of services, and a good administrator must work with his or her team of student service providers (school nurse, psychologist, counselor and others) to maintain a current knowledge base of community partnerships. These may include but are not limited to mental health and social service agencies, vocational training programs, food banks, substance abuse prevention and treatment programs, support groups, advocacy networks, government-sponsored aid programs, and enrichment activities.

SKILL 3.5 Knowledge of community and stakeholder partnerships standard as related to student and parental rights and responsibilities

1. Given the student-parent handbook, identify rights and responsibilities of students, parents, and guardians per Florida Statutes (i.e., notification, due process hearings, student academic progress, school choice preference, health examinations/immunizations, student academic improvement plan, truancy procedures, instructional materials).

In Skill 1.14, the value of knowing the Florida Statutes that govern student and parent rights and responsibilities (Chapter 1002) is discussed. School leaders must be conversant with these laws as they inform many aspects of governance. In terms of community and stakeholder partnerships, one area that frequently arises is related to student records. In utilizing outside resources, school leaders must also be aware of the limitations and constraints on sharing student information.

FERPA

In 1973, Congress passed a federal statute called FERPA to clarify the legal rights of students and parent/guardian(s) concerning access to student records. Also known as the "Buckley Amendment, FERPA stands for Family Educational Rights and Privacy Act (20 U.S.C. § 1232g; 34 CFR Part 99). (Go to nces.ed.gov/forum/FERPA_links.asp for more information about FERPA.)

Schools that receive funds from the federal government must comply with FERPA. The rights afforded by FERPA apply to parent/guardian(s) of students under the age of eighteen. Once a student turns eighteen, these rights are then transferred to the "eligible" student.

Under 34 CFR Part 99.7, FERPA states that parent/guardian(s) be notified on an annual basis about their rights to have access to or review their student's records. The following criteria must be included in the annual notification:

1. Parent/guardian(s) have the right to review their child's records
2. Parent/guardian(s) can advocate for changes to be made to the record should any information be incorrect.
3. Parent/guardian(s) can provide or withhold consent for the disclosure of personal information located with their child's record.
4. The way in which a parent/guardian can file a complaint with the Department of Education concerning a school or institution's failure to comply with FERPA.
5. Define which school officials that may have access to school records.

School employees, on a need-to-know basis, may have access to student records. These individuals may include principals, assistant principals, school psychologists, school counselors, and special education professionals. Regardless of his or her position, each employee must maintain the confidentiality of student information.

Schools may use a variety of ways to inform parents about their rights such as the school or community newspaper, bulletin boards, and student handbooks. Schools are not required to individually inform parents of their rights. Schools must procure parental consent to share student personal information with anyone other than the student and his/her parent/guardians. Examples include getting consent forms signed to release any information to a mental health provider in the community, or having a consent form on file before providing information to a college concerning a student's academic background.

SKILL 3.6 Knowledge of diversity standard as related to federal and State law for education and schooling and organizational communication

1. Given a scenario, apply legal interpretations of the purpose and intent of federal statutes related to equal access and the prohibition of all forms of discrimination in public schools.

2. Given a scenario, identify effective, research-based communication strategies

Cultural Competence

Educational leaders have a duty and responsibility to become attuned to the specific needs and issues relevant to all socio-cultural groups represented in their school district and community. Without such attunement, administrators are not able to adequately provide leadership and services to some students and families. In order to be effective across many cultural groups, school leaders must develop cultural competence and cross-cultural communication skills.

Developing cultural competence does not happen overnight or simply by attending a training workshop on the topic. It is an ongoing process of self-reflection, learning and skill development. Developing an understanding of one's own values, attitudes and awareness of diversity is a first step. Moving beyond cultural sensitivity to cultural competence in a school setting involves learning about other cultural beliefs and attitudes, particularly in relation to schools and institutions, and then developing skills that enable the counselor to relate and communicate well with people of differing socio-cultural backgrounds.

One area that is important to understand is the significance of cross-cultural interactions: how different groups have historically interacted with each other, especially within the context of institutions such as schools and health care systems. Many minority groups, especially people of color, have been mistreated by and underrepresented in many societal institutions. These negative experiences and the resulting distrust can make cross-cultural communication challenging for school counselors at times.

Acquiring cross-cultural skills aimed at respect, trust-building, and effective communication is essential in achieving cultural competence. Further, institutional policies and practices need to be changed as well. Minority groups need to be represented at all levels of the school administration and staff to reach cultural competence, and school practices need to better accommodate and respond to the cultural needs of all students and families.

Two websites that offer more detailed information about cultural competence are cecp.air.org/cultural/default.htm and www11.georgetown.edu/research/gucchd/nccc/foundations/frameworks.html.

Federal Laws Prohibiting Discrimination

Title VI, The Civil Rights Act of 1964 extends protection against discrimination on the basis of race, color, or national origins in any program or activity receiving federal financial assistance. *Clark v. Huntsville, Tyler v. Hot Springs*

Title VII, The Civil Rights Act of 1964 states that it is unlawful for an employer to discriminate against any individual with respect to compensation, terms, conditions, or privileges of employment because of an individual's race, color, religion, sex, or national origin. Some exceptions are noted in this statute. It does not apply to religious organizations that seek individuals of a particular religion to perform the work of that organization. Where suspect classifications (those classifications having no basis in rationality) represent bona fide occupational qualifications, they are permitted. Classifications based upon merit and seniority are also acceptable under this statute. *Ansonia BOE v. Philbrook*

Title IX, The Educational Amendments of 1972 states that no individual shall be excluded from participation in, be denied the benefits of, or be subjected to discrimination under any educational program or activity that receives or benefits from federal assistance on the basis of sex. This statute covers the areas of admission, education programs and activities, access to course offerings, counseling and the use of appraisal and counseling materials, marital or parental status and athletics. *Marshall v. Kirkland*

Section 504, The Rehabilitation Act of 1973 indicates that "No otherwise handicapped individual... will be excluded from the participation in, be denied the benefits of, or be subjected to discrimination under any program or activity receiving federal financial assistance solely because of his/her handicap. *School Board of Nassau Co v. Arline*

The *Age Discrimination Act of 1967* states that it shall be unlawful for an employer to fail or refuse to hire or discharge any individual or otherwise discriminate against any individual with respect to his/her employment because of an individual's age. This statute does allow an employer or employment to consider age as a bone fide occupational qualification (bfoq). *Geller v. Markham*

Managing the School Climate in a Respectful and Inclusive Manner

Administrators should be aware of the operation of the school grapevine and incorporate its positive aspects into the communication structure. The negative aspect of unsubstantiated rumor-passing will be overridden if the administrator consistently does the following:

- keeps employees informed about matters relevant to the school or district and about issues that impact the employees' jobs

- provides employees the opportunity to express attitudes and feelings about issues

- tests employees' reactions to information before making decisions

- builds morale by repeating positive reactions/comments made by employees to higher level administrators or the community and vice versa

Teaching professionals do not like the feeling that they are being kept in the dark or are getting only partial or untimely information. Telling teachers in a faculty meeting that the district is going to reduce the faculty at their school before transfer provisions have been established will create distrust. It may seem to be an open gesture on the principal's part, but the timing is wrong and such a communication will do more harm than good.

Overcoming Barriers to Communication

Filtering is a barrier that occurs during transmission of information from one level to another. It may be intentional or unintentional. It may be the omission of some of the message or improper encoding for the intended audience. Administrators frequently deliver information only on a need-to-know basis or deliver only positive information, fearing that negative information will damage the decoding process. This succeeds only in causing the receivers to be confused as to the message's intent or to feel patronized.

Biases against race, gender, or status can prejudice receivers against a message. Senders can suggest bias by words, nonverbal clues, or attitudes. A male principal with chauvinist attitudes may alienate female teachers; and a female principal may be tuned out by a male teacher who resents her. Unacknowledged biases frequently interfere unconsciously, underling the importance of developing cultural competence as noted earlier.

Overcoming these barriers is an important administrative responsibility. To establish effective communication, the school leader should:

- Establish trust by sincerely correlating his or her message and behavior. For example, claiming an open-door policy but never being available will not create trust.

- Listen carefully and provide open channels for feedback. Avoid giving non-verbal cues that contradict the message.

- Understand and respect employees' needs, interests, and attitudes. Allow discussion, even disagreement. The important thing is that employees know they are being heard.

- Properly time information delivery. Timing affects the manner in which employees perceive the message. Avoid leaking partial information. Transmit accurate information in time for employees to provide feedback.

- Use appropriate media for transmitting the message. Written or face-to-face communication is necessary when the message is of concern to a single receiver or when the message is of immediate concern to a group with common interests. Oral or video presentations are appropriate for delivery of information that affects a department or faculty, such as safety measures or procedures for reporting abuse.

Summary of Good Communication Practices

- Think first. This means preparing for a formal written, or oral presentation and it means pausing to gather your thoughts before impromptu speaking.

- Stay informed. Never speak or write off-the-cuff or attempt to discuss matters beyond your scope of knowledge. Stay abreast of education issues, especially in leadership and supervision. Read journals and participate in professional organizations. Keep a notebook of newsletters, clippings, and resource lists that can be highlighted and used to add credibility to your communication.

- Assess your audience. Know the addressees interests and attitudes. Show respect for their points-of-view by your tone and pace as well as by your volume and posture when speaking. Demonstrate a genuine liking for people by a willingness to share your ideas and solicit their responses.

- Focus attention on your message, not on yourself. A little nervousness is normal even for practiced writers/speakers. Familiarity with your topic, the ability to develop clear, complete sentences, and the use of concrete examples will enhance delivery.

- Speak/write correctly. Use of proper grammar, word-choice, and sentence structure will allow listeners/readers to concentrate on what you say, rather than on distracting language errors.

- Be concise. Get to the point and then quit. Use words and sentences economically. Being unnecessarily long-winded is a sure way to lose your audience.

- Use delivery techniques to your advantage. In written communication, be sure to state the main idea, give examples or explanations, and link the ideas in a logical manner. In oral communication, use eye contact to establish sincerity and hold listener attention. Use body language to add enthusiasm and conviction to your words, but avoid expansive or repetitive movements that can distract. Modulate the pitch and volume of your voice for emphasis.

Listen thoughtfully to feedback. In face-to-face communication, be aware of nonverbal cues that suggest either active listening or boredom.

SKILL 3.7   Knowledge of vision standard that works to relate State standards, the needs of the students, the community, and the goals of the school

1. Identify effective strategies for communicating relevant information about State standards, student needs, community needs, and the goals of the school to appropriate stakeholders.

2. Identify effective strategies for communicating relevant information about the instructional program to the community, staff, and district personnel.

3. Identify practices and implications of effective communication and interpersonal relationships.

Effective Communication

School administrators spend much of their time communicating – with staff, students, parents, board members, community stakeholders, and others. Good communication skills are an important aspect of successful management. In many instances, everyday communication is verbal, involving both listening and responding. Even with written communication, the basic tenets of good listening and responding skills are often applicable.

Listening is a highly subjective and selective activity. Listening is not just hearing words but grasping the meaning the speaker wishes to impart when those words are uttered. The meaning of the words spoken and interpreted depends upon the subjective world of both the speaker and the listener.

Some barriers to good listening are the following:

1. Hearing what you want to hear, not what is actually said.

2. Not hearing what is said at all due to one's own need to speak. Waiting for the other person to finish so we can speak causes us to think about what we are going to say instead of listening to what is being said.

3. We exhibit biased listening when we form an opinion about the value of what is being said and therefore discount the meaning of the words.

4. Emotions, either negative or positive, can cause interference with our listening abilities.

5. The presence of both internal and external distractions.

Effective listening not only involves tuning into the spoken words of the speaker but perceiving the tone of voice, the nonverbal cues given by the speaker and the emphasis given to the words. A good listener is one who consistently, under many circumstances, accurately understands the speaker's meaning by using their listening skills together with their thinking processes.

Good listening skills include the following:

1. Create a positive atmosphere by being alert, attentive, and concentrating on the speaker.

2. Make eye contact and maintaining an expression of genuine interest.

3. Allow the speaker to finish a thought before responding.

4. Avoid critical judgments in your responses.
5. Make an effort to remember what has been said.

6. Avoid changing the subject unless there is a really good reason to do so. When you must change the subject, explain the reason for the change to the speaker.

7. Be as physically relaxed as possible, as such posture communicates that you have time to listen and are interested.

There are a number of ways one can learn to respond to a speaker to let them know you have heard what he or she is trying to say. If you have listened well and thoughtfully to what the person is saying, your response will be appropriate, you will give good feedback and the speaker will feel good about the fact that you have heard what was said.

Good responding skills include:

1. Clarify the meaning of what was said by checking assumptions you have made as the listener to be sure you understand.

2. Continue to maintain eye contact as you give feedback.

3. Keep anger and other emotions out of the interaction. Try to express your feelings in a non-threatening way.

4. Help the other person in problem solving by responding positively and asking good questions.

5. Directly express your appreciation of the speaker's ideas, even if you disagree with them. You can address disagreements more effectively once you have thanked the speaker for sharing his/her ideas.

6. Be physically alert and use appropriate body language.

7. Reflect the person's feelings back to them.

8. Summarize the major ideas and concepts for further clarifications.

9. Use verbal and nonverbal reinforcers (such as head nods) to let the speaker know his/her message has been received.

10. Maintain a comfortable social distance.

11. Give constructive feedback: this is feedback that is descriptive not evaluative, offered not imposed, and focused on behavior rather than personal characteristics. Pay attention to the timing of feedback as well.

These websites offer useful tips on listening and responding skills:

www.taft.cc.ca.us/lrc/class/assignments/actlisten.html, crs.uvm.edu/gopher/nerl/personal/comm/e.html, www.nasua.org/informationandreferral/TipSheet1ActiveListening.pdf , and www.psu.edu/dus/cfe/actvlstn.htm.

Understanding the Needs of Parent/Guardian(s)

Having an understanding of what parents and guardians need can be helpful in developing and maintaining positive relationships with them and other community stakeholders. The three basic things that parents need from school personnel are respect, validation and support, and information. By keeping these needs in mind, school administrators help to communicate the vision of the school by modeling appropriate and collaborative behavior.

Respect
Respect is a key element in all effective communication. Parents and guardians may or may not be respectful of school personnel. The parents' history with members of the school community, their own experiences as a student, the current stresses in their lives and their general approach to life may influence how they respond to school counselors. Nonetheless, it is essential that administrators (indeed, all school personnel) act respectfully in all of their interactions with parents and guardians.

Respect is conveyed through word choice, voice tone, and content. Positive, inclusive statements express respect. Questions that invite collaboration also suggest respect. A lack of reactivity helps maintain respectful interactions. School leaders need to remember that some people respond to any contact by someone from their child's school with fear and/or anger. Being non-reactive to the parent's response will aid in communicating respect and concern, and helps avoid unnecessary conflict.

Validation and Support
Parents and guardians need validation and support, especially when the school is addressing difficult issues on an individual basis. Direct comments such as "I know you want the best for your child" and "I'm sure you are doing your best to help your child" can be useful. It also may be helpful to introduce a sensitive concern with "You probably know this, but I wanted to tell you…." This takes into account that the parent may be aware of what is going to be disclosed and communicates that school personnel believe that the parent is tuned into his or her child. While this may not always be the case, it is better to err in this direction.

In spite of any failings, parents and guardians are doing their best. From the school's perspective, parents may not be meeting the student's needs. They may even be abusive and neglectful. When necessary, school personnel may have to directly confront a parent or guardian, or file an abuse report. However, most of the time, parents and guardians are doing the best they can. Support and validation may also aid them in positively changing their behavior.

Information

The third thing parents and guardians need is clear information. School leaders need to be direct in communicating his or her concerns about a student, or when discussing school budgets, curriculum changes, test results, or other matters. Direct, up-to-date information that is stated without aggression, blame, apology, or condescension goes a long way in building positive relationships with parents and other community members.

When discussing a specific student with a parent or guardian, principals should remember that the parent may or may not be aware of the school's concerns. Parent/guardians have the right and need to be informed. They also need to hear what the principal, counselor and other school personnel are proposing as an action plan. This information needs to be conveyed in a non-judgmental way, without direct or implied criticism of the parent, even when school leaders are asking the parent to do something differently, or are implementing a non-optional disciplinary action.

SKILL 3.8   Knowledge of vision standard as related to data analysis

> 1. Given school data, develop and organize a school action plan that includes methods and approaches to communicate the need for the plan to teachers, students, and the community.

Schools, teachers, principals, students, and parents all feel the push for higher standards and for better performance on standardized tests. Principals must continually nurture a school climate that focuses on achieving the vision that the campus believes is most important. Many schools, in addition to working toward higher achievement on standardized tests, want students to be able to access and apply research from a variety of sources. Other schools are concerned with developing caring and responsible citizens. These goals should not be reduced for the sake of achievement tests. In many ways, the more we work to encourage the things we really believe in, the more motivated the campus community will be to succeed in the other areas.

How do we create a campus climate that encourages staff, students, families, and the community to work toward specific, deeply-held goals? There are many ways, but they all center on the importance of providing stakeholders with a voice and providing information in useful, accessible ways. This includes sharing relevant data on student achievement, budgeting, planning, and other issues.

School leaders are responsible for identifying which data can be helpful to share with different stakeholder groups. Some might be most appropriate for teachers; other information may be specifically designed to be shared with students or community members. Developing specific ways to communicate this information is then the next step. Both verbal and written formats can work, depending on the information to be shared.

The current thinking on stakeholder voice in public schools is that all stakeholders should be able to see how decisions are made (through very transparent processes) and should be given multiple opportunities for comment and critique. Because schools are so heavily involved in a family's life (after all, parents entrust schools to care for their children for approximately six hours per day), providing parents, especially, with open, transparent rationales for decisions is crucial. Furthermore, policies and decisions should take parent and student concerns and needs seriously. The more they feel accepted, the more they will see their place in the system.

Teachers need to feel that they have a voice, as well. Teachers want to be considered professionals, but when administrators seem to take advantage of them or leave them out of critical decisions, they feel as if their levels of expertise are not valued. While their needs cannot always be met fully, the more administrators show them that their concerns are important, the more they will accept the rationales for decisions they are not happy with.

Finally, beyond helping stakeholder groups see that a school values them, the mission and vision must be front and center in the daily operations of the school. A vision cannot simply be something that is written on a banner and hung in a hallway. It has to be talked about, referred to, valued, and considered regularly, especially when decisions must be made.

SKILL 3.9   Effective writing and data analysis for a school-based application

> 1. Given a scenario including data, analyze, interpret, and evaluate data for a specific target audience.

Effective Writing

To write effectively, a school leader should decide what information is to be conveyed. The following strategies can be employed whether writing a memo to the staff or a report for the superintendent:

- List each item to be discussed
- Put them in order -- from most to least important
- Write a brief summary of the entire document -- this will be the first paragraph.
- Expand on each item on the list
- If any action needs to be taken by the recipient, state this in the closing paragraph.

Proofreading is one of the most important actions in writing. Since most writing is done on computers, automated spelling and grammar checkers are readily available. Beware though -- some words, used in the wrong context, may be missed by computerized spell checkers. For example, the sentence "To employees attended too meetings two learn about the gnu curriculum," would pass through the spell check without any misspellings being detected. If possible, have someone else proofread your document and if time allows, put your composition away, and proofread it later, or even better, re-read it on the next day.

In many cases, there can be legal consequences to poor writing. Not documenting or clearly articulating an issue can be problematic at a later time. Good administrators put essential communications and decision in writing, but are careful to write very clearly and thoughtfully. This means the writing should be straightforward, lacking in jargon, spells out concerns and consequences, and includes enough but not too many details. As with proofreading, consulting with a colleague can be useful in writing significant documents and letters.

Report Writing

When writing a report that involves data analysis and interpretation, care needs to be given to think through precisely what needs to be communicated and how this can best be achieved. The intended audience needs to be considered, as different groups and individuals will have varying knowledge bases from which to understand the report. Tone and style can vary depending upon the topic and the writer's personality, but the goal should always be to write in a way that is succinct, clear, free of jargon as much as possible, and limited in personal judgments and opinions.

The format of the report and any accompanying charts or graphs should be chosen thoughtfully. The goal is to ensure that the format and visual depictions clarify and explicate the information, thus enhancing the reader's ability to understand the content. Similarly, direct quotes should only be included when they increase the clarity of the report or provide information that cannot be stated in any other way. References should be available but not interrupt the flow of the text.

The following guidelines provide a basic structure for a report.

- Introduction: Introduce the topic or main idea, state a point a view when relevant, and tell the reader briefly what the main points are.

- Main Points (3 or more): Each paragraph or section should include a lead-in sentence that states the main point. This sentence is followed by supporting detail and evidence regarding the point. Information about the source of data, methodologies and results may be reported in this section. At times, questions may be posed regarding the data to identify gaps in information or the need for further data-gathering or review.

- Summary: Restate the main idea and sum up the main points addressed in the report. Add any comments about future action that may be relevant.

Some key concepts to consider when presenting an analysis and interpretation of data are:

- Analyze: examine the parts
- Compare: look at similarities
- Contrast: look at differences
- Discuss: examine in detail
- Explain: provide reasons or examples, or clarify meaning

For more ideas about writing effective reports and articles, see **APPENDIX: General Strategies for Writing and Essay**.

APPENDIX: General Strategies for Writing the Essay In Subtest #3

* Budget your time. You will not have time to revise your essay. It is important that you write a good first draft.
* Read the question carefully. Make sure you understand what the question is asking you to do.
* Take time to pre-write.
* Write a thesis statement by restating the question.
* Keep your purpose in mind as you write your essay.
* Connect the ideas of your essay in a brief conclusion.
* Leave enough time to quickly proofread and edit your essay.

The essay must demonstrate your ability to write on a specific topic. As you prepare for this test, please keep in mind that this review will not teach you how to address content. It is expected that the fundamentals of educational leadership have been a focus of your course of study. The following steps in writing an essay in a timed situation will aid you in preparing to write the essay in the most time-efficient manner possible.

It is important to keep in mind that a good essay has focus, organization, support for the points being made, and correct word-usage.

Part I - Understanding the question

When you receive your question, the first step is decide what the question is asking you to do. Look for key words that will establish the purpose of your essay. Examine the chart and review the key words and the purpose each word establishes.

PRACTICE - Examine the chart on the next page. The chart identifies some of the key words you might find on an essay test. Please note that for each key word the purpose and an example are illustrated.

KEY WORD	PURPOSE	EXAMPLE
Analyze	to examine the parts of a news release	Read a passage and analyze how the author achieves effective communication using good communication practices
Compare	to identify the similarities	Read two memoranda concerning the handling of a safety issue and compare the similarities in each writer's methods for explaining the procedures for handling safety concerns
Contrast	to identify differences	Read two newsletters to parents and contrast how each writer uses communication techniques to elicit feedback
Discuss	examine in detail	Read a personnel evaluation and discuss how the writer conveys constructive criticism by addressing appropriate and specific job descriptors.
Explain	provide reasons/ examples or clarify the meaning	Read the opening passage of a school annual report and explain how the author provides specific directions to the contents.

When writing an essay, consider the following things before you begin to pre-write.

    ** Identifying the elements for analysis.

    ** Deciding on your main idea. Use the question as a guideline. However, do not merely restate the question. Make sure that in restating the topic you have taken a position on how you will answer the prompt. For example, you might be asked to read a superintendent's letter on facing a budget crisis and discuss not only the tone of the letter, but also the way the writer created the tone. It is important, if you wish to receive a high score on the essay, that your main idea clearly states your interpretation of the tone and how it was created.

    ** Considering Audience, Purpose, and Tone. Keep in mind that as you write an essay for a test, your purpose is to demonstrate knowledge of leadership skills by addressing an issue or solving a problem. Remember to match the style of writing to the proposed audience identified in the prompt. In on-the-job writing, you must use good encoding skills to create your own messages.

Part 2 - Prewriting for ideas and planning your essay

Prior to writing, you will need to pre-write for ideas and details as well as decide how the essay will be organized. In the time you have to write, you should spend no more than a tenth of the time (5-6 minutes for an hour's writing) for prewriting and organizing your ideas. As you pre-write, it might be helpful to remember you should have at least three main points and at least two to three details to support each point. There are several types of graphic organizers that you should practice using as you prepare for the essay portion of the test.

On the next page is a graphic illustration of how to organize ideas for an essay.

VISUAL ORGANIZER: GIVING REASONS

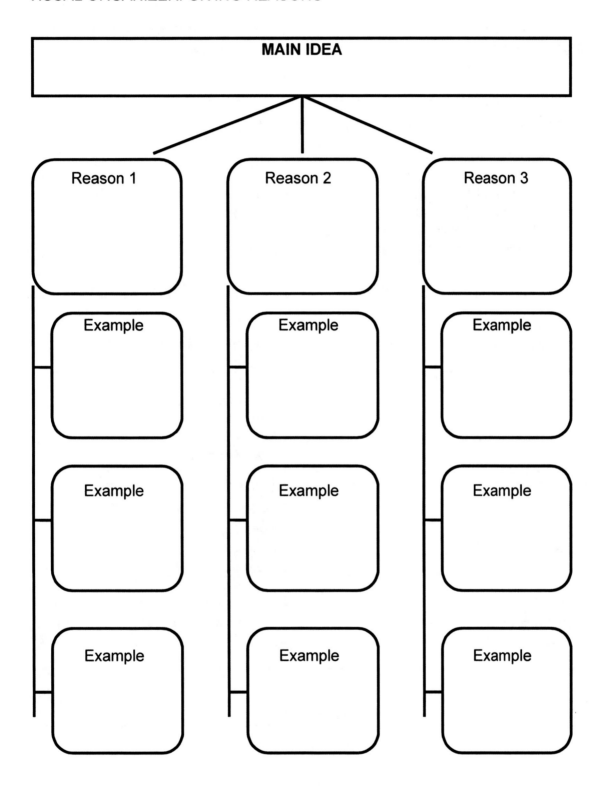

STEP 3: PREWRITE TO ORGANIZE IDEAS

After you have completed a graphic organizer, you need to decide how you will organize your essay. You might consider one of the following patterns to structure your writing.

Examine individual elements such as knowledge of audience, conciseness, specificity of information, timeliness of content, etc.

SINGLE ELEMENT OUTLINE
Intro - main idea statement
Main point 1 with at least two supporting details
Main point 2 with at least two supporting details
Main point 3 with at least two supporting details
Conclusion (restates main idea(s) and summary of main points)

POINT BY POINT	BLOCK
Introduction Statement of main idea about A and B	Introduction Statement of main idea A Statement of main idea B
Main Point 1 Discussion of A Discussion of B	Discussion of A Main Point 1 Main Point 2 Main Point 3
Main Point 2 Discussion of A Discussion of B	Discussion of B Main Point 1 Main Point 2 Main Point 3
Main Point 3 Discussion of A Discussion of B	Conclusion Restatement or summary of main idea A Restatement or summary of main idea B
Conclusion Restatement or summary of main idea	

PRACTICE:

Using the cluster on the next page, choose an organizing chart and complete the chart for your topic.

VIISUAL ORGANIZER: GIVING INFORMATION

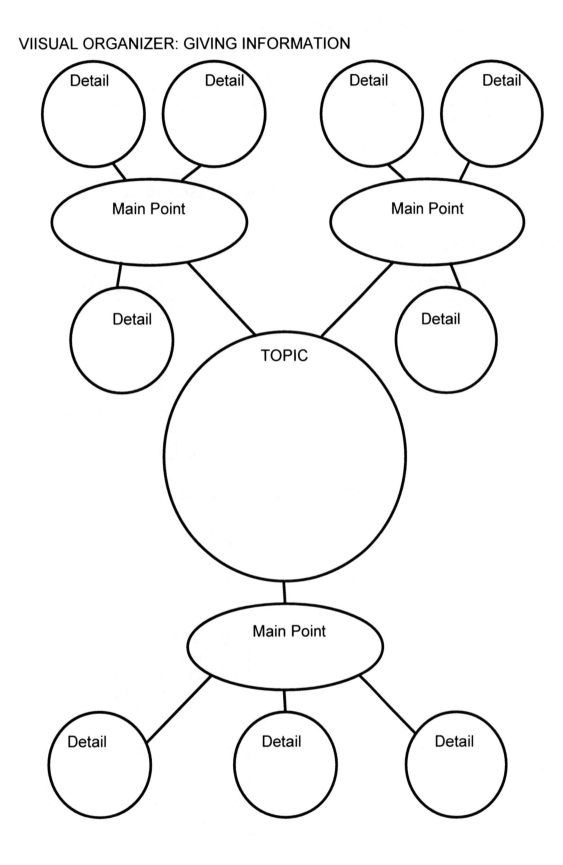

Part 4 - Write The Thesis Statement

First: Identify the topic.

I am going to write about the using good communication practices in news releases in order to raise the standards for athletic eligibility.

Second: State your point of view about the topic.

The positive and optimistic tone of the superintendent's release is created by his word choice, structure, and tone.

Third: Summarize the main points you will make in your essay.

The superintendent creates an optimistic tone by examining specific benefits to be gained with a clear, concise word choice and a positive tone.

PRACTICE:
Using the topic and prewriting you completed on the previous page, write the Thesis Statement for your essay. Follow the steps outlined above.

Part 5: State the main point of each body paragraph and organize support.

PARAGRAPH	PURPOSE	SUPPORT
1-Intro	Main Idea Statement	
2- First Body Paragraph	Main Point 1	Quotes or specific concepts from the text with analysis or explanation of how each detail supports your main point.
3- Second Body Paragraph	Main Point 2	Quotes or specific concepts from the text with analysis or explanation of how each detail supports your main point.
4 - Third Body Paragraph	Main Point 3	Quotes or specific concepts from the text with Analysis or explanation of how each detail supports Your main point.
5-Closing	Summarize Ideas	

<u>PRACTICE:</u> Using the given information cluster, complete your own organizing chart like the one above.

Part 6 - Write the introduction of your essay.

Remember that your introduction should accomplish the following things:

1. It should introduce the topic.
2. It should capture your reader's interest.
3. It should state your thesis.
4. It should prepare the reader for the main points of your essay.

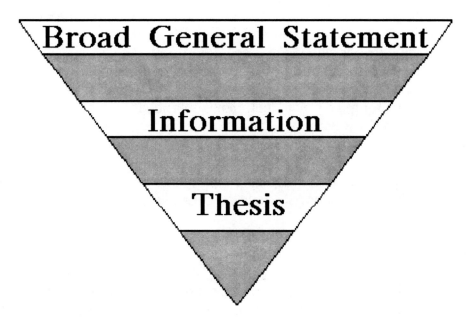

INVERTED TRIANGLE INTRODUCTION

Try to imagine the introduction as an inverted triangle. To write the introduction, follow the steps below.

1. On your prewriting sheet, write down your thesis. Check to see you have made it specific, prepared the reader for what will follow, and clearly addressed the topic.

2. Open your introduction with a broad general statement.

3. Follow the broad general statement with one or more sentences that add interest and information about the topic.

4. Write your thesis at the end of the introduction.

<u>PRACTICE</u>:

Now, you are ready to write your introduction. Complete the steps for writing an introduction using the ideas from your prewriting and organizing chart.

Part 7 - Writing the body paragraphs

Once you have written your introduction, move on to the body paragraphs. Remember the following guidelines as you write your body paragraphs.

Suggestions for Writing Body Paragraphs

* Write at least three body paragraphs.
* For each paragraph, write a main idea sentence, supporting sentences that provide details, and a closing sentence.
* Use transitions between and within each paragraph.
* Vary your sentence structure by using participial phrases, gerunds, infinitives, and adjective and noun clauses. Vary the length of sentences— simple sentences for main points, complex sentences for explanations.

<u>PRACTICE</u>:

Using your prewriting cluster and organizing chart, write the body paragraphs for your essay. Try to follow the suggestions listed above when writing your paragraphs.

Part 8 - Writing the conclusion

The closing paragraph of an essay summarizes the essay and reinforces the principal ideas of the essay. A good conclusion usually restates the thesis and main ideas from each body paragraph. It often ends with a clincher statement, an unforgettable sentence that ends the paper.

<u>PRACTICE</u>:

Now, take out the essay for which you have already written an introduction and the body paragraphs. Write a conclusion to your essay and be sure to include a clincher sentence.

Part 9 - Editing and proofreading

In a testing situation, you will be assessed on your ability to write an essay that demonstrates structural and grammatical skill in a limited amount of time; you will not have time to revise. However, correct usage will be factored into your score. It is important to leave five minutes to reread, edit, and proofread your paper.

In on-the-job writing, you will usually have more time for pre-writing and editing, though we are all occasionally pressured by deadlines. The more accurate you can make the first draft, the more time saved from editing.

Editing occurs when you change words or phrases to clarify your ideas. If you make any changes, cross out the word or words once and write the new word or phrase directly above it. Make sure that any changes you make are clear.

Proofreading is checking your essay for any errors in mechanics or punctuation. Although you are writing in a timed situation, you are expected to follow the standards of correct usage. If you find an error, cross it out with a single line and write the correction directly above the error.

PRACTICE:

Take out the essay for which you have written an introduction, a body, and a conclusion. Take five minutes to edit and proofread your essay.

Sample Test

Select the most appropriate answer for each question.

1. **You have recently been appointed principal of Sunshine State Middle School. During the summer you reviewed the FCAT scores and found that in reading, 90% of 7th and 80% of 8th grade students scored at a level 3 or above; however, 50% of the 6th grade students scored at a level 1 or 2 on this portion of the exam. When you reviewed the instructional records you realized that the school had not aligned its curriculum, instruction, and assessment. In order to achieve this alignment, which of the following is the BEST strategy and why?** *(Skill 1.1) (Rigorous)*

   A. Identify the goals and objectives yourself and then require teachers to meet these goals and objectives; the faculty is aware of the serious nature of meeting AYP requirements and it is your job to create a plan of action

   B. Work with a committee of faculty members, parents, and community leaders to help you develop goals and objectives to address the problem in order to get the necessary buy-in and community-wide commitment necessary to achieve this lofty goal

   C. You identify a team of stakeholders to advise you on goals and objectives; however, you inform them that you reserve the right to determine what the plan will be. As the instructional leader, your priorities need to carry more weight than others in the school

   D. You recruit a team of stakeholders and at the first meeting you break members into three groups. One will tackle the curriculum, one will address the instructional techniques, and the third will work on the assessment practices. You believe this is the most efficient way to get a lot of work done

2. **Which sequence best describes the order of a needs assessment?**
   (Skill 1.1) (Average Rigor)

   A. Survey of needs, goals and objectives development, problem identification, implementation planning, process evaluation

   B. Problem identification, survey of needs, goals and objectives development, implementation planning, process evaluation

   C. Problem identification, survey of needs, goals and objectives development, process evaluation, implementation planning

   D. Survey of needs, problem identification, goals and objectives development, implementation planning, process evaluation

3. **Which of the following refers to the horizontal organization of the elements of the curriculum?**
   (Skill 1.1) (Average Rigor)

   A. The knowledge and skills students learn are useful in life situations

   B. The knowledge and skills that students learn at one grade level are relevant and useful as they progress to other grades

   C. Everything the student learns contributes to fulfillment of the curriculum

   D. What students learn in one class supports and reinforces what they learn in other classes

4. **Which of the following refers to the vertical organization of the elements of the curriculum?** *(Skill 1.1) (Average Rigor)*

   A. Everything the student learns contributes to fulfillment of the curriculum

   B. The knowledge and skills that students learn at one grade level are relevant and useful as they progress to other grades

   C. What students learn in one class supports and reinforces what they learn in other classes

   D. The knowledge and skills students learn are useful in life situations

5. **_____ is based on the clustering of subjects into categories of study.** *(Skill 1.1) (Average Rigor)*

   A. Process-centered curriculum design

   B. Subject-centered curriculum design

   C. Discipline-centered curriculum design

   D. Broad fields curriculum design

6. **Which of the following statements best describes process evaluation?** *(Skill 1.1) (Average Rigor)*

   A. It is concerned with the needs of the program

   B. It is concerned with the adequacy of resources to implement the program

   C. It is concerned with recording procedures and continuous monitoring

   D. It is concerned with the attainment of the goals for the program

7. **According to the Florida Bureau of School Improvement, a school improvement plan should include which of the following:** *(Skill 1.1) (Easy)*

   A. Staff improvement strategies, including professional development plans

   B. Clear goals for readings, mathematics and science, with accompanying budget figures

   C. A coordination and integration component required for Title I

   D. All of the above

8. At the national level, administrators are impacted by entities such as the United States Department of Education. Which of the following is a local entity that has a similar impact on Florida's administrators? *(Skill 1.1) (Easy)*

   A. The Florida Department of Education

   B. The Florida Department of Corrections

   C. The Florida Legislature

   D. The Florida State Bar

9. The _____ is to national educational policy as the _____ is to statewide educational policy. *(Skill 1.1) (Easy)*

   A. Florida Department of Education; United States Department of Education

   B. United States Department of Education; Superintendent

   C. United States Department of Education; Florida Department of Education

   D. Superintendent; Florida Department of Education

10. Your school is committed to drawing on scientifically-based research (SBR) for curriculum development. According to five studies, students have increased math achievement when teachers use a curriculum with four components: manipulatives, memory cards, videos, and a proprietary computer program. However, your school's curriculum committee only has sufficient funds for the manipulatives, memory cards, and videos. Due to this, what should be your biggest concern? *(Skill 1.2) (Average Rigor)*

   A. The program may not be a good match for your school's unique conditions and needs

   B. You only have a limited amount of time to review the research studies supporting this curriculum

   C. The research supports the curriculum with four components; without one element, the program is no longer research-based

   D. None of the above

11. Which of the following resources is MOST efficient in helping educators to locate evidence-based practices? *(Skill 1.2) (Easy)*

   A. Print-based journals

   B. The What Works Clearinghouse

   C. The Recent Trends Website

   D. References from colleagues

12. The following table presents an excerpt of questions from your recent school climate survey. The table also shows, for each question, the percent of staff members who agreed/strongly agreed and the percent of staff who disagreed/strongly disagreed. In order to increase morale and performance, which area should you address first? *(Skill 1.3) (Average Rigor)*

Question	Agree/Strongly Agree	Disagree/Strongly Disagree
I feel as though I am working as part of a team	90%	10%
There are open lines of communication with the administration	80%	20%
The principal supports me in conflicts with parents	60%	40%
The administration has effectively addressed the gang activity in front the school building	20%	80%

   A. Increasing the camaraderie and team-spirit among staff members

   B. Creating better lines of communication between the administration and other stakeholders

   C. Working to support staff members when they have conflicts with parents

   D. Addressing the gang activity in front the school building

13. **Positive school environments have all of the following characteristics except:** *(Skill 1.3) (Easy)*

    A. Strict rules

    B. Clear adult leadership

    C. Respect for diversity

    D. Policies and procedures to ensure the safety of everyone in the school community

14. **For self-efficacy to emerge, which two things must be attached to a task:** *(Skill 1.3) (Rigorous)*

    A. Expectation and value

    B. Emotion and success

    C. Perseverance and ranking

    D. Cognition and Trials

15. **Which of the following definitions correctly identifies self-efficacy theory?** *(Skill 1.3) (Average Rigor)*

    A. Success is the result of applying causal explanations regarding achievement efforts and influence on the effects of expectancies

    B. A person's judgment about his or her ability to perform an activity at a specific level of performance

    C. The causes of success or failure are due to uncontrollable factors

    D. Attaching logic to emotional reactions engenders pride and responsibility

16. **The basic postulate of this theory of motivation is that intentions to achieve a goal form the primary motivating force behind work behavior. Select the theory that best conforms to this postulate.** *(Skill 1.3) (Average Rigor)*

    A. Goal theory

    B. Feedback theory

    C. Attribution theory

    D. Controllability theory

17. Your elementary school will expand its pre-school classes to include a group of three-year-olds in the fall. Which of the following will you need to adjust? *(Skill 1.4) (Easy)*

   A. The lunch schedule, since young children do not have a regular lunch time

    B. The location of classes to make sure the three-year-olds are on the first floor, since not all three-year-olds can climb stairs

   C. The type of supplies purchased, since toddlers need different materials from other children

   D. The parking spaces assigned to teachers so that the new pre-school teacher feels welcomed

18. All of the following are among the six core domains of instructional strategy and functioning except: *(Skill 1.4) (Easy)*

   A. Team Work

   B. Planning

   C. Management of student conduct

   D. Presentation of subject

19. Which of the following best describes the purpose of student assessment? *(Skill 1.4) (Average Rigor)*

   A. To analyze performance at various stages of goal attainment

   B. To appraise curriculum goals and objectives

   C. To determine outcome in terms of cost and achievement related to cost

   D. To analyze various alternatives or program options

20. Which of the following is the best formative assessment practice for students? *(Skill 1.4) (Rigorous)*

   A. Provide a comprehensive multiple choice test at the end of the chapter

   B. Provide several teacher-made quizzes during the chapter

   C. Provide guided practice during the unit

   D. Provide a combination of test formats in the chapter test

21. **Students designated as having mental retardation are likely to have social skills at varying levels of development, depending on an individual's mental age. This means that teachers should do all of the following except:** *(Skill 1.5) (Easy)*

    A. Model desired behavior

    B. Provide clear instructions

    C. Expect appropriate behaviors fo the child's chronological age

    D. Adjust the physical environment when necessary

22. **The term IEP stands for which of the following?** *(Skill 1.5) (Easy)*

    A. Individualized Educational Progress

    B. Individualized Education Plan

    C. Inclusive Education Progress

    D. Inclusive Educational Plan

23. **At a school board meeting, the superintendent is addressing the sections of the *Florida Constitution, Article IX, Uniform System of Public Schools.* She has listed four sections: uniform system of free public schools, makeup of the State Board of Education, terms of service for appointed board members, and scope and duties of school districts. However, she has forgotten the other sections. To assist her, you would add which of the following to that list?** *(Skill 1.6) (Rigorous)*

    A. Terms of office of superintendents

    B. Use of the income from the state school fund

     C. Both A and B

    D. None of the above

24. **The Individuals Disability Education Act (IDEA) was enacted to:**
(Skill 1.6) (Average Rigor)

A. Ensure students overcome language barriers that impede equal participation in instructional programs

B. Provide equal educational opportunities for students of any race, color, or national origin

C. Improve accountability, expand services, simplify parental involvement, and provide earlier access to services and supports for students with special needs

D. Ensure confidentiality of records and other information about students, parents, or staff members with disabilities

25. **One of your staff members has been named as the defendant in a court case. The lawsuit claims that the student became physically ill because of constant fear of the teacher's imposing manner and verbal abuse. The student and her parents are claiming which of the following:**
(Skill 1.7) (Rigorous)

A. Battery

 B. Assault

C. Negligence

D. In Loco Parentis

26. **F.S. 237 Financial Accounts and Expenditures for Public Schools describes guidelines for uniform record keeping and the handling of accounts. It sets forth the procedures for all of the following EXCEPT:**
(Skill 1.7) (Easy)

A. Establishing budgets

B. Auditing procedures

C. Disbursing lottery winnings

D. Levying taxes

27. In reviewing the financial records of your predecessor, you realize that he created the school budget by engaging in the following process:
1) use the categories from the current budget;
2) mark all categories as blank and unfunded;
3) allocate funding to categories that he decided would continue in the coming budget cycle.
Your predecessor was using which technique of school financial management?
(Skill 1.8) (Easy)

A. Zero-based budgeting

B. Planning, Programming, Budgetary, and Evaluation System

C. Incremental budgeting

D. Planning, Programming, Budgetary Justification System

28. Which of the following statements is true of school accounting practices?
(Skill 1.8) (Average Rigor)

A. All purchases from internal funds must be authorized by the principal or a person designated by the principal

B. The principal is the only person authorized to sign checks for the school checking account

C. Principals can pre-sign checks that a designated administrator can use when the principal is unavailable

D. Administrators must record, present, summarize, and interpret accurate records to preserve the school's owner equity

29. General principles of school cost accounting require schools to use a(an) _____ basis for accounting.
(Skill 1.8) (Easy)

A. Single-entry

B. Cash basis

C. Consolidation

D. Accrual

30. **Which of the following is one of the characteristics of the foundation program of funding?** *(Skill 1.8) (Average Rigor)*

A. The state and district work together to define the level of funding

B. The state works alone to define the level of funding

C. A non-profit foundation works alone to define the level of funding

D. None of the above

31. **Who regulates the use of internal school funds?** *(Skill 1.8) (Easy)*

A. State Board of Education

B. Local School Board

C. School Site-Based Management Team

D. School Principal

32. **The calculation of the base student allocation formula is best expressed by which of the following:** *(Skill 1.8) (Rigorous)*

A. The FTE plus program cost factor, times base student allocation, times district cost differential

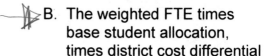
B. The weighted FTE times base student allocation, times district cost differential

C. The FTE times weighted FTE, times base student allocation, times district cost differential

D. The weighted FTE times program cost factor, times base student allocation, times district cost factor

33. **Mr. Price, principal at Wilson High School, wants to make preparation of the campus budget a more collaborative process. The first thing he should do is:** *(Skill 1.8) (Rigorous)*

   A. Contact various stakeholders to gather information.

   B. Form a Budget Committee with representatives from all stakeholder groups.

   C. Articulate a vision statement that shows a relationship between the school's budget and its improvement goals.

   D. Draft a budget that can be used as a basis for discussion, assuming it will be modified by input from stakeholders.

34. **A school principal faced with inadequate funds to achieve school goals can:** *(Skill 1.8) (Average Rigor)*

   A. Use discretionary funds to support the school's mission and vision.

   B. Seek help from all stakeholders.

   C. Approach the Site Based Management Committee for help.

   D. All of the above

35. **The "Financial and Program Cost Accounting for Florida Schools" is a publication that reflects the requirements of Rule 6A-1.001 of Florida's Administrative Code and Sections 237.01 and 237.02 of Florida's Statutes. It is also known as the _____.** *(Skill 1.9) (Easy)*

   A. Money Book

   B. Green Book

   C. FPCA Book

   D. Red Book

36. **Which of the following is a principle of accrual accounting?** *(Skill 1.9) (Rigorous)*

   A. Transactions are recorded when a cash receipt or reimbursement occurs

   B. Transactions are recorded as assets or liabilities when the cash receipt or reimbursement occurs

   C. Transactions are recorded in a cash account and then moved to an asset or liability column when the cash funds are received

    D. Transactions are recorded as assets or liabilities at the time they occur

37. The school administrator should ensure that the building is always safe and comfortable. Which of the following is the most efficient method for achieving this goal? *(Skill1.10) (Rigorous)*

A. Establishing a system for teachers to complete daily logs of building conditions

B. Conducting brief daily walk-throughs of the building, either personally or through a designee

C. Allowing students to come to the office and report problems they encounter

D. Holding monthly rallies for stakeholders to discuss their concerns and requests

38. A fellow principal tells you that her school has been dealing with break-ins during the lunch period. They believe the culprits are neighborhood youth breaking into the gym while it is unused during lunch. To prevent the problem the school has begun locking the doors during lunch and reopening them when gym classes are back in session. What should be your opinion of this plan? *(Skill 1.10) (Average Rigor)*

A. It is an effective method to address the problem; there are no major concerns

B. This is an ineffective plan and should not be used

 C. The plan may prevent break-ins; however, it may prevent egress at any time

D. None of the above

39. The death of a fourth grader in a swimming accident has prompted the implementation of the school crisis response plan. Which of the following would not be included as an appropriate activity in the plan:
(Skill 1.11) (Easy)

A. Getting accurate information out to all members of the school community

B. Sharing the latest media reports about the accident with staff and students

C. Offering crisis/grief counseling to all students

D. Providing information to parents and guardians about common stress and grief reactions

40. A bomb threat is reported at the high school, and the school is evacuated. In order to function appropriately as a crisis responder in this situation, school personnel need all of the following except:
(Skill 1.11) (Average Rigor)

A. A chance to debrief and get support from colleagues

B. Clarity about roles and responsibilities

C. Mandatory post-trauma counseling

D. Adequate training and follow-up

41. A school administrator is asked to develop a crisis management plan for her school. She includes all of the following in the plan except:
(Skill 1.11) (Average Rigor)

A. Specific lines of communication

B. The name of the crisis team leader

C. Goals of the plan

D. Intervention strategies

42. The following letter has been sent to your office by a parent of a kindergarten student.

Dear Ms. Valdes,

My son, Joey Brown, has recently been diagnosed with asthma. In order to control his asthma attacks, the doctor has prescribed the following medication that must be taken EVERY two hours. Please advise me on the best strategy to ensure that he receives his medication according to the prescribed regimen.

Sincerely, Mr. Andrew Brown

According to Florida Statute 232.46, what should be your response to this letter? *(Skill 1.11) (Average Rigor)*

A. Dear Mr. Brown: The school is not permitted to administer medication. As John is 6 years old, the teachers will remind him to take his medication every two hours

B. Dear Mr. Brown: Please provide us with the medication in its original container along with a statement giving us 1) permission to assist in its administration and 2) an explanation of the necessity of the medication

C. Dear Mr. Brown: The school is not permitted to administer medication. In order to use the medication on school grounds, John must 1) keep it in a secured locker and 2) ask permission to leave class every two hours

D. Dear Mr. Brown: Please provide us with the name of John's doctor and of the medication so that we can research whether this is a medication we are allowed to administer to students

43. You are a vice-principal at a large, urban high school. The student population has many teenage parents, including several who have chosen to remain as a couple and raise their child. One of your after-school programs is aimed at increasing the graduation rate of these students. Therefore, you provide them with mentors and meet with their parents to make sure they are on track to graduate. One particularly supportive mother likes to review her son's folder each month. He is a senior, and turned 18 just before Thanksgiving. What are your responsibilities to the parent and to the child according to FERPA? *(Skill 1.12) (Rigorous)*

A. When a student becomes the legal guardian for a child, he or she is viewed as an independent individual under the FERPA legislation

B. The mother has the right to view her son's records as long as he is under her care, regardless of his age

C. The mother's right to view her son's record continues until the end of the school year in which he turns 18

D. Her son in the only individual who has a right to view his records since he is already 18

44. The father of a former student calls you concerning his daughter's progress in college. He is concerned that the now 17-year-old college student has switched majors without telling him. Therefore, he wants to know the best way to obtain her records. You should advise the parent that the Buckley Amendment: *(Skill 1.12) (Average Rigor)*

A. Does not permit colleges to provide student records to parents

B. Allows parents access to college student's records only if the parent pays the tuition

C. Transfers the parent's rights of consent to the student once he/she enters 12th grade

D. Both A and C

45. **Which of the following is NOT a major category in the Florida statutes?** *(Skill 1.12) (Average Rigor)*

    A. Compensatory education, truancy, and home schooling

    B. Educational choice, special and charter schools

    C. Health, immunization and medication issues

    D. Religious issues

46. **A new student has arrived from Italy and you know that he speaks very little English. As the school principal, you realize that his right to a translator and other resources are covered under which of the following?** *(Skill 1.13) (Average Rigor)*

    A. Title VI

    B. EEOC

    C. Both A and B

    D. Neither A nor B

47. **During a meeting with fellow superintendents you overhear a heated exchange between two colleagues. One believes that the META consent decree is similar to IDEA in numerous ways. The other administrator believes that such a comparison is incorrect and borders on discrimination. They ask your opinion. Which of the following the most appropriate response:** *(Skill 1.14) (Average Rigor)*

    A. I just came for the snacks; I'd rather not be involved in a weighty debate

    B. They are not similar, since the META consent decree deals with English language learners and IDEA deals with students with special needs

    C. They are quite similar in that they are both aimed at providing equal access to students

    D. They are quite similar in that they both receive the largest allocations of federal funds

48. Which of the following best illustrates an educational goal?
(Skill 1.14) (Average Rigor)

A. Provide good health and physical fitness

B. By the year 2010, the high school graduation rate will increase to at least 90%

C. Develop self-realization

D. The students will complete a reading comprehension examination within 30 minutes with 80% accuracy

49. Which of the following is a major benefit of the FCAT exam?
(Skill 1.15) (Rigorous)

A. It identifies important educational topics that can drive instruction

B. It is used by the legislature to determine per pupil funding

C. It serves as a benchmark for comparing students with their colleagues in other states

D. It permits educators to monitor how much students learn from one year to the next

50. The most recent FCAT scores has resulted in your school being awarded a grade of "B" by the state. After celebrating this achievement, you turn your attention to addressing the areas that reduced your performance. In mathematics, 100 students earned levels 1, 2, or 3 on the assessment. In reading, 50 students earned levels 1, 2, or 3. For the school to make "adequate progress" you will need to do which of the following?
(Skill 1.15) (Rigorous)

A. Make sure at least 50% of the lowest-performing math students make learning gains in math

B. Make sure at least 50% of the lowest-performing reading students make learning gains in reading

C. Make sure at least 50 of the lowest-performing math students and 25 of the lowest performing reading students make learning gains in their respective subjects

D. All of the above

51. Identify the type of evaluation that occurs before instruction:
(Skill 1.16) (Average Rigor)

 A. Formative

 B. Diagnostic

 C. Summative

 D. Normative

52. While observing your first-year teachers, you noticed that they do not understand the basics of creating appropriate assessments. Therefore, you have created a graphic to help them understand the importance of validity and reliability. What terms should you write next to Line One and Line Two below?
(Skill 1.16) (Average Rigor)

Line Two

Line One

 A. Line One represents reliability

 B. Line Two represents reliability

 C. Line One represents validity

 D. None of the above

53. If the United States Department of Education requires a national test to determine where each student performs compared to other similar students, they would require students to take _____ assessments. If the State of Florida wants to determine how well its students are performing relative to the Sunshine State Standards, they must administer a _____ assessment.
(Skill 1.16) (Easy)

 A. Criterion-referenced, Norm-referenced

 B. Norm-referenced, Criterion-referenced

 C. Norm-referenced, Norm-referenced

 D. Criterion-referenced, Criterion-referenced

54. Data show that at your school, ESOL students are having problems in understanding literary techniques. Particularly challenging for 75% of these students are comparisons such as similes and metaphors. You would like to diagnose the exact source of the problem so that students can learn what the state standards require. Which of the following represents the best series of strategies that teachers should use? *(Skill 1.17) (Average Rigor)*

A. Administer diagnostic assessments, individualize instruction according to the results of the diagnosis, identify strengths and weaknesses, reassess

B. Identify strengths and weaknesses, administer diagnostic assessments, individualize instruction according to the results of the diagnosis, reassess

C. Reassess, administer diagnostic assessments, individualize instruction according to the results of the diagnosis, identify strengths and weaknesses

D. Administer diagnostic assessments, identify strengths and weaknesses, individualize instruction according to the results of the diagnosis, reassess

55. The faculty of the mathematics department has submitted their proposal for the school's technology plan. In it, they have requested a high-tech package that combines various powerful CAI tools. After investigating the proposed purchase, Mrs. Griffin, your technology directory, agrees that it is a worthwhile investment. However, she advises that the processors you currently have are too slow to execute the tasks required. In order for the math students to use the package you must purchase both items in this coming finance cycle. In your budget, the CAI tools would be in category 1, while the processor would be listed under category 2. Of the four options below, which one provides the correct answers for categories1 and 2? *(Skill 2.1) (Easy)*

A. Hardware, 2. Software

B. 1. Software, 2. Peripherals

C. 1. Software, 2. Hardware

D. 1. Peripherals, 2. Hardware

56. What is the MAIN reason for the slow pace of technology's diffusion and integration into teachers' practice?
(Skill 2.1) (Rigorous)

A. Teachers and administrators were not prepared to manage technology in schools

B. Teachers were afraid of technology

C. Administrators did not want to pay for the expensive equipment

D. Students were not interested in technology

57. Which of the following best describes the superintendent's role in assessing hardware and software needs:
(Skill 2.1) (Average Rigor)

A. Researching the use of all appropriate hardware and software packages in educational settings

B. Hiring a consultant to identify what the district needs to buy at this point in time

C. Working closely with a technology committee to identify current needs and possible solutions, including specific purchases

D. Asking each principal what is needed in his or her school

58. The algebra teacher will use a software application for students to calculate several math equations. Which of the following would best complete the task?
(Skill 2.1) (Average Rigor)

A. Communications

B. Word processor

C. Database

D. Spreadsheet

59. Last year, the school created a Technology Committee composed of one representative from the faculty and administration plus one parent, student, and business person. This year, the School Advisor Committee (SAC) has voted to increase the faculty membership. The new requirement mandates that the TC includes one teacher from each department. The SAC is MOST likely accounting for which of the steps in the software evaluation process?
(Skill 2.2) (Rigorous)

A. Determining that the features and capabilities of the software match administrative goals and objectives

B. Determining if the software actually does what it describes and if what it does is what is needed

C. Ascertaining that the software is compatible to the computer system operating at the school

D. Both A and B

60. **All of the following are examples of copyright infringement except:**
    (Skill 2.2) (Average Rigor)

    A. When teachers take home software from school computer labs

    B. Reselling copies of computer programs purchased by one school to another school

    C. Running software applications on computers that are too slow to handle those applications

    D. The illegal duplication of software

61. Mr. Horowitz, the principal, has asked you to review applications in order to hire one new foreign language teacher. You have received the staffing requirements and found that the least critical need is Spanish and the greatest need is in Swahili followed by Arabic. As you assess the applications you have narrowed your choice to two teachers. One has taught in Florida for two years but has not earned her license to teach Swahili in Florida. However, she was licensed in another state and taught Swahili there for ten years. In addition, due to her instructional leadership in the school district, she has received stellar reviews and recommendations from her former principal and the district superintendant. The second candidate graduated three years ago with a major in Spanish. This year he earned his Florida teaching license and his principal has rated him as average for the past two years. Which of these two teachers should you hire and why?
(Skill 2.3) (Rigorous)

A. Hire the candidate who teaches Swahili; this is an area of high-needs and her teaching record indicates that she is experienced and highly-qualified; you can then support her in attaining certification

B. Hire the candidate who teaches Spanish and has attained certification; federal and state laws require that a candidate have a state licensure before being hired to teach in Florida

C. Both candidates should be hired. The Swahili teacher can fill the need for that language; the Spanish teacher's certification can be useful in reports required by *No Child Left Behind*

D. Either teacher can be hired; your school would be well-served to hire either the Swahili or Spanish teacher

62. In selecting instructional personnel, most public school principals are responsible for all of the following EXCEPT: *(Skill 2.3) (Easy)*

    A. Establishing a committee

    B. Initiating the process

    C. Determining the recommendations for employment

    D. Making the offer of employment

63. A school needs a reading specialist; however, the applicant pool is small and no applicant meets all position requirements. The principal should: *(Skill 2.3) (Rigorous)*

    A. Select the best person and provide him or her with support

    B. Leave the position unfilled and advertise the position again

    C. Re-assign teachers to cover the position during their planning periods

    D. Inform parents that reading will not be taught until a qualified person is hired

64. When using site-based management, why should a principal involve a diverse group of stakeholders in the planning and decision-making processes? *(Skill 2.3) (Rigorous)*

    A. Law requires that diverse groups participate in all parts of school management

    B. It avoids conflict when choices are made because every person is represented by individuals on the committee

    C. A committee of diverse individuals cannot represent everyone; however, they are more likely to bring different perspectives compared to a non-diverse committee

    D. This guarantees that special-interest groups will not be upset at the administration

65. Which of the following is MOST LIKELY to assist participants in staff development activities to retain information? *(Skill 2.3) (Average Rigor)*

    A. Cover the topic in a single-session workshop

    B. Cover the topic in a three to four session workshop

    C. Cover the topic throughout the school year, allowing teachers to try the strategies then report back

    D. Cover the topic daily at informal meetings

66. Which of the following is an appropriate district level orientation activity for a group of new teachers: *(Skill 2.3) (Easy)*

    A. A review of their individual school's philosophy

    B. An introduction to faculty

    C. Getting information about school board policies

    D. A statement of their individual school's vision

67. During the interview process, the principal may ask about the applicant's: *(Skill 2.3) (Easy)*

    A. Reasons for applying for the job

    B. Mother's maiden name

    C. Ages of children

    D. Handicapping conditions

68. **Mr. Blanchard has taken care to match the qualifications of new teachers he hires with school needs and district policies. However, by the end of the first semester, he has received numerous complaints about two of his new hires, and some community leaders have criticized him for the teachers he hired. From the information provided, what is a likely explanation for this criticism?**
(Skill 2.3) (Rigorous)

A. The new teachers did not buy into the school mission and vision

B. Students dislike the school vision and have complained to their parents about how the new teachers promote it

C. He inadequately communicated his actions to community stakeholders

D. Mr. Blanchard's hiring process is inadequate for his staffing needs

69. **When new teachers attend a school-level orientation, which of the following would be an appropriate topic:** *(Skill 2.3) (Easy)*

A. Retirement benefits

B. Insurance benefits

C. Introduction to the district payroll system

D. The school's faculty handbook

70. **The Florida Department of Education (FLDOE) has mandated that all teachers receive ongoing evaluations and that all salary increases be tied to learning. Your administrative team has developed an intensive instructional assessment instrument with the following categories: classroom management and discipline, knowledge of subject matter, instructional strategies and pedagogical techniques, integration of technology, cultural competency and incorporation of diversity, and professional development and self-reflection. When submitted to the FLDOE for approval, the instrument was returned, noting that a key element was missing. Which of the following categories should you add?** *(Skill 2.4) (Average Rigor)*

   A. Teacher disposition

   B. Student achievement

   C. Team work

   D. Parental and community involvement

71. **Which of the following criteria should be used to evaluate personnel in schools?** *(Skill 2.4) (Average Rigor)*

   A. How well the parents like the teacher

   B. How well the children like the teacher

   C. How well the other teachers relate to the teacher

   D. Test score gains by the students

72. **In performance-based assessments, the principal ties teachers' performance to which of the following:** *(Skill 2.4) (Average Rigor)*

   A. Student learning

   B. Parental feedback

   C. Administrative ratings

   D. Student surveys

73. **The building level principal should perform which of the following performance appraisal tasks?** *(Skill 2.4) (Easy)*

    A. Develop appraisal criteria

    B. Design the appraisal process

    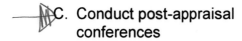C. Conduct post-appraisal conferences

    D. Assess the appraisal system

74. **The district is attempting to streamline the way it handles personnel information. As the superintendent, you have reviewed all the available options and would like to invest in a computerized system. At your last board meeting, 75% of the school board members expressed concern that the system was too expensive. In addition, they could not understand why you could not simply perfect the filing system currently in use. Which of the following points would you use to convince the board members to approve the computerized system?** *(Skill 2.5) (Easy)*

    A. It will allow for more precise access to sensitive personnel information with access being limited and monitored

    B. It can provide administrative staff with an efficient way to enter, share, and use personnel data as they see fit

    C. It can eliminate the need for paper files on employees.

    D. A and C

75. One of your teacher's has received negative ratings on each of her evaluations for the past four years. As principal, you have referred her to the Employee Assistance Program but she has used their services. The superintendent's office has reviewed her folder and decided to dismiss her. Which of the following must happen next? *(Skill 2.6)* *(Average Rigor)*

A. The teacher must be notified in writing

B. The teacher is allowed an appeal

C. The teacher must be allowed to examine any evidence

D. The teacher must be permitted counsel of his or her choice

76. Which of the following is NOT required when bringing punitive action against a teacher? *(Skill 2.6) (Easy)*

A. A videotape of the hearing

B. Notification of charges in writing

C. A transcript of the hearing

D. An impartial hearing

77. An employee has not performed well throughout the year although you have followed all steps to help her, and her previous recommendations had been excellent. You have documented her work and your evaluation process. She recently disclosed that she has had a number of personal stressors this past year and knows she did not perform well. What will be your recommendation for her employment next year? *(Skill 2.6) (Rigorous)*

A. Terminate her, based on the objective evaluation criteria

B. Conduct a hearing before an impartial tribunal prior to making a decision

C. Rehire her because she has acknowledged her problems

D. Request that she take a leave of absence for the next year

78. One of your teachers is threatening legal action against you and the school district. He asserts that he has been unfairly overlooked during the process of raises and promotions. Your position is that the district has required that teacher raises be tied to student achievement. His students have consistently performed poorly on the state achievement tests. In addition, he refuses to attend professional development sessions that are not required in his contract. The attorney's office has advised you that your position may not be supported in court. She has shown you that the teacher's unions have been able to resist efforts to include pay-for-performance measures in its contracts. Therefore, the district has decided to give the teacher the raise he wants. After talking with other principals in your district, you realize this is an ongoing problem. What is the most effective way for you to solve the discrepancy between the pay-for-performance requirement and the contract stipulations?
(*Skill 2.7*) (*Rigorous*)

A. Compose a resolution, obtain the signatures of your fellow principals, and submit the document to the superintendent

B. Mobilize parents to petition the school board on this issue

C. Work with the school district as it engages in collective bargaining with the teacher's union

D. Lobby the state Department of Education to legislate that the discrepancy be corrected

79. **Why is collective bargaining beneficial for both the teachers' union and the school district?** *(Skill 2.7)* *(Rigorous)*

A. Working together allows both sides to consider each other's needs and can bring unity and effective action once a decision is reached

B. Discussing the issues with small groups of teachers allows individual perspectives to be considered in the decision-making process

C. Using collective bargaining allows the teachers' union and the school district to avoid conflict because one side has to give in to the other's wishes

D. Engaging in collective bargaining is never beneficial for either the union or the district

80. **Your teachers have agreed that they will set student achievement goals tied to the FCAT assessment. To aid them, you have provided ongoing professional development on setting S.M.A.R.T goals, improving instructional strategies, and using continuous assessments to gauge student learning. Which of the following teachers appear to have been impacted by your strategy?** *(Skill 2.8) (Rigorous)*

A. Mrs. Johnson set her goal to have 65% of her students achieve a level 3 or above on the FCATs; 40% achieved this goal during the first year, 56% the second year, and 68% last year. This year she made her goal 70% and 75% achieved it

B. Ms. Marta determined her goal would be for 60% of her students to achieve a level 3 or above on the FCATs. The first year she achieved 50%, the second year she achieved 60%, and the third and fourth year she achieved 55%

C. Mr. Williams chose his goal to have 100% of his students achieve either a level 3 or above on the FCATs. During the first year, 70% of his students achieved this level. In the second year 65% achieved it, and during the past two years 60% achieved it

D. None of these teachers had over ¾ of their students achieve at a level 3; Therefore, none of them have been truly been impacted by your strategy

81. You are a high school assistant principal charged with handling personnel problems. Students in a physics class complain that the teacher employs teaching strategies and evaluation procedures that make it impossible for any student to earn an A in his class. After checking student records and consulting with the science department chair, you determine that the students have a legitimate concern. The least threatening initial approach in dealing with the teacher is to: *(Skill 2.8) (Average Rigor)*

A. Stress the negative effects his grading policy will have on the grade point averages of the more able students

B. Encourage the teacher to do a self-evaluation of his teaching methods and propose solutions to help students achieve greater success

C. Recommend procedures for the teacher to adopt if he intends to remain on staff

D. Schedule a classroom evaluation and give a copy of the results to the teacher as well as filing it in his permanent record

82. F.S. 231 (Personnel of School Systems) does not cover which of the following topics? *(Skill 2.9) (Easy)*

A. Personnel reappointment

B. Certification processes

C. Operational elements of the US Department of Education

D. The operation of the Educational Standards Commission

83. An employee has been incompetent all year in spite of your efforts to help her. You have documented her work and your efforts to help her improve. Now, she has instituted a grievance against you for allegedly harassing her and claims that she is an excellent teacher as demonstrated by her work at other schools. Further, you learn through the grapevine that she has been under personal stress. What should you do to decide her fate for the upcoming school year? *(Skill 2.9) (Average Rigor)*

A. Terminate her

B. Discuss the matter with another principal

C. Rehire her because she had problems

D. Evaluate her using the district's pre-selected criteria

84. As chair of a personnel committee considering applicants for an administrative position in the central office, one member of the committee advises you that the superintendent has expressed difficulty in working with female administrators. What action should you take? *(Skill 2.9) (Average Rigor)*

A. Advise the committee member to introduce this consideration into the committee's deliberations

B. Advise the committee member that consideration of the superintendent's expressed difficulty in working with women should not influence the selection of an applicant

C. Advise the committee member that the superintendent's expressed difficulty in working with women should be shared with the rest of the selection process

D. Advise the committee member that the superintendent's expressed difficulty in working with women should be a primary consideration in determining the applicant to be recommended

85. One of your students came to school with a dark circle on her cheek. Although she has stated that the bruise is a sports injury, you are concerned about it. Her mother is one of your most dedicated teachers and she has corroborated the story that her daughter was hit in the face while playing softball. Therefore, you take the story on face-value but make a mental note to be on alert if another incident occurs. Is this a correct course of action? Why or why not?   (Skill 2.10) (Average Rigor)

A. Yes: The student and her mother are credible individuals, which is the main criterion you should consider. You should accept the current explanation and maintain your plan to look out for suspicious marks or explanations in the future

B. Yes: Your duty of care has been met. You informally inquired about the matter and received a satisfactory response

C. No: You have not sufficiently attended to the issue. The duty of care to the student requires that you investigate further and submit, to the school district, a written statement of your findings

D. No: Because you are not a social worker, the duty of care placed on you is much less than would be required for someone certified to recognize child abuse

86. The state requires that teachers report indications of child abuse or indications that the student has attempted suicide. The state considers this requirement to be which of the following: (Skill 2.10) (Rigorous)

A. A standard of professional ethics

B. A standard of religious conviction

C. A standard of personal ethics

D. A consideration for certified teachers

87. A school received a grant to cover the cost of putting computers and peripherals in every classroom. The district's technology coordinator and some teachers want the money to be spent to equip two computer labs. The principal is adamant that the money will be used to put computers and peripherals in classrooms. Select the conflict management style of the administrator in this scenario. *(Skill 2.10)* (*Average Rigor*

A. Accommodating

B. Collaborating

C. Competing

D. Compromising

88. The state requires that teachers report indications of child abuse or indications that the student has attempted suicide. The state considers this requirement: *(Skill 2.10)* (*Average Rigor*)

A. A standard of professional ethics

B. A standard of religious conviction

C. A standard of personal ethics

D. A consideration for certified teachers

89. A student has worn shirts with slogans that you consider inflammatory. In addition, her choice of dress has caused other students to be distracted during instructional time. It is your belief that these shirts should be banned while on school grounds. Which of the following Constitutional rights should be studied and discussed prior to a decision being made? *(Skill 2.11)* (*Easy*)

A. Freedom of Speech

B. Freedom of Religion

C. Freedom from Unreasonable Searches

D. Freedom of Attire

90. Why should administrators have a basic grounding in relevant law?
(Skill 2.11) (Average Rigor)

A. So they can act ethically when quick action is required

B. So they can advise parents of the best solution to concerns they raise

C. So they can act as their own counsel if necessary

D. So they can decide when to abide by the rules and when to bend them

91. When a teacher stepped out the room to call a parent, the unsupervised students began throwing items. The incident resulted in the serious injury of a student. The court found the school system to be negligent in this incident. Identify the element of negligence that best supports the court's judgment.
(Skill 2.12) (Rigorous)

A. Dereliction of duty of care

B. Dereliction of standard of care

C. Dereliction of proximate cause

D. Actual loss or injury

92. It is the day before Middlebrook High School is scheduled to participate in the state level basketball tournament. The parents had chartered buses to transport the team; however, the bus-charter contract has fallen through. A proactive, "take-charge" principal should do which of the following:
(Skill 2.12) (Average Rigor)

A. Call a meeting with the administrative team, parent association, executive committee, and the basketball coaches

B. Rent cars so that the athletes can drive to the tournament

C. Use the buses available for transporting students on a daily basis

D. Withdraw from the tournament

93. **Compulsory school attendance law requires which of the following:** *(Skill 2.12) (Average Rigor)*

    A. Students who are married or become pregnant shall be prohibited from attending school

    B. Mandatory school attendance ends at the age of sixteen

    C. No child can be admitted or promoted to the first grade in a public school unless he or she has successfully completed kindergarten in a public school

    D. No special education service be provided to children over the age of sixteen

94. **Effective school leaders must be willing and able to do all of the following EXCEPT:** *(Skill 2.13) (Average Rigor)*

    A. Stick to an original decision regardless of new information

    B. Clearly delineate expectations for all stakeholders

    C. Manage the school by walking around and being visible

    D. Be consistent yet fair

95. **Two principals have recently been hired at high schools within the most diverse neighborhood in the city. Their schools have rich histories of activism during the civil-rights era and many former students who are now neighborhood residents. They are also well known for providing venues for activities ranging from business meetings to community assistance programs. Principal A has decided that he would like to display the achievements of current students. To make space, he has had to move a display highlighting the civil-rights era activities of his school's student government body. Principal B believes that parents are the backbone of the school; therefore, in the past four months, he has decided to grant the PTA meeting space over other groups, even if the other groups had submitted their applications first. According to the "four organizational frames" theory proposed by Bolman and Deal, which of the frames is each of these principals ignoring?** *(Skill 2.13) (Rigorous)*

    (See next page for answer options.)

A. Principal A is ignoring the symbolic frame; Principal B is also ignoring the symbolic frame

B. Principal A is ignoring the political frame; Principal B is also ignoring the political frame

C. Principal A is ignoring the symbolic frame; Principal B is ignoring the political frame

D. Principal A is ignoring the political frame; Principal B is ignoring the symbolic frame

96. **At the beginning of the year, the principal has implemented a change in the way exams are submitted to the main office. Even after the changes are shared, some teachers submit the exams in the way they choose. At the end of the year, the principal gives a bad review to those teachers who did not submit the reports as specified and teachers are very upset by the bad reviews. The principal could have avoided this conflict by doing which of the following:**
(Skill 2.13) (Rigorous)

A. Not requiring adherence to the established policy

B. Providing feedback during the year so that teachers were reminded of the policy

C. Changing the policy in the middle of the year

D. Going to each classroom to collect the exams

97. Trinity School will initiate its International Baccalaureate Program this fall. The principal has provided clearly stated tasks, expected outcomes, and timelines for accomplishment, and then designated an assistant principal as coordinator for this program. At the initial meeting for the program, the assistant principal organized and ran the meeting, and all the staff participated in the discussion. This principal's behavior demonstrates which of the following: *(Skill 2.13) (Average Rigor)*

A. Organizing the activity of a group to develop a plan

B. Delegating authority and responsibility

C. Failing to trust the assistant principal

D. Showing a developmental orientation toward the assistant principal

98. Bolman and Deal argue that leaders often forget two of four important organizational frames. Which of these is the one that focuses on the organizational culture and history, a frame very important to employees, students, and others? *(Skill 2.13) (Easy)*

A. Structural

B. Human Resources

C. Political

D. Symbolic

99. A school is interested in a new math series for students. A committee has been charged with the responsibility for making a decision and doing what is necessary regarding this matter. Several meetings have taken place to consider the advantages and disadvantages of adopting the materials. If the committee has adopted the math series and is now distributing it to students, in what stage of change is the committee? *(Skill 2.13) (Average Rigor)*

A. The committee is in the integration stage because a decision to adopt the math series has been made

B. The committee has gone through all three stages so its work is now complete

C. The committee is now in the second stage of change

D. The committee is poised between the second and third stages of change

100. At a recent town-hall meeting, parents expressed concern that recent graduates have been unable to find employment in fields requiring knowledge of web-design and website creation software. This gap exists in the students skills because the school administration failed to: *(Skill 2.13) (Rigorous)*

A. Maintain the status-quo in course offerings

B. Appeal to student interests

C. Respond to changing environmental conditions, particularly job-market requirements

D. Administer surveys about the jobs held by parents

101. **What should a principal who is new to a school do to promote necessary change?** *(Skill 2.13)* *(Average Rigor)*

   A. Identify areas of need and thoroughly research new programs that could impact the problem

   B. Spend a short time observing school procedures, then make the most important changes immediately

   C. Involve teachers and other stakeholders in the planning and development process

   D. Impose ideas because many teachers are afraid of change and will not cooperate unless an authority figure requires their participation

(See next page for question 102.)

102. Middle School 71 has analyzed its standardized testing data and found serious shortcomings. The overall school performance is commendable: 75% of students achieved a level 3 or 4 on the FCAT. However, there are alarming trends when the data are disaggregated. To address the achievement gaps, the school has developed and implemented an improvement plan for the following subgroups of students:
1) Those from lower socio-economic (SES) backgrounds, which is measured by eligibility for Free and Reduced Lunch (FRL),
2) Those who are learning English as a Second Language (ESOL), and
3) Those with certain special needs who are still required to be tested.

The following table highlights the goals section of the schools' improvement plan.

Percentage of Students Who Attain Level 3 or 4 on the FCAT

Subgroup	Current Percentage	Anticipated Percentage	Team Responsible
FRL	40	50	Mr. Watson
ESOL	30	45	Ms. Tanner
Special Needs	35	40	Mr. Jamison

According to the table above, the school improvement plan would recognize which group as making satisfactory learning gains? *(Skill 2.14) (Rigorous)*

A. The Special Needs group, if 50% or more of these students achieve a level 3 or 4 on the FCAT

B. The ESOL group if 40% or more of these students achieve a level 3 or 4 on the FCAT

C. Both A and B

D. Neither A nor B

103. The students at Cornwell Elementary School have consistently surpassed district and state achievement test levels. During the current year, the scores are in the lower quartile. The MOST appropriate action for the principal to take at the school site would be to: *(Skill 2.14) (Rigorous)*

A. Meet with the parents to get their support

B. Call an emergency faculty meeting to decide what to do

C. Analyze test results to determine areas and patterns of poor performance by students

D. Get assistance from her district supervisor on action that has worked elsewhere

104. You recently learned that your school district has been affected by negative market conditions and falling property tax revenues. For this reason, next year your school will be allocated 25% less money than you received in the current year. In a second meeting you were given a copy of the school choice trends for the past two years. Records indicate that enrollment at your school has dropped by 10% each year and that it has risen at the same rate for a neighboring charter school. Informal data suggests that parents are moving children out of your school and are enrolling them in the charter school. News of the budget cuts are certain to accelerate the rate at which parents leave the school in favor of their other "choice" options. Which of the following is an effective strategy to communicate the challenges faced by your school?
(Skill 3.1) (Rigorous)

(See the next page for answer options.)

A. Try to down-play the problems and minimize any internal or external communication: the more attention you put on the issue, the more stakeholders will panic and the worse will be the outcome

B. Hold an internal meeting with staff and inform them of the issues; encourage them to work as a team within the new budget while continuing to provide a top-notch education to students; minimize external communications

C. Hold internal meetings to decide on an approach that will include parents and external stakeholders. Next, hold events during which all parties can be informed of the news and can participate in finding solutions

D. Call an emergency meeting of all internal and external stakeholders and inform everyone at the same time. Next obtain solutions from those present and develop a plan that will address the problem

105. A three-member committee planned a pep rally to increase attendance at school basketball games. During the month following the rally, attendance increased by 10% at the first game and 15% at the second game. The coach felt that the planned strategy was a success, the PTA representative thought it was a failure, and the principal could not decide how to view the attendance changes. What is the MOST likely reason for this disagreement?
(Skill 3.1) (Rigorous)

A. The coach, the PTA representative, and the principal each measured success differently

B. The committee did not establish clear attendance goals

C. The three members of the committee did not get student feedback on the attendance changes

D. Both A and C

106. This is the second year your school has been identified as one of the lowest performing in your district; you have decided that in the next year you will meet AYP. What is the BEST strategy to increase support systems to accomplish school goals AND decrease those elements that can have a negative influence on its functioning?
(Skill 3.1) (Average Rigor)

A. Ban students from text-messaging each other during class time

B. Holding town-hall meetings to solicit parental involvement and enforcing a zero-tolerance policy for disruptive behaviors

C. Having fund-raisers to collect money for new textbooks and encouraging teachers to stay after school with students

D. Conduct a series of meetings with stakeholders to develop a plan of action

107. Your school was put on the critically low school list by the state. No measurable gains were recorded the next year and you are on the list two consecutive years. How would you get your school off the list? *(Skill 3.1) (Average Rigor)*

A. Involve the community

B. Have a meeting with teachers and establish a strategic plan that involves the parents and community

C. Secure advice from the state and district and work on the problem

D. Conduct a series of meeting with teachers, parents, and community members to obtain information to aid in developing a plan of action with the faculty

108. The neighborhood demographics around Peabody High School have markedly changed over the past few years. Single-family homes are now occupied by multiple families. The first language of most adults has changed from English to Spanish. The businesses in the community are also changing and are requiring different types of skilled employees. You, as principal, have been asked to redesign your program to better meet the needed work force. Your first step to meet this need is to:

(Skill 3.1) (Average Rigor)

A. Talk to the new residents at a town meeting you hold at the school

B. Conduct a survey of the business owners to determine their needs

C. Plan to enlarge the school to meet increased student enrollment

D. Discuss the matter with your area supervisor

109. Your assessment officer has just brought two sets of reports with FACT scores to your office. He states that they require your signature so they can go in the mail today. One group will go to parents and the other will be given to the teachers. Unfortunately, before he could identify which was which, you were called away to a meeting. As you wait for the meeting to begin, you pull out the reports. You notice that Group A has the student scores as percentage ranks; the reports in Group B provide raw scores for each student. From your understanding of how to communicate with different audiences, which reports are intended for parents and which does he plan to give to the teachers?
(Skill 3.2) (Average Rigor)

A. Group A will go to parents and Group B will go to teachers

B. Group A will go to teachers and Group B will go to parents

C. Group A will go to both parents and teachers; Group B will not be shared

D. Group B will go to both parents and teachers; Group A will not be shared

110. You are the superintendent of a small school district and your secretary has told you that the district attendance records show that three siblings were listed on the Northwest Regional Data Center (NWRDC) database of missing children. What steps should you take? *(Skill 3.3) (Rigorous)*

A. Call the local law enforcement agency which originated the case and then call the Florida Department of Education

B. Call the Florida Department of Education and then call the local law enforcement agency which originated the case

C. Use form ESE 092 to update the NWRDC database

D. Use form ESE 092 to report this information to the local law enforcement agency which originated the case and to the Florida Department of Education

111. Jake has not met the specified levels of proficiency in either reading or math. Therefore you are aware that a Progress Monitoring Plan (PMP) must be in place to improve his achievement. In a phone conference with the counselor at his previous school, you were told that Jake also had a PMP there. He had received one diagnostic assessment, an Academic Improvement Plan (AIP), and frequent monitoring of his progress, and monthly academic updates were given to him and his parents. She also tells you that they have left the PMP open for the past three years. Where has the previous school not adhered to state Statute 1008.25? *(Skill 3.4) (Rigorous)*

A. They only administered one diagnostic assessment and the state mandates three

B. They have left the PMP open for three years

C. They should not provide academic updates to Jake, only to his parents

D. None of the Above

112. You have been dealing with a lunchroom fight that has resulted in one student being hospitalized and two students being expelled. As you investigated the matter, you learned that the incident resulted from racial tensions that you and your staff have downplayed for the past two months. Which of the following is a communications decision you should AVOID and why? (*Skill 3.4*) (*Rigorous*)

A. Provide a statement to parents that follows your strategy of downplaying the issue; this will minimize overreactions while the situation is resolved

B. Send all required documentation to the district immediately; they must be kept abreast of the incident through ongoing upward communication

C. Make notes of the important facts as soon as possible; you will need to remember the facts as you communicate to various stakeholders

D. Send a clear statement to all stakeholders so that they are aware of the situation and can understand your commitment to resolving the issue

113. A mutually beneficial relationship can exist between schools and community partners such as resource centers. The centers can assist schools with training, resources, and information. Which of the following is the most significant benefit schools can provide in return? (*Skill 3.4*) (*Average Rigor*)

A. Schools do not provide any benefit to the centers; the relationship is only beneficial to the schools, not the centers

B. Schools provide access to sensitive student information that the centers would not otherwise be able to obtain

C. Schools allow the resource centers to engage in their practice, to perfect their outreach, and to continue functioning

D. Schools are able to pay resource centers for their services, which increases the income brought in by these centers

114. The top student at your school is among the finalists for a full scholarship to the state university. The University's admissions office just called because the committee must make a decision today and they need the student's 3rd quarter report card. Unfortunately, the student is on a class trip and her parents have not returned your phone calls. According to the Buckley Amendment, what should you do?
(Skill 3.5) (Average Rigor)

A. You should provide the report card to the University so that the student can be awarded the scholarship

B. The University can send a representative to view the student's records; however, the student's information cannot leave your office without her parent's permission

C. The University must provide the request in writing; upon receipt of the document, you are able to provide them with a copy of the report card

D. You are not permitted to release the student's information to the University without written consent

115. The guidelines established by the Buckley Amendment (or FERPA), give access to a student's records to all of the following individuals EXCEPT?
(Skill 3.5) (Average Rigor)

A. The student

B. Parents or legal guardians

C. All school-level teaching staff

D. Appropriate district-level personnel

116. When an administrator wants to overcome the negative effects of the school grapevine she should:
(Skill 3.6) (Average Rigor)

A. Identify the leaders of the grapevine and pass information through them

B. Keep teachers and staff informed of key policy changes or issues relevant to staff, the school, and/or the district

C. Attempt to minimize the amount of information that is shared about a particular topic until all the facts are clear

D. Redirect negative attitudes and feelings to avoid any confrontations regarding unfavorable policy changes

117. A school principal is confused by his repeated inability to connect with the parents and students of races other than his own. He feels that he is respectful and interested in them, but they never seem to respond positively, either one-on-one or in group settings. He attends a workshop on cultural competence and learns all of the following except: *(Skill 3.6) (Average Rigor)*

A. The best way to become more culturally competent is to attend a series of workshops on the topic

B. He needs to learn more about his students' cultural backgrounds

C. He has made assumptions about what his students feel and think that are probably inaccurate

D. Just being sensitive to differences isn't enough; it's only a first step

118. Effective communication is a key component in building relationships with faculty, students, parents and community members. The keys to effective communication include all of the following except: *(Skill 3.7) (Average Rigor)*

A. Being able to anticipate what the speaker is going to say

B. Paying attention to nonverbal communication

C. Asking for clarification

D. Expressing oneself clearly and directly

119. You are experimenting with a new teaching strategy that is supposed to increase professional and interpersonal relationships among teachers. It is also shown to lead to better student achievement. You select one group of 10th grade Social Studies teachers to work collaboratively. The teachers assign their students a similar end-of-unit writing project. They utilize the same assignment, have the same standards, and assess the work according to the same rubric. Then as a group, the teachers score these essays together, discuss similar problems they notice, seek help from one another, and brainstorm solutions so that they can better prepare students for the next assessment. What type of strategy are they using? *(Skill 3.7) (Easy)*

A. Take, Pair, Share

B. Professional Learning Community

C. Silo-style classrooms

D. Social studies teacher hierarchy

120. School data show that student test scores have been decreasing for the past two years. From Informal surveys with teachers, parents, and students you realize that during that period many parents have been working overtime and are interact less with their children during the week. You have hired several educational consultants who developed a plan that will utilize parental involvement to reinforce and review information taught. Which of the following strategies would be most likely to both communicate the need for the change AND gain parental support for the plan? *(Skill 3.8) (Average Rigor)*

A. Provide and discuss a chart showing the trend of scores going down as parental involvement goes down at a meeting; then address ideas for changes and adaptations to meet the needs of the parents and teachers

B. Send out a memo with a chart showing the trend of scores going down as parental involvement goes down, letting parents know you are available to meet with them if they would like that

C. Both A and B

D. Neither A nor B

121. Which two elements should be central in the daily operations of the school and drive all planning, activities, and school climate:
(Skill 3.8) (Average Rigor)

    A. Staff and parents

    B. Mission and vision

    C. Classes and activities

    D. Aims and objectives

122. In today's educational climate it is believed that all stakeholders should be valued, be able to see how decisions are made, and should feel welcomed in every part of the school's operations. The BEST way to achieve this is through:*(Skill 3.8) (Rigorous)*

    A. Transparent processes that give multiple opportunities for comment and critique

    B. Careful planning and strategies to communicate decisions made by the administration

    C. Presenting a unified front between the district, administration, and teachers

    D. Sharing information on a need-to-know basis and deciding which items require stakeholder input

123. To write effectively, a school leader should use strategies to organize his or her thoughts. Which of the following lists these strategies in the correct order:
(Skill 3.9) (Rigorous)

    A. State any actions to be taken, list items to be discussed, expand on each item, put items in order, write a brief summary

    B. Write a brief summary, state any actions to be taken, list items to be discussed, expand on each item, put items in order,

    C. List items to be discussed, put items in order, state any actions to be taken, expand on each item, write a brief summary

    D. List items to be discussed, put items in order, write a brief summary, expand on each item, state any actions to be taken

124. Administrators must understand key concepts when analyzing and interpreting data. These concepts include the ability to *contrast*, *explain*, *discuss*, *analyze*, and *compare* information..

1. _____ = examine the parts

2. _____ = look at similarities

3. _____ = look at differences

4. _____ = examine in detail

5. _____ = provide reasons or examples, or clarify meaning

Select the option below that places the key concepts in correct blanks in the list above.
(Skill 3.9) (Rigorous)

A. 1. contrast, 2. explain, 3. discuss, 4. analyze, 5. compare

B. 1. analyze, 2. compare, 3. discuss, 4. contrast, 5. explain

C. 1. analyze, 2. compare, 3. contrast, 4. discuss, 5. explain

D. 1. discuss, 2. compare, 3. contrast, 4. analyze, 5. explain

125. You constantly engage in self-reflection in all areas of your professional practice. This week you have been thinking about a comment made by a PTA member. She stated that many of her fellow parents complained that your memos are too long and incoherent. They are also concerned because you mailed information on the recent test scores, but they could not understand what the numbers meant. As you reviewed your prior memos about the test scores, you see why parents could not understand your memo and why they could not understand the data. Which of the following is the most time-efficient approach to correcting this problem?
(Skill 3.9) (Average Rigor)

A. Inform your secretary that he will need to edit your documents so that they are not as wordy or difficult for parents to understand

B. Register for the district's course on "effective communication for administrators"

C. Hold a parent's night during which a presenter shows parents how to understand important assessment data

D. Both B and C

Answer Key

1. B	33. A	65. C	97. B
2. D	34. D	66. C	98. D
3. D	35. D	67. A	99. C
4. B	36. D	68. C	100. C
5. D	37. B	69. D	101. C
6. C	38. C	70. B	102. A
7. D	39. B	71. D	103. C
8. A	40. C	72. A	104. C
9. C	41. B	73. C	105. B
10. C	42. B	74. A	106. B
11. B	43. D	75. B	107. D
12. D	44. A	76. A	108. B
13. A	45. A	77. B	109. A
14. A	46. C	78. C	110. D
15. B	47. C	79. A	111. B
16. A	48. B	80. A	112. A
17. B	49. D	81. B	113. C
18. A	50. D	82. C	114. D
19. A	51. B	83. D	115. C
20. B	52. A	84. B	116. B
21. C	53. B	85. B	117. A
22. B	54. D	86. A	118. A
23. C	55. C	87. C	119. B
24. C	56. A	88. A	120. A
25. B	57. C	89. A	121. B
26. C	58. D	90. A	122. A
27. A	59. B	91. B	123. D
28. A	60. C	92. C	124. C
29. D	61. A	93. B	125. D
30. A	62. D	94. A	
31. A	63. A	95. C	
32. B	64. C	96. B	

Rigor Table

	Easy - 22%	Average Rigor - 48%	Rigorous – 30 %
Question #	1, 7, 8, ,11,13,17, 18, 21, 22, 26, 27, 29, 31, 35, 39, 53, 55, 62, 66, 67, 69, 73, 74, 82, 89, 98, 119	2, 3, 4, 5, 6, 10, 12, 15, 16, 19, 24, 28, 30, 34, 38, 40, 41, 42, 44, 45, 46, 47, 48, 51, 52, 54, 57, 58, 65, 70, 71, 72, 75, 76, 81, 83, 84, 85, 87, 88, 90, 92, 93, 94, 97, 99, 101, 106,107, 108, 109, 113, 114, 115, 116, 117, 118, 120, 121, 125	14, 20, 23, 25, 32, 33, 36, 37, 43, 49, 50, 56, 59, 60, 61, 63, 64, 68, 77, 78, 79, 80, 86, 91, 95, 96, 100, 102, 103, 104, 105, 110, 111, 112, 122, 123, 124

Answer/Rationales

1. **You have recently been appointed principal of Sunshine State Middle School. During the summer you reviewed the FCAT scores and found that in reading, 90% of 7th and 80% of 8th grade students scored at a level 3 or above; however, 50% of the 6th grade students scored at a level 1 or 2 on this portion of the exam. When you reviewed the instructional records you realized that the school had not aligned its curriculum, instruction, and assessment. In order to achieve this alignment, which of the following is the BEST strategy and why? (Skill 1.1) (Rigorous)**

A. Identify the goals and objectives yourself and then require teachers to meet these goals and objectives; the faculty is aware of the serious nature of meeting AYP requirements and it is your job to create a plan of action

B. Work with a committee of faculty members, parents, and community leaders to help you develop goals and objectives to address the problem in order to get the necessary buy-in and community-wide commitment necessary to achieve this lofty goal

C. You identify a team of stakeholders to advise you on goals and objectives; however, you inform them that you reserve the right to determine what the plan will be. As the instructional leader, your priorities need to carry more weight than others in the school

D. You recruit a team of stakeholders and at the first meeting you break members into three groups. One will tackle the curriculum, one will address the instructional techniques, and the third will work on the assessment practices. You believe this is the most efficient way to get a lot of work done.

Answer: B. Work with a committee of faculty members, parents, and community leaders to help you develop goals and objectives to address the problem in order to get the necessary buy-in and community-wide commitment necessary to achieve this lofty goal
Raising the reading achievement of the 6th grade students is a big goal. Your first task should be to identify measurable goals and objectives so your intent is clear. This must be a process that involves not only faculty, but also parents, students, staff, and other members of the school community to obtain buy-in and ownership. Only response B takes this into account. Response A uses a top-down approach to curriculum planning which can be detrimental for a new principal. Response C may back-fire. Often, stakeholders take offense when they are not asked for their input; however, they take greater offense when their input is ignored or devalued. Response D has completely overlooked that setting goals and objectives should be the first step in tackling a problem.

2. Which sequence best describes the order of a needs assessment?
(Skill 1.1) (Average Rigor)

A. Survey of needs, goals and objectives development, problem identification, implementation planning, process evaluation

B. Problem identification, survey of needs, goals and objectives development, implementation planning, process evaluation

C. Problem identification, survey of needs, goals and objectives development, process evaluation, implementation planning

D. Survey of needs, problem identification, goals and objectives development, implementation planning, process evaluation

Answer: D. Survey of needs, problem identification, goals and objectives development, implementation planning, process evaluation
In order to determine what the problem is, the administrator along with the teacher (s) should perform a needs assessment. This will help define the problem and lead to goal setting. To effectively solve the problems, there should be goals to ensure that pertinent information is gathered. Once this is done and the data gathered, the stakeholders should determine which solution would be most effective and then set about planning how best to implement it.

3. **Which of the following refers to the horizontal organization of the elements of the curriculum?**
   (Skill 1.1) (Average Rigor)

   A. The knowledge and skills students learn are useful in life situations

   B. The knowledge and skills that students learn at one grade level are relevant and useful as they progress to other grades

   C. Everything the student learns contributes to fulfillment of the curriculum

   D. What students learn in one class supports and reinforces what they learn in other classes

Answer: D. What students learn in one class supports and reinforces what they learn in other classes

Horizontal organization refers to utilizing the connections between the various subjects of the curriculum. Teachers of different subject areas plan together so that they can teach and reinforce the same skills. For example, Social Studies and Language Arts courses are quite often grouped together. Not only does the Social Studies teacher ensure that students have the essential knowledge of the concepts, but also reinforces the writing and reading skills taught in Language Arts. Similarly, the Language Arts teacher uses books that reinforce the concepts of the Social Studies course.

4. **Which of the following refers to the vertical organization of the elements of the curriculum?**
(Skill 1.1) (Average Rigor)

   A. Everything the student learns contributes to fulfillment of the curriculum

   B. The knowledge and skills that students learn at one grade level are relevant and useful as they progress to other grades

   C. What students learn in one class supports and reinforces what they learn in other classes

   D. The knowledge and skills students learn are useful in life situations

Answer: B. The knowledge and skills that students learn at one grade level are relevant and useful as they progress to other grades
Each area of the curriculum is designed so that the outcomes for one grade form the basis and the foundation for the learning that will take place in the next. Outcomes start out with the basics and build on them as students progress through the grade levels. If you look at a single outcome, you will easily see how it develops naturally as students are able to process more and more information. In Mathematics, for example an outcome for Grade 8 may be that students are able to pictorially represent the square root of a number and in Grade 9, they are expected to solve problems using the square root of a number. This horizontal organization of the curriculum ensures that students have the knowledge they need to be successful at each grade level.

5. _____ is based on the clustering of subjects into categories of study.

(Skill 1.1) (Average Rigor)

  A. Process-centered curriculum design

  B. Subject-centered curriculum design

  C. Discipline-centered curriculum design

  D. Broad fields curriculum design

Answer: D. Broad fields curriculum design
In the broad fields curriculum design, two or more subjects are blended into a broader field of study. Language Arts, for example, combines the major communication skills of reading, writing, listening, speaking, viewing and representing. The basis of using this curriculum design in elementary and middle schools is to cut down on fragmenting the curriculum into separate subject areas. It also allows teachers to provide students with a greater integration of learning activities.

6. Which of the following statements best describes process evaluation? *(Skill 1.1) (Average Rigor)*

  A. It is concerned with the needs of the program

  B. It is concerned with the adequacy of resources to implement the program

  C. It is concerned with recording procedures and continuous monitoring

  D. It is concerned with the attainment of the goals for the program

Answer: C. It is concerned with recording procedures and continuous monitoring
Process evaluation is concerned with the implementation of curriculum. In the case of new curricula, it will look at the type of teacher professional development necessary for teachers to implement new ideas in their classrooms. Problems are dealt with as they occur, which means there is continuous evaluation of the programs.

7. **According to the Florida Bureau of School Improvement, a school improvement plan should include which of the following:**
   (Skill 1.1) (Easy)

   A. Staff improvement strategies, including professional development plans

   B. Clear goals for readings, mathematics and science, with accompanying budget figures

   C. A coordination and integration component required for Title I

   D. All of the above

Answer: D. All of the above
In addition to all of these, the school improvement plan should also include:
- School vision/mission/belief statements
- School profile demographics
- A match between schools needing assistance with high performance schools in order to learn improvement strategies
- A plan for recruiting and retaining high quality administrators and teachers
- A School Wide Improvement Model selected by the school for use in its change efforts
- Information for parents about public school choice options, as required by the No Child Left Behind Act
- Appropriate use of school and student assessment data, including formal and informal sources
- Teaching strategies required by the state including direct instruction, School Learning Communities, parental involvement, and academic and career planning
- Attention to discipline, school safety, and student health and fitness
- Reporting issues

8. At the national level, administrators are impacted by entities such as the United States Department of Education. Which of the following is a local entity that has a similar impact on Florida's administrators? *(Skill 1.1) (Easy)*

   A. The Florida Department of Education

   B. The Florida Department of Corrections

   C. The Florida Legislature

   D. The Florida State Bar

Answer: A. The Florida Department of Education
At the local level, task forces of parents, educators, and community groups impact school curriculum as well. The Florida Department of Education is a statewide entity that impacts Florida's administrators in ways that are similar to the national impact of the United States Department of Education

9. The _____ is to national educational policy as the _____ is to statewide educational policy. *(Skill 1.1) (Easy)*

   A. Florida Department of Education; United States Department of Education

   B. United States Department of Education; Superintendent

   C. United States Department of Education; Florida Department of Education

   D. Superintendent; Florida Department of Education

Answer: C. United States Department of Education; Florida Department of Education
The United States Department of Education sets and enforces national educational policy; similarly, the Florida Department of Education sets and enforces statewide educational policy

10. Your school is committed to drawing on scientifically-based research (SBR) for curriculum development. According to five studies, students have increased math achievement when teachers use a curriculum with four components: manipulatives, memory cards, videos, and a proprietary computer program. However, your school's curriculum committee only has sufficient funds for the manipulatives, memory cards, and videos. Due to this, what should be your biggest concern? *(Skill 1.2) (Average Rigor)*

    A. The program may not be a good match for your school's unique conditions and needs

    B. You only have a limited amount of time to review the research studies supporting this curriculum

    C. The research supports the curriculum with four components; without one element, the program is no longer research-based

    D. None of the above

Answer: C. The research supports the curriculum with four components; without one element, the program is no longer research-based
There are a number of concerns in utilizing SBR such as the small number of experimental studies, overreliance on SBR, poor matching with a school's specific conditions and needs, and the time-consuming nature of literature review. For this question, however, the biggest problem is that the research supports the curriculum with all four elements. When any component is removed, the research no longer supports the truncated program.

11. Which of the following resources is MOST efficient in helping educators to locate evidence-based practices? *(Skill 1.2) (Easy)*

    A. Print-based journals

    B. The What Works Clearinghouse

    C. The Recent Trends Website

    D. References from colleagues

Answer: B. The What Works Clearinghouse
A good resource for identifying evidence-based practices is the What Works Clearinghouse (WWC), sponsored by the U.S. Department of Education

12. The following table presents an excerpt of questions from your recent school climate survey. The table also shows, for each question, the percent of staff members who agreed/strongly agreed and the percent of staff who disagreed/strongly disagreed. In order to increase morale and performance, which area should you address first? *(Skill 1.3)* *(Average Rigor)*

Question	Agree/Strongly Agree	Disagree/Strongly Disagree
I feel as though I am working as part of a team	90%	10%
There are open lines of communication with the administration	80%	20%
The principal supports me in conflicts with parents	60%	40%
The administration has effectively addressed the gang activity in front the school building	20%	80%

A. Increasing the camaraderie and team-spirit among staff members

B. Creating better lines of communication between the administration and other stakeholders

C. Working to support staff members when they have conflicts with parents

D. Addressing the gang activity in front the school building

Answer: D. Addressing the gang activity in front the school building
Several factors contribute to a positive school climate. The survey data show that improvements can be made on all fronts; however, because gang activity threatens security and the sense of safety, it has a negative impact on morale and performance. Thus, you see that only 20% of respondents agreed that the gang activity had been effectively addressed, this is compared with the other areas where 90%, 80%, and 60% of the respondents felt positively. Therefore, to increase morale you should work to effectively address and eliminate the gang activity in front of the school building.

13. Positive school environments have all of the following characteristics except: *(Skill 1.3) (Easy)*

A. Strict rules

B. Clear adult leadership

C. Respect for diversity

D. Policies and procedures to ensure the safety of everyone in the school community

Answer: A. Strict rules

While clear policies and strong leadership are essential, strict rules generally do not contribute to creating positive school environments. At times, they may even have a detrimental effect, depending on the nature of the rules.

14. For self-efficacy to emerge, which two things must be attached to a task:
(Skill 1.3) (Rigorous)

A. Expectation and value

B. Emotion and success

C. Perseverance and ranking

D. Cognition and trials

Answer: A. Expectation and value

When there is the expectation that one can succeed at a task, and value is attached to achieving that task, then a feeling of self-efficacy emerges. In organizations, leaders need to ask what can be done to help bring about a sense of self-efficacy in its members.

15. **Which of the following definitions correctly identifies self-efficacy theory?**
(Skill 1.3) (Average Rigor)

   A. Success is the result of applying causal explanations regarding achievement efforts and influence on the effects of expectancies

   B. A person's judgment about his or her ability to perform an activity at a specific level of performance

   C. The causes of success or failure are due to uncontrollable factors

   D. Attaching logic to emotional reactions engenders pride and responsibility

Answer: B. A person's judgment about his or her ability to perform an activity at a specific level of performance.
A person's success in situations will greatly depend on that person's belief in his or herself. It is a person's perception of his or her ability to plan and take action to reach a particular goal.

16. **The basic postulate of this theory of motivation is that intentions to achieve a goal form the primary motivating force behind work behavior. Select the theory that best conforms to this postulate.**
(Skill 1.3) (Average Rigor)

   A.   Goal theory

   B.   Feedback theory

   C.   Attribution theory

   D.   Controllability theory

Answer: A. Goal theory
Goal theory revolves around the manner in which individuals determine their goals in achievement. There are three factors: achievement goals, perceived ability, and achievement behavior.

17. **Your elementary school will expand its pre-school classes to include a group of three-year-olds in the fall. Which of the following will you need to adjust?** *(Skill 1.4) (Easy)*

 A. The lunch schedule, since young children do not have a regular lunch time

 B. The location of classes to make sure the three-year-olds are on the first floor, since not all three-year-olds can climb stairs

 C. The type of supplies purchased, since toddlers need different materials from other children

 D. The parking spaces assigned to teachers so that the new pre-school teacher feels welcomed

Answer: B. The location of classes to make sure the three-year-olds are on the first floor, since not all three-year-olds can climb stairs
Development depends on maturation or the sequential characteristic of biological growth and progress. Biological changes occur in sequential order and give children new abilities. For instance, by the age of three children can typically walk and run; however, they have not mastered walking up and down stairs. Therefore, the principal must make sure that these classes are held on the first floor.

18. **All of the following are among the six core domains of instructional strategy and functioning except:** *(Skill 1.4) (Easy)*

 A. Team Work

 B. Planning

 C. Management of student conduct

 D. Presentation of subject

Answer: A. Team work
There exist six core domains of instructional strategy and functioning. They are planning, management of student conduct, instructional organization and development, presentation of subject, communication, and testing. Each should be part of evaluating teacher effectiveness.

19. **Which of the following best describes the purpose of student assessment?** *(Skill 1.4) (Average Rigor)*

    A. To analyze performance at various stages of goal attainment

    B. To appraise curriculum goals and objectives

    C. To determine outcome in terms of cost and achievement related to cost

    D. To analyze various alternatives or program options

Answer: A. To analyze performance at various stages of goal attainment
Assessment at regular intervals is essential for both students and teachers. This testing can be formal or informal in that the teacher can keep a record of the marks or just make notes regarding how the students are doing. As students are assessed, the teacher can decide whether or not they are experiencing success or difficulty, and how best to proceed to help them be successful. Assessment guides instruction. While grading is a necessary element in schools, assessment and grading are different. Grading occurs at the end of assessment.

20. **Which of the following is the best formative assessment practice for students?** *(Skill 1.4) (Rigorous)*

    A. Provide a comprehensive multiple choice test at the end of the chapter

    B. Provide several teacher-made quizzes during the chapter

    C. Provide guided practice during the unit

    D. Provide a combination of test formats in the chapter test

Answer: B. Provide several teacher-made quizzes during the chapter
Formative assessment takes place during the process of teaching a lesson. It can be both formal and informal, with the teacher assigning marks or making a simple note in the teacher's grade book. It could also be a note to the student reminding him or her of mistakes to watch out for. On another occasion, the teacher may look for the same things to see whether the student has improved. Formative assessment tells the teacher how well the students have mastered the objectives, and, if students are having difficulties, the teacher can adjust the instruction accordingly.

21. **Students designated as having mental retardation are likely to have social skills at varying levels of development, depending on an individual's mental age. This means that teachers should do all of the following except:** *(Skill 1.5) (Easy)*

    A. Model desired behavior

    B. Provide clear instructions

    C. Expect appropriate behaviors for the child's chronological age

    D. Adjust the physical environment when necessary

Answer: C. Expect appropriate behaviors for the child's chronological age
Chronological-age appropriateness refers to behavior that is appropriate for the numerical age of the student. In contrast, age appropriate means mental age appropriateness. When teaching students with mental retardation, educators must expect behaviors that are age appropriate, not what might be chronologically appropriate.

22. **The term IEP stands for which of the following?** *(Skill 1.5) (Easy)*

    A. Individualized Educational Progress

    B. Individualized Education Plan

    C. Inclusive Education Progress

    D. Inclusive Educational Plan

Answer: B. Individualized Education Plan
An IEP is an Individualized Education Plan developed for a student with specialized learning needs.

23. **At a school board meeting, the superintendent is addressing the sections of the *Florida Constitution, Article IX, Uniform System of Public Schools.* She has listed four sections: uniform system of free public schools, makeup of the State Board of Education, terms of service for appointed board members, and scope and duties of school districts. However, she has forgotten the other sections. To assist her, you would add which of the following to that list?**
(Skill 1.6) (Rigorous)

A. Terms of office of superintendents

B. Use of the income from the state school fund

C. Both A and B

D. None of the above

Answer: C. Both A and B
Florida Constitution, Article IX, Uniform System of Public Schools focuses specifically on education and contains six sections. The first section states that adequate provision shall be made by law for a uniform system of free public schools. Section 2 describes the makeup of the State Board of Education. Section 3 states the terms of service for appointed board members. Section 4 identifies the scope and duties of school districts. Section 5 states the manner in which, superintendents come to office and the terms of office. Section 6 identifies the use of the income from the state school fund.

24. The Individuals Disability Education Act (IDEA) was enacted to
(Skill 1.6) (Average Rigor)

A. Ensure students overcome language barriers that impede equal participation in instructional programs

B. Provide equal educational opportunities for students of any race, color, or national origin

C. Improve accountability, expand services, simplify parental involvement, and provide earlier access to services and supports for students with special needs

D. Ensure confidentiality of records and other information about students, parents, or staff members with disabilities

Answer: C. Improve accountability, expand services, simplify parental involvement, and provide earlier access to services and supports for students with special needs
IDEA specifically addresses the needs of individuals with disabilities. It does not focus on (A) language learning, (B) general equality of opportunity, or (D) confidentiality.

25. One of your staff members has been named as the defendant in a court case. The lawsuit claims that the student became physically ill because of constant fear of the teacher's imposing manner and verbal abuse. The student and her parents are claiming which of the following: *(Skill 1.7) (Rigorous)*

A. Battery

B. Assault

C. Negligence

D. *In Loco Parentis*

Answer: B. Assault
Negligence is the failure to exercise ordinary prudence and foresight, resulting in injury to another person to whom some duty is owed. The relationship between the educator and the student rises to *In loco parentis*, which by its very nature implies a heightened duty of care. Battery is the unpermitted and unprivileged contact with another person. Actual harm is not necessary. Assault is the act of placing someone in apprehension of immediate harm; physical contact is not required. Said another way, battery requires contact but not harm; assault requires harm, but not contact.

26. *F.S. 237 Financial Accounts and Expenditures for Public Schools describes guidelines for uniform record keeping and the handling of accounts. It sets forth the procedures for all of the following EXCEPT: (Skill 1.7) (Easy)*

   A. Establishing budgets

   B. Auditing procedures

   C. Disbursing lottery winnings

   D. Levying taxes

Answer: C. Disbursing lottery winnings
F.S. 237 Financial Accounts and Expenditures for Public Schools describes guidelines for uniform record keeping and the handling of accounts. It sets forth the procedures for establishing budgets, levying taxes, incurring indebtedness, the obligation to eliminate emergency conditions, handling school funds, and auditing procedures.

27. In reviewing the financial records of your predecessor, you realize that he created the school budget by engaging in the following process: 1) use the categories from the current budget; 2) mark all categories as blank and unfunded; 3) allocate funding to categories that he decided would continue in the coming budget cycle. Your predecessor was using which technique of school financial management? *(Skill 1.8)* *(Easy)*

   A. Zero-based budgeting

   B. Planning, Programming, Budgetary, and Evaluation System

   C. Incremental budgeting

   D. Planning, Programming, Budgetary Justification System

Answer: A. Zero-based budgeting
School financial management utilizes three commonly used techniques. Incremental budgeting examines each line item in a current budget against expected revenues. By addressing expenditures by items and categories, there is a failure to observe the impact of the budget as a whole on the goals of the organization and the needs of children. It also hinders creativity and change. Zero-based budgeting focuses on the current budgetary cycle and begins with zero dollars in all accounts to then justify the continuation of a program, activities, or expenditure.

In contrast, the Planning, Programming, Budgetary, and Evaluation System (PPBES) integrates long-range planning and uses annual fund allocations to obtain resources to achieve institutional goals. This process requires the periodic collection and analysis of data to inform the decisions to be made about programs and to plan for needs to be met.

28. **Which of the following statements is true of school accounting practices?** *(Skill 1.8) (Average Rigor)*

A. All purchases from internal funds must be authorized by the principal or a person designated by the principal

B. The principal is the only person authorized to sign checks for the school checking account

C. Principals can pre-sign checks that a designated administrator can use when the principal is unavailable

D. Administrators must record, present, summarize, and interpret accurate records to preserve the school's owner equity

Answer: A. All purchases from internal funds must be authorized by the principal or a person designated by the principal
Principals, or their designee, must authorize all purchases from internal funds. (B) is wrong because checks must be signed by two people. (C) is inappropriate because principals should never pre-sign checks. (D) is incorrect because schools do not have owner equity; they are publicly owned by the taxpayers.

29. **General principles of school cost accounting require schools to use a(an) _____ basis for accounting.** *(Skill 1.8) (Easy)*

A. Single-entry

B. Cash basis

C. Consolidation

D. Accrual

Answer: D. Accrual
Schools use accrual accounting.

30. **Which of the following is one of the characteristics of the foundation program of funding?** *(Skill 1.8) (Average Rigor)*

    A. The state and district work together to define the level of funding

    B. The state works alone to define the level of funding

    C. A non-profit foundation works alone to define the level of funding

    D. None of the above

Answer: A. The state and district work together to define the level of funding

Unlike the flat grant model, where the state alone provides per-pupil funding, in the foundation program the state and the districts act in partnership to determine the required level of local participation.

31. **Who regulates the use of internal school funds?** *(Skill 1.8) (Easy)*

    A. State Board of Education

    B. Local School Board

    C. School Site-Based Management Team

    D. School Principal

Answer: A. State Board of Education
The State Board of Education sets rules for the use of internal school funds.

32. **The calculation of the base student allocation formula is best expressed by which of the following:**
(Skill 1.8) (Rigorous)

   A. The FTE plus program cost factor, times base student allocation, times district cost differential

   B. The weighted FTE times base student allocation, times district cost differential

   C. The FTE times weighted FTE, times base student allocation, times district cost differential

   D. The weighted FTE times program cost factor, times base student allocation, times district cost factor

Answer: B. The weighted FTE times base student allocation, times district cost differential
To arrive at the weighted FTE, you multiply the FTE by the program cost factor. Then you multiply this by the base student allocation and the district cost differential to arrive at the base student funding.

33. **Mr. Price, principal at Wilson High School, wants to make preparation of the campus budget a more collaborative process. The first thing he should do is:** *(Skill 1.8) (Rigorous)*

   A. Contact various stakeholders to gather information

   B. Form a Budget Committee with representatives from all stakeholder groups

   C. Articulate a vision statement that shows a relationship between the school's budget and its improvement goals

   D. Draft a budget that can be used as a basis for discussion, assuming it will be modified by input from stakeholders

Answer: A. Contact various stakeholders to gather information
The order of collaborative budgeting is: 1) Gather information from stakeholders; 2) Select a committee with representatives from each stakeholder group; 3) Have the committee create a common vision; 4) Train committee members, explain school budgetary statutes, and provide all necessary information; 5) Present data and accept input; 6) Create a budget; and 7) Present the budget to the district.

34. **A school principal faced with inadequate funds to achieve school goals can:** *(Skill 1.8) (Average Rigor)*

    A. Use discretionary funds to support the school's mission and vision.

    B. Seek help from all stakeholders.

    C. Approach the Site Based Management Committee for help.

    D. All of the above

Answer: D. All of the above
All of these choices could contribute to procuring additional funding.

35. **The "Financial and Program Cost Accounting for Florida Schools" is a publication that reflects the requirements of Rule 6A-1.001 of Florida's Administrative Code and Sections 237.01 and 237.02 of Florida's Statutes. It is also known as the _____.** *(Skill 1.9) (Easy)*

    A. Money Book

    B. Green Book

    C. FPCA Book

    D. Red Book

Answer: D. Red Book
Methods for cost accounting and reporting are contained in the Florida Department of Education's publication "Financial and Program Cost Accounting for Florida Schools" which is also known as The Red Book. The content of this publication also reflects the requirements of Rule 6A-1.001 of Florida's Administrative Code and Sections 237.01 and 237.02 of Florida's Statutes.

36. **Which of the following is a principle of accrual accounting?**
   (Skill 1.9) (Rigorous)

   A. Transactions are recorded when a cash receipt or reimbursement occurs

   B. Transactions are recorded as assets or liabilities when the cash receipt or reimbursement occurs

   C. Transactions are recorded in a cash account and then moved to an asset or liability column when the cash funds are received

   D. Transactions are recorded as assets or liabilities at the time they occur

Answer: D. Transactions are recorded as assets or liabilities at the time they occur

General principles of school cost-accounting use an accrual rather than a cash basis accounting system. When using accrual accounting, financial transactions must be recorded as revenues or expenditures at the time the transaction occurs. There should never be cash exchanged for goods or services. In this process, revenues earned at the time of the transaction become assets, and expenditures become liabilities, regardless of when the cash receipt or reimbursement occurs.

37. **The school administrator should ensure that the building is always safe and comfortable. Which of the following is the most efficient method for achieving this goal? (Skill1.10) (Rigorous)**

   A. Establishing a system for teachers to complete daily logs of building conditions

   B. Conducting brief daily walk-throughs of the building, either personally or through a designee

   C. Allowing students to come to the office and report problems they encounter

   D. Holding monthly rallies for stakeholders to discuss their concerns and requests

Answer: B. Conducting brief daily walk-throughs of the building, either personally or through a designee

While district decisions and funding levels play significant parts in the aesthetics of a school building, basic safety and comfort are the responsibility of a school's administrative team. Various strategies can promote building safety and efficiency. Walk-throughs are a good example of such practices. They provide information to the principal about what is going on in the school as well as provide teachers and students with a sense of the principal's presence.

38. **A fellow principal tells you that her school has been dealing with break-ins during the lunch period. They believe the culprits are neighborhood youth breaking into the gym while it is unused during lunch. To prevent the problem the school has begun locking the doors during lunch and reopening them when gym classes are back in session. What should be your opinion of this plan?**
(Skill 1.10) (Average Rigor)

   A. It is an effective method to address the problem; there are no major concerns

   B. This is an ineffective plan and should not be used

   C. The plan may prevent break-ins; however, it may prevent egress at any time

   D. None of the above

Answer: C. The plan may prevent break-ins; however, it may prevent egress at any time
As an administrator, your concern about safety and security should cause you to question the propriety of this plan. By locking the school doors, your fellow principal is violating the rules and statutes governing proper facilities management. Although it may appear that the break-ins are a large enough concern to justify locking the doors, there is no justification for locking exits that would allow egress at any time. If the locks could be opened from the inside at any time, then the plan would be viable.

39. **The death of a fourth grader in a swimming accident has prompted the implementation of the school crisis response plan. Which of the following would not be included as an appropriate activity in the plan: (Skill 1.11) (Easy)**

    A. Getting accurate information out to all members of the school community

    B. Sharing the latest media reports about the accident with staff and students

    C. Offering crisis/grief counseling to all students

    D. Providing information to parents and guardians about common stress and grief reactions

Answer: B. Sharing the latest media reports about the accident with staff and students. Although the media may provide some useful information, for the most part, attending to news reports if not helpful in providing good crisis intervention. Crisis responders need to get information from reliable sources, such as emergency management or law enforcement personnel. Further, the sensationalistic nature of news reports can feed fear and create unnecessary anxiety.

40. **A bomb threat is reported at the high school, and the school is evacuated. In order to function appropriately as a crisis responder in this situation, the school personnel need all of the following except: (Skill 1.11) (Average Rigor)**

    A. A chance to debrief and get support from colleagues

    B. Clarity about roles and responsibilities

    C. Mandatory post-trauma counseling

    D. Adequate training and follow-up

Answer: C. Mandatory post-trauma counseling.
Most crisis responders, with adequate training and support, will recover from the effects of providing crisis intervention. In some cases, professional counseling may be helpful or necessary. However, mandating such counseling is inappropriate.

41. **A school administrator is asked to develop a crisis management plan for her school. She includes all of the following in the plan except: (Skill 1.11) (Average Rigor)**

    A. Specific lines of communication

    B. The name of the crisis team leader

    C. Goals of the plan

    D. Intervention strategies

Answer: B. The name of the crisis team leader
Although designating a crisis team leader is an important part of a crisis management plan, the team leader's name may change over time or in different situations. Writing the plan so it can be used in varied events will make it most useful and comprehensive.

42. **The following letter has been sent to your office by a parent of a kindergarten student.**

    Dear Ms. Valdes,

    My son, Joey Brown, has recently been diagnosed with asthma. In order to control his asthma attacks, the doctor has prescribed the following medication that must be taken EVERY two hours. Please advise me on the best strategy to ensure that he receives his medication according to the prescribed regimen.
    Sincerely, Mr. Andrew Brown

    According to Florida Statute 232.46, what should be your response to this letter? *(Skill 1.11) (Average Rigor)*

    A. Dear Mr. Brown: The school is not permitted to administer medication. As John is 6 years old, the teachers will remind him to take his medication every two hours

    B. Dear Mr. Brown: Please provide us with the medication in its original container along with a statement giving us 1) permission to assist in its administration and 2) an explanation of the necessity of the medication

    C. Dear Mr. Brown: The school is not permitted to administer medication. In order to use the medication on school grounds, John must 1) keep it in a secured locker and 2) ask permission to leave class every two hours

    D. Dear Mr. Brown: Please provide us with the name of John's doctor and of the medication so that we can research whether this is a medication we are allowed to administer to students

Answer: B. Dear Mr. Brown: Please provide us with the medication in its original container along with a statement giving us 1) permission to assist in its administration and 2) an explanation of the necessity of the medication
Florida Statute 232.46 addresses the administration of medication by school district personnel. Each school district must develop a policy based on the statute which states that the medication must be in its original container and explicit, written parental permission is necessary prior to administering any medication.

43. **You are a vice-principal at a large, urban high school. The student population has many teenage parents, including several who have chosen to remain as a couple and raise their child. One of your after-school programs is aimed at increasing the graduation rate of these students. Therefore, you provide them with mentors and meet with their parents to make sure they are on track to graduate. One particularly supportive mother likes to review her son's folder each month. He is a senior, and turned 18 just before Thanksgiving. What are your responsibilities to the parent and to the child according to FERPA?** *(Skill 1.12) (Rigorous)*

A. When a student becomes the legal guardian for a child, he or she is viewed as an independent individual under the FERPA legislation

B. The mother has the right to view her son's records as long as he is under her care, regardless of his age

C. The mother's right to view her son's record continues until the end of the school year in which he turns 18

D. Her son in the only individual who has a right to view his records since he is already 18

Answer: D. Her son in the only individual who has a right to view his records since he is already 18

The Family Rights and Privacy Act of 1964 (FERPA) (also know as the Buckley Amendment) states that no funds will be made available under any applicable program to any state or local educational agency, any institution of higher education, any community college, any school, agency offering a preschool program, or any other educational institution which has a policy of denying parents of students the right to inspect and review any and all official records, files, and data directly related to their children. However, according to FERPA, students who are 18 years of age or attending a post-secondary educational institution acquire the right of consent formerly held by the parent.

44. The father of a former student calls you concerning his daughter's progress in college. He is concerned that the now 17-year-old college student has switched majors without telling him. Therefore, he wants to know the best way to obtain her records. You should advise the parent that the Buckley Amendment: *(Skill 1.12) (Average Rigor)*

   A. Does not permit colleges to provide student records to parents

   B. Allows parents access to college student's records only if the parent pays the tuition

   C. Transfers the parent's rights of consent to the student once he/she enters 12th grade

   D. Both A and C

Answer: A. Does not permit colleges to provide student records to parents
Students who are 18 years of age or attending a post-secondary educational institution acquire the right of consent formerly held by the parent. Thus, the father has no rights to his daughter's college records.

45. Which of the following is NOT a major category in the Florida statutes? *(Skill 1.12) (Average Rigor)*

   A. Compensatory education, truancy, and home schooling

   B. Educational choice, special and charter schools

   C. Health, immunization and medication issues

   D. Religious issues

Answer: A. Compensatory education, truancy, and home schooling
Compensatory education is not discussed in the Florida statutes. Major categories of the Florida statutes include the following topics:
   - Compulsory education, truancy and home schooling
   - Educational choice, special and charter schools
   - Health, immunization and medication issues
   - Instructional environment guidelines
   - Disabilities and special needs students
   - Student records
   - Disciplinary actions
   - Religious issues
   - Athletics and other extracurricular activities
   - Parental notification, progress reports and due process
   - Student-parent handbooks

46. **A new student has arrived from Italy and you know that he speaks very little English. As the school principal, you realize that his right to a translator and other resources are covered under which of the following?** *(Skill 1.13) (Average Rigor)*

   A. Title VI

   B. EEOC

   C. Both A and B

   D. Neither A nor B

Answer: C. Both A and B
Public school children who receive assistance to learn English are protected by Title VI (of the Civil Rights Act). This act states "school systems are responsible for assuring that students of a particular race, color, or national origin are not denied the opportunity to obtain the education generally obtained by other students in the system". Additionally, a section of the U.S. Equal Educational Opportunities Act (EEOC), the federal agency responsible for interpreting and enforcing Title VI, adds that states are mandated also to protect and help students "overcome language barriers that impede equal participation by its students in its instructional programs."

47. During a meeting with fellow superintendents you overhear a heated exchange between two colleagues. One believes that the META consent decree is similar to IDEA in numerous ways. The other administrator believes that such a comparison is incorrect and borders on discrimination. They ask your opinion. Which of the following the most appropriate response? *(Skill 1.14) (Average Rigor)*

A. I just came for the snacks; I'd rather not be involved in a weighty debate

B. They are not similar, since the META consent decree deals with English language learners and IDEA deals with students with special needs

C. They are quite similar in that they are both aimed at providing equal access to students

D. They are quite similar in that they both receive the largest allocations of federal funds

Answer: C. They are quite similar in that they are both aimed at providing equal access to students
The META consent decree and IDEA are similar. Although one deals with English language learners and the other deals with students with special needs, both are aimed at providing equal access to students.

48. **Which of the following best illustrates an educational goal?**
    (Skill 1.14) (Average Rigor)

    A. Provide good health and physical fitness

    B. By the year 2010, the high school graduation rate will increase to at least 90%

    C. Develop self-realization

    D. The students will complete a reading comprehension examination within 30 minutes with 80% accuracy

Answer: B. By the year 2010, the high school graduation rate will increase to at least 90%
Goals can be broad and take a long time to achieve, which is why they are further broken down into manageable outcomes. Goals must be specific and measurable. In this case, the parameters are set using the year 2010 and the graduation rate of 90%. When stakeholders examine the graduation results of students in 2010, they can compare them with the results of the year this goal was formed and determine whether or not the 90% has been achieved. Option (D) is an example of an educational objective.

49. **Which of the following is a major benefit of the FCAT exam?**
    (Skill 1.15) (Rigorous)

    A. It identifies important educational topics that can drive instruction

    B. It is used by the legislature to determine per pupil funding

    C. It serves as a benchmark for comparing students with their colleagues in other states

    D. It permits educators to monitor how much students learn from one year to the next

Answer: D. It permits educators to monitor how much students learn from one year to the next
Since FCAT reading and mathematics exams are given in grades 3 – 10, it is possible to monitor how much students learn from one year to the next. Students can demonstrate learning gains in any one of three ways: *Improve* achievement levels from 1-2, 2-3, 3-4, or 4-5; **or** *Maintain* within the relatively high levels of 3, 4, or 5; **or** *Demonstrate more than one year's growth* within achievement levels 1 or 2 (this does not include retained students).

50. **The most recent FCAT scores has resulted in your school being awarded a grade of "B" by the state. After celebrating this achievement, you turn your attention to addressing the areas that reduced your performance. In mathematics, 100 students earned levels 1, 2, or 3 on the assessment. In reading, 50 students earned levels 1, 2, or 3. For the school to make "adequate progress" you will need to do which of the following?** *(Skill 1.15) (Rigorous)*

   A. Make sure at least 50% of the lowest-performing math students make learning gains in math

   B. Make sure at least 50% of the lowest-performing reading students make learning gains in reading

   C. Make sure at least 50 of the lowest-performing math students and 25 of the lowest performing reading students make learning gains in their respective subjects

   D. All of the above

Answer: D. All of the above
To make "adequate progress" your school must show learning gains for the lowest-performing students in math and the lowest-performing students in reading. There must be learning gains for 50% of the students in each group. Thus, in our example, 50 individuals equal 50% of the lowest performing math students. Likewise, 25 students equal 50% of the lowest performing reading students. For "adequate progress," all the answer choices are required.

51. **Identify the type of evaluation that occurs before instruction:** *(Skill 1.16) (Average Rigor)*

   A. Formative

   B. Diagnostic

   C. Summative

   D. Normative

Answer: B. Diagnostic
Diagnostic evaluation is provided prior to instruction to identify problems, to place students in certain groups, and to make assignments that are appropriate to their needs. *Formative* evaluation is used to obtain feedback during the instructional process. *Summative evaluation* is used to culminate a unit or series of lessons to arrive at a grade.

52. **While observing your first-year teachers, you noticed that they do not understand the basics of creating appropriate assessments. Therefore, you have created a graphic to help them understand the importance of validity and reliability. What terms should you write next to Line One and Line Two below?** *(Skill 1.16) (Average Rigor)*

A. Line One represents reliability

B. Line Two represents reliability

C. Line One represents validity

D. None of the above

Answer: A. Line One represents reliability
Reliability refers to the consistency of the test to measure what it should measure. This is represented by line one. For example, the items on a true or false quiz, given by a classroom teacher, are reliable if they convey the same meaning every time the quiz is administered to similar groups of students under similar situations. In other words, there is no ambiguity or confusion with the items on the quiz. *Validity* is the extent to which a test measures what it is intended to measure. This is represented by line two. For example, a test may lack validity if it was designed to measure the creative writing of students, but it is also used to measure handwriting even though it was not designed for the latter.

53. If the United States Department of Education requires a national test to determine where each student performs compared to other similar students, they would require students to take _____ assessments. If the State of Florida wants to determine how well its students are performing relative to the Sunshine State Standards, they must administer a _____ assessment. *(Skill 1.16) (Easy)*

A. Criterion-referenced, Norm-referenced

B. Norm-referenced, Criterion-referenced

C. Norm-referenced, Norm-referenced

D. Criterion-referenced, Criterion-referenced

Answer: B. Norm-referenced, Criterion-referenced
Standardized, norm-referenced achievement tests are designed to measure what a student knows in a particular subject in relation to other students of similar characteristics. The test batteries provide a broad scope of content area coverage so that it may be used on a larger scale in many different states and school districts. However, the questions may not measure the goals and content emphasized in a particular local curriculum. Criterion-Referenced Standardized Achievement Tests are designed to indicate the student's performance that is directly related to specific educational objectives, thus indicating what the student can or cannot do.

54. Data show that at your school, ESOL students are having problems in understanding literary techniques. Particularly challenging for 75% of these students are comparisons such as similes and metaphors. You would like to diagnose the exact source of the problem so that students can learn what the state standards require. Which of the following represents the best series of strategies that teachers should use?   *(Skill 1.17) (Average Rigor)*

   A. Administer diagnostic assessments, individualize instruction according to the results of the diagnosis, identify strengths and weaknesses, reassess

   B. Identify strengths and weaknesses, administer diagnostic assessments, individualize instruction according to the results of the diagnosis, reassess

   C. Reassess, administer diagnostic assessments, individualize instruction according to the results of the diagnosis, identify strengths and weaknesses

   D. Administer diagnostic assessments, identify strengths and weaknesses, individualize instruction according to the results of the diagnosis, reassess

Answer: D. Administer diagnostic assessments, identify strengths and weaknesses, individualize instruction according to the results of the diagnosis, reassess

To determine students' current level of achievement, first diagnostic assessments should be administered. The scores will then identify strengths and weaknesses. With this information teachers can individualize instruction to maximize each student's learning. Finally, students should be reassessed to ensure that they are learning and that the individualized instruction is effective.

55. The faculty of the mathematics department has submitted their proposal for the school's technology plan. In it, they have requested a high-tech package that combines various powerful CAI tools. After investigating the proposed purchase, Mrs. Griffin, your technology directory, agrees that it is a worthwhile investment. However, she advises that the processors you currently have are too slow to execute the tasks required. In order for the math students to use the package you must purchase both items in this coming finance cycle. In your budget, the CAI tools would be in category 1, while the processor would be listed under category 2. Of the four options below, which one provides the correct answers for categories1 and 2?   *(Skill 2.1)* *(Easy)*

   A. 1. Hardware, 2. Software

   B. 1. Software, 2. Peripherals

   C. 1. Software, 2. Hardware

   D. 1. Peripherals, 2. Hardware

Answer: C. 1. Software, 2. Hardware
The physical components of a computer system are called the hardware. The software consists of the program applications that tell a computer what to do. In effect, a computer system is delineated by the software which provides instructions to the computer and the hardware which executes the commands. In our example, the CAI programs would fall under the software category and the processors are among the hardware purchases.

56. What is the MAIN reason for the slow pace of technology's diffusion and integration into teachers' practice? *(Skill 2.1)* *(Rigorous)*

   A. Teachers and administrators were not prepared to advance and manage technology in schools

   B. Teachers were afraid of technology

   C. Administrators did not want to pay for the expensive equipment

   D. Students were not interested in technology

Answer: A. Teachers and administrators were not prepared to advance and manage technology in schools
There are many reasons why technology has been slow in diffusing through schools and into teachers' practices. The MAIN reason is that teachers and administrators were not prepared. Most of the other reasons, such as fear of using technology, stem from this lack of preparation and background.

57. **Which of the following best describes the superintendent's role in assessing hardware and software needs:** *(Skill 2.1) (Average Rigor)*

    A. Researching the use of all appropriate hardware and software packages in educational settings

    B. Hiring a consultant to identify what the district needs to buy at this point in time

    C. Working closely with a technology committee to identify current needs and possible solutions, including specific purchases

    D. Asking each principal what is needed in his or her school

Answer: C. Working closely with a technology committee to identify current needs and possible solutions, including specific purchases

Assessing technology needs and determining a course of action is a complex task. The superintendent must effectively utilize district personnel, including appropriate administrators, teachers, and possibly community members, who can tackle the various aspects of needs assessment and selection of hardware and software. The superintendent needs to be well-informed but cannot be "the expert" on technology issues as he or she has many other duties, and the field of technology is vast.

58. **The algebra teacher will use a software application for students to calculate several math equations. Which of the following would best complete the task?** *(Skill 2.1) (Average Rigor)*

    A. Communications

    B. Word processor

    C. Database

    D. Spreadsheet

Answer: D. Spreadsheet

A spreadsheet contains rows and columns and can be used for easy organization of large amounts of information.

59. Last year the school created a Technology Committee (TC) composed of one representative from the faculty and administration plus one parent, student, and business person. This year, the School Advisor Committee (SAC) has voted to increase the faculty membership. The new requirement mandates that the TC includes one teacher from each department. The SAC is MOST likely accounting for which of the steps in the software evaluation process?   *(Skill 2.2) (Rigorous)*

    A. Determining that the features and capabilities of the software match administrative goals and objectives

    B. Determining if the software actually does what it describes and if what it does is what is needed

    C. Ascertaining that the software is compatible to the computer system operating at the school

    D. Both A and B

Answer: B. Determining if the software actually does what it describes and if what is does is what is needed.
The acquisition of software is an expensive proposition. Mistakes in the selection of software programs prevent the school from accomplishing intended objectives. Software evaluation is a critical skill for administrators; therefore, they should follow these steps when selecting software:
1. Identify the objectives that are to be accomplished by introducing the software in the school environment
2. Determine if the features and capabilities of the software match administrative goals and objectives
3. Determine if the software actually does what it describes and if what it does is what is needed
4. Ascertain that the software is compatible to the computer system in operation at the school

Of these four steps, teacher representation is most likely to affect step three. While teachers will also bring a good perspective on step one; this can likely be address by any mix of faculty members on the TC. By requiring that there be one teacher from each department, the SAC MOST likely wants the TC to consider the needs of each subject-area and the subject-specific standards that must be reinforced by the software.

60. All of the following are examples of copyright infringement except:
(Skill 2.2) (Average Rigor)

    A. When teachers take home software from school computer labs

    B. Reselling copies of computer programs purchased by one school to another school

    C. Running software applications on computers that are too slow to handle those applications

    D. The illegal duplication of software

Answer: C. Running software applications on computers that are too slow to handle those applications
Unless the entity, whether it is a school or an individual teacher, purchases the software, it does not have a license to use it. Piracy is theft of software invented and sold by someone else and duplicating it does not give the inventor any credit or pay for his or her work.

61. Mr. Horowitz, the principal, has asked you to review applications in order to hire one new foreign language teacher. You have received the staffing requirements and found that the least critical need is Spanish and the greatest need is in Swahili followed by Arabic. As you assess the applications you have narrowed your choice to two teachers. One has taught in Florida for two years but has not earned her license to teach Swahili in Florida. However, she was licensed in another state and taught Swahili there for ten years. In addition, due to her instructional leadership in the school district, she has received stellar reviews and recommendations from her former principal and the district superintendant. The second candidate graduated three years ago with a major in Spanish. This year he earned his Florida teaching license and his principal has rated him as average for the past two years. Which of these two teachers should you hire and why?   *(Skill 2.3) (Rigorous)*

   A. Hire the candidate who teaches Swahili; this is an area of high-needs and her teaching record indicates that she is experienced and highly-qualified; you can then support her in attaining certification

   B. Hire the candidate who teaches Spanish and has attained certification; federal and state laws require that a candidate have a state licensure before being hired to teach in Florida

   C. Both candidates should be hired. The Swahili teacher can fill the need for that language; the Spanish teacher's certification can be useful in reports required by *No Child Left Behind*

   D. Either teacher can be hired; your school would be well-served to hire either the Swahili or Spanish teacher

Answer: A. Hire the candidate who teaches Swahili; this is an area of high-needs and her teaching record indicates that she is experienced and highly-qualified; you can then support her in attaining certification
Hiring criteria have become quite stringent due to regulations imposed by *No Child Left Behind* and state laws. Newly hired teachers must possess the credential of being licensed, highly-qualified, or experienced. For example, all secondary subject-area teachers must have a degree in the subject they are teaching or they must demonstrate extensive competency, usually through a very rigorous exam. Schools and districts must also fill their "high needs" vacancies as promptly as possible. The scenario above suggests that both candidates bring qualifications required under *No Child Left Behind* regulations. When comparing the two individuals, the Spanish teacher only brings a state teaching license. In contrast, the Swahili teacher fills an area of high-needs, can be classified as highly qualified, and has many years of experience in teaching. Therefore, since you can only hire one teacher, the Swahili teacher should be selected.

62. In selecting instructional personnel, most public school principals are responsible for all of the following EXCEPT: *(Skill 2.3) (Easy)*

   A. Establishing a committee

   B. Initiating the process

   C. Determining the recommendations for employment

   D. Making the offer of employment

Answer: D. Making the offer of employment
The principal is responsible for all stages of hiring instructional personnel except extending the offer of employment; typically the school district main office performs this function.

63. A school needs a reading specialist; however, the applicant pool is small and no applicant meets all position requirements. The principal should: *(Skill 2.3) (Rigorous)*

   A. Select the best person and provide him or her with support

   B. Leave the position unfilled and advertise the position again

   C. Re-assign teachers to cover the position during their planning periods

   D. Inform parents that reading will not be taught until a qualified person is hired

Answer: A. Select the best person and provide him or her with support
It is important to have a certified person in each classroom. However, if time does not allow for a continued search, the principal should hire the best candidate and provide a mentor and additional resources to help the teacher develop skills during his or her first year.

64. When using site-based management, why should a principal involve a diverse group of stakeholders in the planning and decision-making processes?   *(Skill 2.3) (Rigorous)*

    A. Law requires that diverse groups participate in all parts of school management

    B. It avoids conflict when choices are made because every person is represented by individuals on the committee

    C. A committee of diverse individuals cannot represent everyone; however, they are more likely to bring different perspectives compared to a non-diverse committee

    D. This guarantees that special-interest groups will not be upset at the administration

Answer: C. A committee of diverse individuals cannot represent everyone; however, they are more likely to bring different perspectives compared to a non-diverse committee
Site-based management involves more people in the decision-making process, and results in more accountability and ownership in school operations.

65. Which of the following is MOST LIKELY to assist participants in staff development activities to retain information?   *(Skill 2.3) (Average Rigor)*

    A. Cover the topic in a single-session workshop

    B. Cover the topic in a three to four session workshop

    C. Cover the topic throughout the school year, allowing teachers to try the strategies then report back

    D. Cover the topic daily at informal meetings

Answer: C. Cover the topic throughout the school year, allowing teachers to try the strategies then report back
The new model of staff development focuses on sustaining learning. Instead of providing teachers with a single training session, the topic is brought up throughout a school year. This allows for ongoing learning and long-term change.

66. Which of the following is an appropriate district level orientation activity for a group of new teachers:
(Skill 2.3) (Easy)

A. A review of their individual school's philosophy

B. An introduction to faculty

C. Getting information about school board policies

D. A statement of their individual school's vision

Answer: C. Getting information about school board policies.
Information about school board policy is relevant at the district orientation since it does not relate to a specific school and includes teachers from different schools.

67. During the interview process, the principal may ask about the applicant's: *(Skill 2.3) (Easy)*

A. Reasons for applying for this job

B. Mother's maiden name

C. Ages of children

D. Handicapping conditions

Answer: A. Reasons for applying for this job
The principal may ask only about reasons for applying for the job. Answers B, C and D are not appropriate topics for questions in a job interview. They violate discrimination statutes.

68. Mr. Blanchard has taken care to match the qualifications of new teachers he hires with school needs and district policies. However, by the end of the first semester, he has received numerous complaints about two of his new hires, and some community leaders have criticized him for the teachers he hired. From the information provided, what is a likely explanation for this criticism?
(Skill 2.3) (Rigorous)

A. The new teachers did not buy into the school mission and vision

B. Students dislike the school vision and have complained to their parents about how the new teachers promote it

C. He inadequately communicated his actions to community stakeholders

D. Mr. Blanchard's hiring process is inadequate for his staffing needs

Answer: C. He inadequately communicated his actions to community stakeholders
It is likely Mr. Blanchard made his hiring decisions without communicating with stakeholders. Since all types of resources carry emotional and personal weight with school community members, forgetting the political elements of running a school often damages relationships. It's unlikely the new teachers were not onboard (A) if Mr. Blanchard took care in hiring them to meet school needs; (B) students would not single out new teachers regarding the school vision if all teachers support it; and (D) according to the information given, Mr. Blanchard gave careful thought to his hiring process.

69. When new teachers attend a school-level orientation, which of the following would be an appropriate topic: *(Skill 2.3) (Easy)*

A. Retirement benefits

B. Insurance benefits

C. Introduction to the district payroll system

D. The school's faculty handbook

Answer: D. The school's faculty handbook
School orientations are designed to make teachers familiar with all school policies and expectations after they have been hired. Answers A, B, and C are usually discussed during the hiring process or at the district's orientation.

70. The Florida Department of Education (FLDOE) has mandated that all teachers receive ongoing evaluations and that all salary increases be tied to learning. Your administrative team has developed an intensive instructional assessment instrument with the following categories: classroom management and discipline, knowledge of subject matter, instructional strategies and pedagogical techniques, integration of technology, cultural competency and incorporation of diversity, and professional development and self-reflection. When submitted to the FLDOE for approval, the instrument was returned, noting that a key element was missing. Which of the following categories should you add? *(Skill 2.4) (Average Rigor)*

A. Teacher disposition

B. Student achievement

C. Team work

D. Parental and community involvement

Answer: B. Student achievement
In Florida, teacher evaluations are required by law, and are linked to compensation increases. Teacher performance ratings should be directly tied to student achievement, so student achievement data should be included in determining appraisal scores. The driving motto should be that teaching has not happened unless students have learned!

71. Which of the following criteria should be used to evaluate personnel in schools?   *(Skill 2.4) (Average Rigor)*

A. How well the parents like the teacher

B. How well the children like the teacher

C. How well the other teachers relate to the teacher

D. Test score gains by students

Answer: D. Test score gains by students
Test scores of students are one objective measure of how well a teacher is performing. Options A, B, and C may provide useful information but are not objective measures and could be misleading.

72. **In performance-based assessments, the principal ties teachers' performance to which of the following:** *(Skill 2.4) (Average Rigor)*

A. Student learning

B. Parental feedback

C. Administrative ratings

D. Student surveys

Answer: A. Student learning
In performance-based assessments, the principal must tie teachers' performance to student learning.

73. **The building level principal should perform which of the following performance appraisal tasks?** *(Skill 2.4) (Easy)*

A. Develop appraisal criteria

B. Design the appraisal process

C. Conduct post-appraisal conferences

D. Assess the appraisal system

Answer: C. Conduct post-appraisal conferences
The principal is responsible for having a post-appraisal conference with all personnel to discuss the strengths and weaknesses revealed by the appraisal, and set professional goals and objectives for improvement. The other options are tasks that are the responsibility of other administrators.

74. **The district is attempting to streamline the way it handles personnel information. As the superintendent, you have reviewed all the available options and would like to invest in a computerized system. At your last board meeting, 75% of the school board members expressed concern that the system was too expensive. In addition, they could not understand why you could not simply perfect the filing system currently in use. Which of the following points would you use to convince the board members to approve the computerized system?**
(Skill 2.5) (Easy)

A. It will allow for more precise access to sensitive personnel information with access being limited and monitored

B. It can provide administrative staff with an efficient way to enter, share, and use personnel data as they see fit

C. It can eliminate the need for paper files on employees.

D. A and C

Answer: A. It will allow for more precise access to sensitive personnel information, with access being limited and monitored.
While computerization will not eliminate all paper files, it will allow more precise and monitored access to personnel information. Ultimately, it will also be more efficient, and facilitate appropriate control and access, providing greater confidentiality to employees.

75. One of your teacher's has received negative ratings on each of her evaluations for the past four years. As principal, you have referred her to the Employee Assistance Program but she has used their services. The superintendent's office has reviewed her folder and decided to dismiss her. Which of the following must happen next? *(Skill 2.6)* *(Average Rigor)*

A. The teacher must be notified in writing

B. The teacher is allowed an appeal

C. The teacher must be allowed to examine any evidence

D. The teacher must be permitted counsel of his or her choice

Answer: B. The teacher is allowed an appeal
The teacher is allowed an appeal when there is a decision to terminate her. Before the decision is made, the teacher should have been notified of the charges in writing, been allowed to examine any evidence during an impartial hearing, and have consulted with a counsel of her choice.

76. Which of the following is NOT required when bringing punitive action against a teacher? *(Skill 2.6)* *(Easy)*

A. A videotape of the hearing

B. Notification of charges in writing

C. A transcript of the hearing

D. An impartial hearing

Answer: A. A videotape of the hearing
If an issue requires punitive action, the teacher must be notified of charges in writing and adequate time must be given for the teacher to prepare a rebuttal. The teacher must be permitted counsel of his or her choice. During an impartial hearing, the teacher must be able to examine any evidence. When a decision is made based on the evidence, a transcript of the hearing must be given to the teacher. Lastly, he or she is allowed an appeal if there is a decision to terminate him or her or if there is a severe loss to the teacher

77. **An employee has not performed well throughout the year although you have followed all steps to help her, and her previous recommendations had been excellent. You have documented her work and your evaluation process. She recently disclosed that she has had a number of personal stressors this past year and knows she did not perform well. What will be your recommendation for her employment next year?** *(Skill 2.6) (Rigorous)*

   A. Terminate her, based on the objective evaluation criteria

   B. Conduct a hearing before an impartial tribunal prior to making a decision

   C. Rehire her because she has acknowledged her problems

   D. Request that she take a leave of absence for the next year

Answer: B. Conduct a hearing before an impartial tribunal before a final decision is made

This approach would be most fair for the teacher and would ensure that others are involved in the decision to renew or dismiss her.

78. One of your teachers is threatening legal action against you and the school district. He asserts that he has been unfairly overlooked during the process of raises and promotions. Your position is that the district has required that teacher raises be tied to student achievement. His students have consistently performed poorly on the state achievement tests. In addition, he refuses to attend professional development sessions that are not required in his contract. The attorney's office has advised you that your position may not be supported in court. She has shown you that the teacher's unions have been able to resist efforts to include pay-for-performance measures in its contracts. Therefore, the district has decided to give the teacher the raise he wants. After talking with other principals in your district, you realize this is an ongoing problem. What is the most effective way for you to solve the discrepancy between the pay-for-performance requirement and the contract stipulations? *(Skill 2.7) (Rigorous)*

A. Compose a resolution, obtain the signatures of your fellow principals, and submit the document to the superintendent

B. Mobilize parents to petition the school board on this issue

C. Work with the school district as it engages in collective bargaining with the teacher's union

D. Lobby the state Department of Education to legislate that the discrepancy be corrected

Answer: C. Work with the school district as it engages in collective bargaining with the teacher's union

Collective bargaining is the process of negotiating a contract between the management of a school district and the teachers' union, which represents the teachers within a district. Although monetary matters comprise the majority of issues in most collective bargaining sessions, other facets of working conditions (such as job duties, hours on campus, etc.) are negotiated, as well.

A principal may serve on the school district's management team during a collective negotiation. The negotiation process is usually lengthy, involves multi-year contracts, team determination, unit recognition, planning and preparation, agreement and implementation, strategies to reach agreement, and counterproposals. As a principal, this would be the best avenue for you to work to address this discrepancy.

79. **Why is collective bargaining beneficial for both the teachers' union and the school district?** *(Skill 2.7) (Rigorous)*

   A. Working together allows both sides to consider each other's needs and can bring unity and effective action once a decision is reached

   B. Discussing the issues with small groups of teachers allows individual perspectives to be considered in the decision-making process
   C. Using collective bargaining allows the teachers' union and the school district to avoid conflict because one side has to give in to the other's wishes

   D. Engaging in collective bargaining is never beneficial for either the union or the district

Answer: A. Working together allows both sides to consider each other's needs and can bring unity and effective action once a decision is reached
While collective bargaining has historically been viewed as a divisive process, both progressive unions and sensitive school districts have found that working together can be more beneficial to both sides.

80. Your teachers have agreed that they will set student achievement goals tied to the FCAT assessment. To aid them, you have provided ongoing professional development on setting S.M.A.R.T goals, improving instructional strategies, and using continuous assessments to gauge student learning. Which of the following teachers appear to have been impacted by your strategy?   *(Skill 2.8) (Rigorous)*

   A. Mrs. Johnson set her goal to have 65% of her students achieve a level 3 or above on the FCATs; 40% achieved this goal during the first year, 56% the second year, and 68% last year. This year she made her goal 70% and 75% achieved it

   B. Ms. Marta determined her goal would be for 60% of her students to achieve a level 3 or above on the FCATs. The first year she achieved 50%, the second year she achieved 60%, and the third and fourth year she achieved 55%

   C. Mr. Williams chose his goal to have 100% of his students achieve either a level 3 or above on the FCATs. During the first year, 70% of his students achieved this level. In the second year 65% achieved it, and during the past two years 60% achieved it

   D. None of these teachers had over ¾ of their students achieve at a level 3; Therefore, none of them have been truly been impacted by your strategy

Answer: A. Mrs. Johnson set her goal to have 65% of her students achieve a level 3 or above on the FCATs; 40% achieved this goal during the first year, 56% the second year, and 68% last year. This year she made her goal 70% and 75% achieved it

Goal setting is one way to bring about change in instructional techniques, and in school growth and improvement. Principals can assist teachers in setting goals that are SMART – Specific, Measurable, Achievable, Relevant, and Time-framed. As a result, teachers have goals that will drive their instruction and add personal ownership to their practices. In this example, Mrs. Johnson has internalized your strategy of using SMART goals. She started with a realistic goal and then constantly made gains toward achieving the goal. Then once she surpassed the initial goal, she set another more challenging goal to strive toward. Ms. Marta also set a realistic goal; however, after she achieved it in the second year, she did not achieve it in the third or fourth year. Rather than showing continued improvement; she leveled off at a lower level than she planned. In contrast to his colleagues, Mr. Williams set an unrealistic goal. Each year he fell further and further from his goal. A possible contributor could be the disheartening consequences of disappointment resulting from unrealistic goals.

81. You are a high school assistant principal charged with handling personnel problems. Students in a physics class complain that the teacher employs teaching strategies and evaluation procedures that make it impossible for any student to earn an A in his class. After checking student records and consulting with the science department chair, you determine that the students have a legitimate concern. The least threatening initial approach in dealing with the teacher is to: *(Skill 2.8) (Average Rigor)*

   A. Stress the negative effects his grading policy will have on the grade point averages of the more able students

   B. Encourage the teacher to do a self-evaluation of his teaching methods and propose solutions to help students achieve greater success

   C. Recommend procedures for the teacher to adopt if he intends to remain on staff

   D. Schedule a classroom evaluation and give a copy of the results to the teacher as well as filing it in his permanent record

Answer: B. Encourage the teacher to do a self-evaluation of his teaching methods and propose solutions to help students achieve greater success
This will be the least threatening first approach to the concern, and will invite the teacher to be aware of the effect of his/her strategies. Involving the teacher as an active participant in the solution will likely prompt a more positive reaction from the teacher.

82. F.S. 231 (Personnel of School Systems) does not cover which of the following topics? *(Skill 2.9) (Easy)*

   A. Personnel reappointment

   B. Certification processes

   C. Operational elements of the US Department of Education

   D. The operation of the Educational Standards Commission

Answer: C. Operational elements of the US Department of Education
F.S. 231 (Personnel of School Systems) spells out personnel qualifications, selection processes, certification processes, the operation of the Educational Standards Commission and the Educational Practices Commission, leave policies, and contractual and termination procedures. The operation of the US Department of Education is not covered by Florida law.

83. An employee has been incompetent all year in spite of your efforts to help her. You have documented her work and your efforts to help her improve. Now, she has instituted a grievance against you for allegedly harassing her and claims that she is an excellent teacher as demonstrated by her work at other schools. Further, you learn through the grapevine that she has been under personal stress. What should you do to decide her fate for the upcoming school year?   *(Skill 2.9)* *(Average Rigor)*

A. Terminate her

B. Discuss the matter with another principal

C. Rehire her because she had problems

D. Evaluate her using the district's pre-selected criteria

Answer: D. Evaluate her using the district's re-selected criteria
By using the districts pre-selected criteria, the principal can remain objective in appraising staff. Additionally, because the personal information was obtained through "the grapevine" it should be deemed unreliable and should not be used. Her grievance should not come into play in the evaluation process.

84. **As chair of a personnel committee considering applicants for an administrative position in the central office, one member of the committee advises you that the superintendent has expressed difficulty in working with female administrators. What action should you take?** *(Skill 2.9) (Average Rigor)*

   A. Advise the committee member to introduce this consideration into the committee's deliberations

   B. Advise the committee member that consideration of the superintendent's expressed difficulty in working with women should not influence the selection of an applicant

   C. Advise the committee member that the superintendent's expressed difficulty in working with women should be shared with the rest of the selection process

   D. Advise the committee member that the superintendent's expressed difficulty in working with women should be a primary consideration in determining the applicant to be recommended

Answer: B. Advise the committee member that consideration of the superintendent's expressed difficulty in working with women should not influence the selection of an applicant
Title VII, The Civil Rights Act of 1964, Section 703(a) specifically states that "It shall be unlawful employment practice for an employer …to discriminate against any individual … because of such individual race, color, religion, sex, or national origin…" Further, discussing this issue with the entire committee would not be productive in any way.

85. One of your students came to school with a dark circle on her cheek. Although she has stated that the bruise is a sports injury, you are concerned about it. Her mother is one of your most dedicated teachers and she has corroborated the story that her daughter was hit in the face while playing softball. Therefore, you take the story on face-value but make a mental note to be on alert if another incident occurs. Is this a correct course of action? Why or why not?   *(Skill 2.10) (Average Rigor)*

A. Yes: The student and her mother are credible individuals, which is the main criterion you should consider. You should accept the current explanation and maintain your plan to look out for suspicious marks or explanations in the future

B. Yes: Your duty of care has been met. You informally inquired about the matter and received a satisfactory response

C. No: You have not sufficiently attended to the issue. The duty of care to the student requires that you investigate further and submit, to the school district, a written statement of your findings

D. No: Because you are not a social worker, the duty of care placed on you is much less than would be required for someone certified to recognize child abuse

Answer: B. Yes: Your duty of care has been met. You informally inquired about the matter and received a satisfactory response
The state of Florida has assembled a variety of statements to guide the professional conduct of school employees. When certain concerns about students arise, educators are mandated by the state to submit reports. For example, indications of child abuse or suicide attempts would require that a teacher follow specified reporting procedures. In this case, you addressed the matter and made a determination based on the facts available.

86. **The state requires that teachers report indications of child abuse or indications that the student has attempted suicide. The state considers this requirement to be which of the following:**
    (Skill 2.10) (Rigorous)

    A. A standard of professional ethics

    B. A standard of religious conviction

    C. A standard of personal ethics

    D. A consideration for certified teachers

Answer: A. A standard of professional ethics
Ideally, teachers should have either personal convictions or ethics that would cause them to report suspected abuse or attempted suicide. However, the state REQUIRES teachers to report abuse as a part of the code of professional ethics.

87. **A school received a grant to cover the cost of putting computers and peripherals in every classroom. The district's technology coordinator and some teachers want the money to be spent to equip two computer labs. The principal is adamant that the money will be used to put computers and peripherals in classrooms. Select the conflict management style of the administrator in this scenario.** *(Skill 2.10)*
    (Average Rigor

    A. Accommodating

    B. Collaborating

    C. Competing

    D. Compromising

Answer: C. Competing
The administrator is adamant about his/her position, with no accommodations, compromises, or collaborations. While such a stance in this example might be perceived as "ethical," it is a rigid leadership style that is ultimately unhelpful and can lead to ethical missteps.

88. **The state requires that teachers report indications of child abuse or indications that the student has attempted suicide. The state considers this requirement:** *(Skill 2.10)* *(Average Rigor)*

    A. A standard of professional ethics

    B. A standard of religious conviction

    C. A standard of personal ethics

    D. A consideration for certified teachers

Answer: A. standard of professional ethics

In order to protect children, teachers should have either personal convictions or personal ethics that would cause them to report suspected abuse or attempted suicide. However, the state REQUIRES teachers to report abuse as a part of the code of professional ethics.

89. **A student has worn shirts with slogans that you consider inflammatory. In addition, her choice of dress has caused other students to be distracted during instructional time. It is your belief that these shirts should be banned while on school grounds. Which of the following Constitutional rights should be studied and discussed prior to a decision being made?** *(Skill 2.11)* *(Easy)*

    A. Freedom of Speech

    B. Freedom of Religion

    C. Freedom from Unreasonable Searches

    D. Freedom of Attire

Answer: A. Freedom of Speech

Fundamental knowledge of key constitutional amendments – such as freedom of expression, citizenship, school desegregation, and freedom from unreasonable searches – is important. See http://www.usconstitution.net/ for the text of the US Constitution and all subsequent amendments. Further, principals should have a basic understanding of Florida education law. An excellent resource regarding Florida statutes and the state board of education can be found at http://www.fldoe.org/ese/pdf/1b-stats.pdf. The issue of student clothing typically falls under "Freedom of Speech."

90. **Why should administrators have a basic grounding in relevant law?** *(Skill 2.11) (Average Rigor)*

    A. So they can act ethically when quick action is required

    B. So they can advise parents of the best solution to concerns they raise

    C. So they can act as their own counsel if necessary

    D. So they can decide when to abide by the rules and when to bend them

Answer: A. So they can act ethically when quick action is required.
Without a basic grounding in relevant law, school leaders cannot act ethically in complex situations where conflicting needs or the pressure for quick action is needed. Administrators should not act their own counsel, advise parents about legal issues, or bend rules at will.

91. **When a teacher stepped out the room to call a parent, the unsupervised students began throwing items. The incident resulted in the serious injury of a student. The court found the school system to be negligent in this incident. Identify the element of negligence that best supports the court's judgment.** *(Skill 2.12) (Rigorous)*

    A. Dereliction of duty of care

    B. Dereliction of standard of care

    C. Dereliction of proximate cause

    D. Actual loss or injury

Answer: B. Dereliction of standard of care
The standard of care that educators must exercise to avoid liability is defined as that of the reasonable and prudent educator charged with similar duties under similar circumstances. The standard of care varies according to such factors as the age of the student, the child's mental capacity, and the environment and circumstances under which the injury occurred. Since adolescent high school students are not adults, they should not be expected to exhibit the degree of discretion associated with mature adults. The school was negligent in not having a schedule of supervision assignments with appropriate instructions if a teacher needs to leave the room.

92. **It is the day before Middlebrook High School is scheduled to participate in the state level basketball tournament. The parents had chartered buses to transport the team; however, the bus-charter contract has fallen through. A proactive, "take-charge" principal should do which of the following:** *(Skill 2.12) (Average Rigor)*

    A. Call a meeting with the administrative team, parent association, executive committee, and the basketball coaches

    B. Rent cars so that the athletes can drive to the tournament

    C. Use the buses available for transporting students on a daily basis

    D. Withdraw from the tournament

Answer: C. Use the buses available for transporting students on a daily basis

Although using the daily service buses is not the first choice, the principal has a responsibility to provide transportation for the athletes in this situation. It is important for the principal to reflect on possible scenarios such as this and always have a back-up plan in the future.

93. **Compulsory school attendance law requires which of the following:** *(Skill 2.12) (Average Rigor)*

    A. Students who are married or become pregnant shall be prohibited from attending school

    B. Mandatory school attendance ends at the age of sixteen

    C. No child can be admitted or promoted to the first grade in a public school unless he or she has successfully completed kindergarten in a public school

    D. No special education service be provided to children over the age of sixteen

Answer: B. Mandatory school attendance ends at the age of sixteen

Chapter 232 of the State's Statutes provides the specific requirements for the fulfillment of the compulsory attendance laws. The mandatory school attendance ages are from six to sixteen.

94. **Effective school leaders must be willing and able to do all of the following EXCEPT:** *(Skill 2.13) (Average Rigor)*

    A. Stick to an original decision regardless of new information

    B. Clearly delineate expectations for all stakeholders

    C. Manage the school by walking around and being visible

    D. Be consistent yet fair

Answer: A. Stick to an original decision regardless of new information
While efficient school leaders must be decisive and strong, they must also be willing to change an original decision in the face of new evidence. They should be known as consistent yet fair. In efforts to be consistent, fair, and proactive, principals also do well to clearly delineate expectations for all stakeholders. It is particularly important that principals "manage by walking around;" this phrase describes a leader who is visible, knows what is going on, and does not hide in an office.

95. Two principals have recently been hired at high schools within the most diverse neighborhood in the city. Their schools have rich histories of activism during the civil-rights era and many former students who are now neighborhood residents. They are also well known for providing venues for activities ranging from business meetings to community assistance programs. Principal A has decided that he would like to display the achievements of current students. To make space, he has had to move a display highlighting the civil-rights era activities of his school's student government body. Principal B believes that parents are the backbone of the school; therefore, in the past four months, he has decided to grant the PTA meeting space over other groups, even if the other groups had submitted their applications first. According to the "four organizational frames" theory proposed by Bolman and Deal, which of the frames is each of these principals ignoring? *(Skill 2.13) (Rigorous)*

A. Principal A is ignoring the symbolic frame; Principal B is also ignoring the symbolic frame

B. Principal A is ignoring the political frame; Principal B is also ignoring the political frame

C. Principal A is ignoring the symbolic frame; Principal B is ignoring the political frame

D. Principal A is ignoring the political frame; Principal B is ignoring the symbolic frame

Answer: C. Principal A is ignoring the symbolic frame; Principal B is ignoring the political frame

In this example Principal A is ignoring the symbolic frame, while Principal B is ignoring the political frame. Bolman and Deal (1997) suggest that people within organizations operate within one (or more) of four frames: structural, human resources, political, and symbolic. Many leaders operate in the structural frame (focusing on hierarchies, rules, regulations, procedures, etc.) or the human resources frame (focusing on the needs of people; within schools, this could either be teachers, students, or both). The two remaining frames, often ignored, are highly important for the proper running of an organization. The political frame focuses on sources of power, and the symbolic frame focuses on the symbols of organizational culture and history.

96. **At the beginning of the year, the principal has implemented a change in the way exams are submitted to the main office. Even after the changes are shared, some teachers submit the exams in the way they choose. At the end of the year, the principal gives a bad review to those teachers who did not submit the reports as specified and teachers are very upset by the bad reviews. The principal could have avoided this conflict by doing which of the following:** *(Skill 2.13)* *(Rigorous)*

    A. Not requiring adherence to the established policy

    B. Providing feedback during the year so that teachers were reminded of the policy

    C. Changing the policy in the middle of the year

    D. Going to each classroom to collect the exams

Answer: B. Providing feedback during the year so that teachers were reminded of the policy
An effective educational leader recognizes that he or she cannot hold teachers accountable at the end of the year if no feedback is provided during the year.

97. **Trinity School will initiate its International Baccalaureate Program this fall. The principal has clearly stated tasks, expected outcomes, and timelines for accomplishment, and then designated an assistant principal as coordinator for this program. At the initial meeting for the program, the assistant principal organized and ran the meeting, and all the staff participated in the discussion. This principal's behavior demonstrates which of the following:**
    (Skill 2.13) *(Average Rigor)*

    A. Organizing the activity of a group to develop a plan

    B. Delegating authority and responsibility

    C. Failing to trust the assistant principal

    D. Showing a developmental orientation toward the assistant principal

Answer: B. Delegating authority and responsibility
Delegating is effective when the principal establishes clear guidelines, assigns another person to do required tasks under his or her supervision, and then allows the person to implement the plan and make appropriate decisions.

98. **Bolman and Deal argue that leaders often forget two of four important organizational frames. Which of these is the one that focuses on the organizational culture and history, a frame very important to employees, students, and others?** *(Skill 2.13) (Easy)*

   A. Structural

   B. Human Resources

   C. Political

   D. Symbolic

Answer: D. Symbolic
The symbolic frame focuses on the symbols of organizational culture and history. These often carry meaning and emotion for employees, students, and others, and therefore the symbolic should not be overlooked by administrators, especially when implementing change.

99. **A school is interested in a new math series for students. A committee has been charged with the responsibility for making a decision and doing what is necessary regarding this matter. Several meetings have taken place to consider the advantages and disadvantages of adopting the materials. If the committee has adopted the math series and is now distributing it to students, in what stage of change is the committee?** *(Skill 2.13) (Average Rigor)*

   A. The committee is in the integration stage because a decision to adopt the math series has been made

   B. The committee has gone through all three stages so its work is now complete

   C. The committee is now in the second stage of change

   D. The committee is poised between the second and third stages of change

Answer: C. The committee is now in the second stage of change
The decision has already been made and the committee is in the implementation stage, or the second stage of change.

100. **At a recent town-hall meeting, parents expressed concern that recent graduates have been unable to find employment in fields requiring knowledge of web-design and website creation software. This gap exists in the students skills because the school administration failed to:** *(Skill 2.13) (Rigorous)*

    A. Maintain the status-quo in course offerings

    B. Appeal to student interests

    C. Respond to changing environmental conditions, particularly job-market requirements

    D. Administer surveys about the jobs held by parents

Answer: C. Respond to changing environmental conditions, particularly job-market requirements
Administrators must facilitate schools changing due to environmental conditions, demographics, and economic issues. For instance, changes in the job market require schools to prepare students accordingly.

101. **What should a principal who is new to a school do to promote necessary change?** *(Skill 2.13) (Average Rigor)*

    A. Identify areas of need and thoroughly research new programs that could impact the problem

    B. Spend a short time observing school procedures, then make the most important changes immediately

    C. Involve teachers and other stakeholders in the planning and development process

    D. Impose ideas because many teachers are afraid of change and will not cooperate unless an authority figure requires their participation

Answer: C. Involve teachers and other stakeholders in the planning and development process
School change is a difficult process. It is most likely to be effective when all stakeholders are involved in the process from the start. Importing new programs (A) is ineffective; trying to effect immediate change (B) doesn't work; and top-down management (D) is also ineffective.

102. **Middle School 71 has analyzed its standardized testing data and found serious shortcomings. The overall school performance is commendable: 75% of students achieved a level 3 or 4 on the FCAT. However, there are alarming trends when the data are disaggregated. To address the achievement gaps, the school has developed and implemented an improvement plan for the following subgroups of students:**
    1) **Those from lower socio-economic (SES) backgrounds, which is measured by eligibility for Free and Reduced Lunch (FRL),**
    2) **Those who are learning English as a Second Language (ESOL), and**
    3) **Those with certain special needs who are still required to be tested.**
    The following table highlights the goals section of the schools' improvement plan.

Percentage of Students Who Attain Level 3 or 4 on the FCAT

Subgroup	Current Percentage	Anticipated Percentage	Team Responsible
FRL	40	50	Mr. Watson
ESOL	30	45	Ms. Tanner
Special Needs	35	40	Mr. Jamison

According to the table above, the school improvement plan would recognize which group as making satisfactory learning gains? (Skill 2.14) (Rigorous)

A. The Special Needs group, if 50% or more of these students achieve a level 3 or 4 on the FCAT

B. The ESOL group if 40% or more of these students achieve a level 3 or 4 on the FCAT

C. Both A and B

D. Neither A nor B

Answer: A. The Special Needs group, if 50% or more of these students achieve a level 3 or 4 on the FCAT
For each subgroup, the table provides the goals set forth by the school improvement plan. It shows both the current and anticipated percentage of students who achieve a level 3 or 4 on the FCAT exam. Therefore, according to the school improvement plan, the Special Needs group should see 40% of its students achieve a level 3 or 4. If 50% of this subgroup attain a level 3 or 4, then they have not only met but surpassed the goals of the school improvement plan. In contrast, the plan proposes that 45% of ESOL students should achieve a level 3 or 4 on the exam. If only 40% of these students achieve to those levels, then the school improvement plan would not recognize that sufficient learning gains have been made within this subgroup of students.

103. **The students at Cornwell Elementary School have consistently surpassed district and state achievement test levels. During the current year, the scores are in the lower quartile. The MOST appropriate action for the principal to take at the school site would be to:** *(Skill 2.14) (Rigorous)*

    A. Meet with the parents to get their support

    B. Call an emergency faculty meeting to decide what to do

    C. Analyze test results to determine areas and patterns of poor performance by students

    D. Get assistance from her district supervisor on action that has worked elsewhere

Answer: C. Analyze test results to determine areas and patterns of poor performance by students
Student assessment data should be used to identify targets for campus instructional improvement. Once targets for improvement are identified, then a search for effective and research based programs can be done.

104. You recently learned that your school district has been affected by negative market conditions and falling property tax revenues. For this reason, next year your school will be allocated 25% less money than you received in the current year. In a second meeting you were given a copy of the school choice trends for the past two years. Records indicate that enrollment at your school has dropped by 10% each year and that it has risen at the same rate for a neighboring charter school. Informal data suggests that parents are moving children out of your school and are enrolling them in the charter school. News of the budget cuts are certain to accelerate the rate at which parents leave the school in favor of their other "choice" options. Which of the following is an effective strategy to communicate the challenges faced by your school?   *(Skill 3.1) (Rigorous)*

A. Try to down-play the problems and minimize any internal or external communication: the more attention you put on the issue, the more stakeholders will panic and the worse will be the outcome

B. Hold an internal meeting with staff and inform them of the issues; encourage them to work as a team within the new budget while continuing to provide a top-notch education to students; minimize external communications

C. Hold internal meetings to decide on an approach that will include parents and external stakeholders. Next, hold events during which all parties can be informed of the news and can participate in finding solutions

D. Call an emergency meeting of all internal and external stakeholders and inform everyone at the same time. Next obtain solutions from those present and develop a plan that will address the problem

Answer: C. Hold internal meetings to decide on an approach that will include parents and external stakeholders. Next, hold events during which all parties can be informed of the news and can participate in finding solutions

The best approach is open, honest communication, particularly when the issues impact all students, their parents, and the community. It is more effective for internal stakeholders learn of problems first. In that way, those closest to the problem can discuss the matter and propose methods to involve other parties. Due to the far-reaching effects of these changes, it is best to plan a series of events during which people can collaborate on a solution. This type of approach will lead to greater camaraderie and will increase stakeholder commitment to the organization. The committee did not attach the plan to achievable goals and objectives.

105. **A three-member committee planned a pep rally to increase attendance at school basketball games. During the month following the rally, attendance increased by 10% at the first game and 15% at the second game. The coach felt that the strategy was a success, the PTA representative thought it was a failure, and the principal could not decide how to view the attendance changes. What is the MOST likely reason for this disagreement?** *(Skill 3.1) (Rigorous)*

   A. The coach, the PTA representative, and the principal each measured success differently

   B. The committee did not establish clear attendance goals

   C. The three members of the committee did not get student feedback on the attendance changes

   D. Both A and C

Answer: B. The committee did not establish clear attendance goals
When a plan is being conceived, it must be attached to achievable goals and objectives. Otherwise, stakeholders will have no basis on which to judge whether the plan is successful or not.

106. **This is the second year your school has been identified as one of the lowest performing in your district; you have decided that in the next year you will meet AYP. What is the BEST strategy to increase support systems to accomplish school goals AND decrease those elements that can have a negative influence on its functioning?**
    (Skill 3.1) (Average Rigor)

    A. Ban students from text-messaging each other during class time

    B. Holding town-hall meetings to solicit parental involvement and enforcing a zero-tolerance policy for disruptive behaviors

    C. Having fund-raisers to collect money for new textbooks and encouraging teachers to stay after school with students

    D. Conduct a series of meetings with stakeholders to develop a plan of action

Answer: B. Holding town-hall meetings to solicit parental involvement and enforcing a zero-tolerance policy for disruptive behaviors
By holding town-hall meetings to solicit parental involvement, you will be increasing support systems AND by enforcing a zero-tolerance policy for disruptive behaviors, you will be decreasing those elements that can have a negative influence on student learning.

107. Your school was put on the critically low school list by the state. No measurable gains were recorded the next year and you are on the list two consecutive years. How would you get your school off the list? *(Skill 3.1) (Average Rigor)*

    A. Involve the community

    B. Have a meeting with teachers and establish a strategic plan that involves the parents and community

    C. Secure advice from the state and district and work on the problem

    D. Conduct a series of meetings with teachers, students, parents, and community members to obtain information to aid in developing a plan of action with the faculty

Answer: D. Conduct a series of meetings with teachers, students, parents, and community members to obtain information to aid in developing a plan of action with the faculty

This serious situation calls for a truly collaborative, long-range plan. Involving all the stakeholders is needed in order to gather key information that can lead to a plan of action to effect change.

108. The neighborhood demographics around Peabody High School have markedly changed over the past few years. Single-family homes are now occupied by multiple families. The first language of most adults has changed from English to Spanish. The businesses in the community are also changing and are requiring different types of skilled employees. You, as principal, have been asked to redesign your program to better meet the needed work force. Your first step to meet this need is to: *(Skill 3.1) (Average Rigor)*

    A. Talk to the new residents at a town meeting you hold at the school

    B. Conduct a survey of the business owners to determine their needs

    C. Plan to enlarge the school to meet increased student enrollment

    D. Discuss the matter with your area supervisor

Answer: B. Conduct a survey of the business owners to determine their needs

The first step in planning change is to conduct a needs assessment to determine the changes needed. After that, pursuing some of the other options may be useful.

109. Your assessment officer has just brought two sets of reports with FACT scores to your office. He states that they require your signature so they can go in the mail today. One group will go to parents and the other will be given to the teachers. Unfortunately, before he could identify which was which, you were called away to a meeting. As you wait for the meeting to begin, you pull out the reports. You notice that Group A has the student scores as percentage ranks; the reports in Group B provide raw scores for each student. From your understanding of how to communicate with different audiences, which reports are intended for parents and which does he plan to give to the teachers?   *(Skill 3.2) (Average Rigor)*

A. Group A will go to parents and Group B will go to teachers

B. Group A will go to teachers and Group B will go to parents

C. Group A will go to both parents and teachers; Group B will not be shared

D. Group B will go to both parents and teachers; Group A will not be shared

Answer: A. Group A will go to teachers and Group B will go to parents
You realize that different audiences would require different types of communications. In the case of sharing assessment results, parents can appreciate the meaning of percentage ranks but some may not understand the meaning of the raw scores. In contrast, while teachers can understand percentage ranks, they can gain more benefit from using the raw scores to guide their instructional decisions.

110. **You are the superintendent of a small school district and your secretary has told you that the district attendance records show that three siblings were listed on the Northwest Regional Data Center (NWRDC) database of missing children. What steps should you take? (Skill 3.3) (Rigorous)**

    A. Call the local law enforcement agency which originated the case and then call the Florida Department of Education

    B. Call the Florida Department of Education and then call the local law enforcement agency which originated the case

    C. Use form ESE 092 to update the NWRDC database

    D. Use form ESE 092 to report this information to the local law enforcement agency which originated the case and to the Florida Department of Education

Answer: D. Use form ESE 092 to report this information to the local law enforcement agency which originated the case and to the Florida Department of Education

Through cooperative efforts with multiple law enforcement agencies, the Northwest Regional Data Center (NWRDC) makes data available on missing children. The Florida Department of Education FLDOE then provides this database to school districts that are responsible for comparing this information with their own student database records. If they establish any matches between the names of children reported as missing and names of students in the district they report possible matches. Using the ESE 092 form, the notification goes to both the local law enforcement agency which originated the case and to the FLDOE. As the children in question are identified and located, the original law enforcement agency can then remove the solved cases from the Florida Crime Information Center (FCIC) database.

111. Jake has not met the specified levels of proficiency in either reading or math. Therefore you are aware that a Progress Monitoring Plan (PMP) must be in place to improve his achievement. In a phone conference with the counselor at his previous school, you were told that Jake also had a PMP there. He had received one diagnostic assessment, an Academic Improvement Plan (AIP), and frequent monitoring of his progress, and monthly academic updates were given to him and his parents. She also tells you that they have left the PMP open for the past three years. Where has the previous school not adhered to state Statute 1008.25?
(Skill 3.4) (Rigorous)

A. They only administered one diagnostic assessment and the state mandates three

B. They have left the PMP open for three years

C. They should not provide academic updates to Jake, only to his parents

D. None of the Above

Answer: B. They have left the PMP open for three years
Florida Statute §1008.25(4), mandates that when students do not meet specified levels of proficiency in reading, writing, mathematics, or science, the school district must develop a Progress Monitoring Plan (PMP). The process involves diagnostic assessments, individualized or school-wide Academic Improvement Plans (AIPs), frequent monitoring, academic progress updates to the student(s) and his or her/their parents, and the "closing" of the PMP annual contract by the last day of school. The previous district has not closed the contract each year as is required by the statute.

112. **You have been dealing with a lunchroom fight that has resulted in one student being hospitalized and two students being expelled. As you investigated the matter, you learned that the incident resulted from racial tensions that you and your staff have downplayed for the past two months. Which of the following is a communications decision you should AVOID and why?** *(Skill 3.4) (Rigorous)*

   A. Provide a statement to parents that follows your strategy of downplaying the issue; this will minimize overreactions while the situation is resolved

   B. Send all required documentation to the district immediately; they must be kept abreast of the incident through ongoing upward communication

   C. Make notes of the important facts as soon as possible; you will need to remember the facts as you communicate to various stakeholders

   D. Send a clear statement to all stakeholders so that they are aware of the situation and can understand your commitment to resolving the issue

Answer: A. Provide a statement to parents that follows your strategy of downplaying the issue; this will minimize overreactions while the situation is resolved
In many cases, there can be legal consequences to poor writing and not communicating effectively. Not documenting or clearly articulating an issue can be problematic at a later time. In addition, downplaying important issues typically results in unwanted consequences including negative gossip, escalation of problems, and distrust of the administration. Good administrators put essential communications and decision in writing, but are careful to write very clearly and thoughtfully. This means the writing should be straightforward, lacking in jargon, spells out concerns and consequences, and includes enough but not too many details.

113. **A mutually beneficial relationship can exist between schools and community partners such as resource centers. The centers can assist schools with training, resources, and information. Which of the following is the most significant benefit schools can provide in return?** (*Skill 3.4*) (*Average Rigor*)

   A. Schools do not provide any benefit to the centers; the relationship is only beneficial to the schools, not the centers

   B. Schools provide access to sensitive student information that the centers would not otherwise be able to obtain

   C. Schools allow the resource centers to engage in their practice, to perfect their outreach, and to continue functioning

   D. Schools are able to pay resource centers for their services, which increases the income brought in by these centers

Answer: C. Schools allow the resource centers to engage in their practice, to perfect their outreach, and to continue functioning
Strong symbiotic relationships can develop between schools and their community partners. This is particularly the case with resource centers, which provide information, training, and resources to enhance the educational outcomes of students. Among them are Learning Resource Centers (LRCs), Diagnostic Resource Centers (DRCs), and School Choice Resource Centers (SCRCs). These organizations serve a range of stakeholders including administrators, teachers, paraprofessionals, and parents.

114. **The top student at your school is among the finalists for a full scholarship to the state university. The University's admissions office just called because the committee must make a decision today and they need the student's 3rd quarter report card. Unfortunately, the student is on a class trip and her parents have not returned your phone calls. According to the Buckley Amendment, what should you do?** *(Skill 3.5) (Average Rigor)*

A. You should provide the report card to the University so that the student can be awarded the scholarship

B. The University can send a representative to view the student's records; however, the student's information cannot leave your office without her parent's permission

C. The University must provide the request in writing; upon receipt of the document, you are able to provide them with a copy of the report card

D. You are not permitted to release the student's information to the University without written consent

Answer: D. You are not permitted to release the student's information to the University without written consent
According to the Buckley Amendment, also known as FERPA, in order to release the student's information to the University, you must obtain written consent.

115. **The guidelines established by the Buckley Amendment/FERPA, give access to a student's records to all of the following individuals EXCEPT?** *(Skill 3.5) (Average Rigor)*

A. The student

B. Parents or legal guardians

C. All school-level teaching staff

D. Appropriate district-level personnel

Answer: C. All school-level teaching staff
School employees, on a need-to-know basis, may have access to student records. These individuals may include principals, assistant principals, school psychologists, school counselors, and special education professionals. Regardless of his or her position, each employee must maintain the confidentiality of student information.

116. **When an administrator wants to overcome the negative effects of the school grapevine she should:** *(Skill 3.6) (Average Rigor)*

    A. Identify the leaders of the grapevine and pass information through them

    B. Keep teachers and staff informed of key policy changes or issues relevant to staff, the school, and/or the district

    C. Attempt to minimize the amount of information that is shared about a particular topic until all the facts are clear

    D. Redirect negative attitudes and feelings to avoid any confrontations regarding unfavorable policy changes

Answer: B. Keep teachers and staff informed of key policy changes or issues relevant to staff, the school, and/or the district
Administrators should be aware of the operation of the school grapevine and incorporate its positive aspects into the communication structure. The negative aspect of unsubstantiated rumor-passing will be overridden if the administrator consistently does the following:

- keeps employees informed about matters relevant to the school or district and about issues that impact the employees' jobs
- provides employees the opportunity to express attitudes and feelings about issues
- tests employees' reactions to information before making decisions
- builds morale by repeating positive reactions/comments made by employees to higher level administrators or the community and vice versa

117. **A school principal is confused by his repeated inability to connect with the parents and students of races other than his own. He feels that he is respectful and interested in them, but they never seem to respond positively, either one-on-one or in group settings. He attends a workshop on cultural competence and learns all of the following except:** *(Skill 3.6) (Average Rigor)*

   A. The best way to become more culturally competent is to attend a series of workshops on the topic

   B. He needs to learn more about his students' cultural backgrounds

   C. He has made assumptions about what his students feel and think that are probably inaccurate

   D. Just being sensitive to differences isn't enough; it's only a first step

Answer: A. The best way to become more culturally competent is to attend a series of workshops on the topic
Although education and training can be helpful in gaining cultural competence, more important is the principal's willingness to be self-reflective, to learn more about different cultures and beliefs, and to find ways to communicate that reflect cultural sensitivity and awareness.

118. **Effective communication is a key component in building relationships with faculty, students, parents and community members. The keys to effective communication include all of the following except:** *(Skill 3.7) (Average Rigor)*

   A. Being able to anticipate what the speaker is going to say

   B. Paying attention to nonverbal communication

   C. Asking for clarification

   D. Expressing oneself clearly and directly

Answer: A. Being able to anticipate what the speaker is going to say
Focusing of what you *think* the speaker is going to say interferes with your ability to actually listen to what the speaker is saying.

119. You are experimenting with a new teaching strategy that is supposed to increase professional and interpersonal relationships among teachers. It is also shown to lead to better student achievement. You select one group of 10th grade Social Studies teachers to work collaboratively. The teachers assign their students a similar end-of-unit writing project. They utilize the same assignment, have the same standards, and assess the work according to the same rubric. Then as a group, the teachers score these essays together, discuss similar problems they notice, seek help from one another, and brainstorm solutions so that they can better prepare students for the next assessment. What type of strategy are they using? *(Skill 3.7) (Easy)*

A. Take, Pair, Share

B. Professional Learning Community

C. Silo-style classrooms

D. Social studies teacher hierarchy

Answer: B. Professional Learning Community
Professional discussion about student learning and teacher techniques is said to take place in Professional Learning Communities (PLCs). PLCs take many different forms, but they all have one thing in common: teachers working as professionals to problem solve, participate in dialogues, and question instructional strategies. A common format for PLCs is group scoring sessions in which teachers assign their students the same assignments, standards, and assessments. They then compare their students' scores to improve learning and instruction.

120. School data show that student test scores have been decreasing for the past two years. From Informal surveys with teachers, parents, and students you realize that during that period many parents have been working overtime and are interact less with their children during the week. You have hired several educational consultants who developed a plan that will utilize parental involvement to reinforce and review information taught. Which of the following strategies would be most likely to both communicate the need for the change AND gain parental support for the plan?
(Skill 3.8) (Average Rigor)

A. Provide and discuss a chart showing the trend of scores going down as parental involvement goes down at a meeting; then address ideas for changes and adaptations to meet the needs of the parents and teachers

B. Send out a memo with a chart showing the trend of scores going down as parental involvement goes down, letting parents know you are available to meet with them if they would like that

C. Both A and B

D. Neither A nor B

Answer: A. Provide a chart showing the trend of scores going down as parental involvement goes down; have a meeting during which the plan is first presented and then discussed for changes and adaptations to meet the needs of the parents and teachers
All stakeholders should be able to see how decisions are made and should be given multiple opportunities for comment and critique. Because schools are so heavily involved in a family's life, it is especially critical that parents receive open, clear rationales for decisions. Furthermore, policies and decisions should take parent and student concerns and needs seriously. The more they feel accepted and valued, the more they will see their place in the system.

121. **Which two elements should be central in the daily operations of the school and drive all planning, activities, and school climate:** *(Skill 3.8) (Average Rigor)*

   A. Staff and parents

   B. Mission and vision

   C. Classes and activities

   D. Aims and objectives

Answer: B. Mission and vision
In addition to helping stakeholder groups see that a school values them, the mission and vision must be front and center in the daily operations of the school. A vision cannot simply be something that is written on a banner and hung in a hallway. It has to be talked about, referred to, valued, and considered regularly, especially when decisions must be made.

122. **In today's educational climate it is believed that all stakeholders should be valued, be able to see how decisions are made, and should feel welcomed in every part of the school's operations. The BEST way to achieve this is through:** *(Skill 3.8) (Rigorous)*

   A. Transparent processes that give multiple opportunities for comment and critique

   B. Careful planning and strategies to communicate decisions made by the administration

   C. Presenting a unified front between the district, administration, and teachers

   D. Sharing information on a need-to-know basis and deciding which items require stakeholder input

Answer: A. Transparent processes that give multiple opportunities for comment and critique
The current thinking on stakeholder voice in public schools is that all stakeholders should be able to see how decisions are made (through very transparent processes) and should be given multiple opportunities for comment and critique.

123. To write effectively, a school leader should use strategies to organize his or her thoughts. Which of the following lists these strategies in the correct order: (Skill 3.9) (Rigorous)

A. State any actions to be taken, list items to be discussed, expand on each item, put items in order, write a brief summary

B. Write a brief summary, state any actions to be taken, list items to be discussed, expand on each item, put items in order,

C. List items to be discussed, put items in order, state any actions to be taken, expand on each item, write a brief summary

D. List items to be discussed, put items in order, write a brief summary, expand on each item, state any actions to be taken

Answer: D. List items to be discussed, put items in order, write a brief summary, expand on each item, state any actions to be taken
To write effectively, a school leader should decide what information is to be conveyed. The following strategies can be employed whether writing a memo to the staff or a report for the superintendent:

- List each item to be discussed
- Put them in order -- from most to least important
- Write a brief summary of the entire document -- this will be the first paragraph.
- Expand on each item on the list
- If any action needs to be taken by the recipient, state this in the closing paragraph.

124. Administrators must understand key concepts when analyzing and interpreting data. These concepts include the ability to *contrast*, *explain*, *discuss*, *analyze*, and *compare* information.

1. _____ = examine the parts
2. _____ = look at similarities
3. _____ = look at differences
4. _____ = examine in detail
5. _____ = provide reasons or examples, or clarify meaning

Select the option below that places the key concepts in correct blanks in the list above. *(Skill 3.9) (Rigorous)*

A. 1. contrast, 2. explain, 3. discuss, 4. analyze, 5. compare

B. 1. analyze, 2. compare, 3. discuss, 4. contrast, 5. explain

C. 1. analyze, 2. compare, 3. contrast, 4. discuss, 5. explain

D. 1. discuss, 2. compare, 3. contrast, 4. analyze, 5. explain

Answer: C. 1. analyze, 2. compare, 3. contrast, 4. discuss, 5. explain
Some key concepts to consider when presenting an analysis and interpretation of data are:
- Analyze: examine the parts
- Compare: look at similarities
- Contrast: look at differences
- Discuss: examine in detail
- Explain: provide reasons or examples, or clarify meaning

125. **You constantly engage in self-reflection in all areas of your professional practice. This week you have been thinking about a comment made by a PTA member. She stated that many of her fellow parents complained that your memos are too long and incoherent. They are also concerned because you mailed information on the recent test scores, but they could not understand what the numbers meant. As you reviewed your prior memos about the test scores, you see why parents could not understand your memo and why they could not understand the data. Which of the following is the most time-efficient approach to correcting this problem?**
(Skill 3.9) (Average Rigor)

   A. Inform your secretary that he will need to edit your documents so that they are not as wordy or difficult for parents to understand

   B. Register for the district's course on "effective communication for administrators"

   C. Hold a parent's night during which a presenter shows parents how to understand important assessment data

   D. Both B and C

Answer: D. Both B and C
The best approach is to polish your own writing while also helping parents to understand more complex assessment data. When communicating basic information you should be clear and concise so that your audience will be able to gain the information you are attempting to share.

XAMonline, INC. 21 Orient Ave. Melrose, MA 02176

Toll Free number 800-509-4128

TO ORDER Fax 781-662-9268 OR www.XAMonline.com

FLORIDA TEACHER CERTIFICATION
EXAMINATIONS   - FTCE - 2008

PO#   Store/School:

Bill to Address 1   Ship to address

City, State Zip

Credit card number_____-_____-_____-_____   expiration____

EMAIL _____

PHONE   **FAX**

13# ISBN 2008	TITLE	Qty	Retail	Total
978-1-58197-900-8	Art Sample Test K-12		$15.00	
978-1-58197-689-2	Biology 6-12		$59.95	
978-1-58197-046-3	Chemistry 6-12		$59.95	
978-1-58197-047-0	Earth/Space Science 6-12		$59.95	
978-1-58197-578-9	Educational Media Specialist PK-12		$59.95	
978-1-58197-347-1	Elementary Education K-6		$28.95	
978-1-58197-292-4	English 6-12		$59.95	
978-1-58197-274-0	Exceptional Student Ed. K-12		$73.50	
978-1-58197-294-8	FELE Florida Ed. Leadership		$59.95	
978-1-58197-619-9	French Sample Test 6-12		$15.00	
978-1-58197-615-1	General Knowledge		$28.95	
978-1-58197-586-4	Guidance and Counseling PK-12		$59.95	
978-1-58197-045-6	Humanities K-12		$34.95	
978-1-58197-640-3	Mathematics 6-12		$32.95	
978-1-58197-597-0	Middle Grades English 5-9		$59.95	
978-1-58197-662-5	Middle Grades General Science 5-9		$59.95	
978-1-58197-286-3	Middle Grades Integrated Curriculum		$59.95	
978-1-58197-284-9	Middle Grades Math 5-9		$59.95	
978-1-58197-590-1	Middle Grades Social Science 5-9		$59.95	
978-1-58197-616-8	Physical Education K-12		$59.95	
978-1-58197-044-9	Physics 6-12		$59.95	
978-1-58197-657-1	Prekindergarten/Primary PK-3		$73.50	
978-1-58197-695-3	Professional Educator		$34.95	
978-1-58197-659-5	Reading K-12		$59.95	
978-1-58197-270-2	Social Science 6-12		$59.95	
978-1-58197-583-3	Spanish K-12		$59.95	
			SUBTOTAL	
/handling $8.25 one title, $11.00 two titles, $15.00 three or more titles				
			TOTAL	

CPSIA information can be obtained at www.ICGtesting.com
Printed in the USA
LVOW09s1923231213

366584LV00009B/1068/P